Success with
Emotional Intelligence

Dr. Shamira Soren Malekar

Dr. Rajendra Prasad Mohanty

Kendall Hunt
publishing company

Cover image © Shutterstock, Inc.

Kendall Hunt
publishing company

www.kendallhunt.com
Send all inquiries to:
4050 Westmark Drive
Dubuque, IA 52004-1840

Copyright © 2017 by Kendall Hunt Publishing Company

ISBN 978-1-5249-5961-6

Published in the United States of America

DEDICATED TO OUR PARENTS

Mrs. Ruby Sassoon Kurulkar

and

Late Mr. Sassoon David Kurulkar

— Dr. Shamira Malekar

Late Mrs. Malli Dei Kunjabihari Mohanty

and

Late Mr. Kunjabihari Mohanty

— Dr. R.P. Mohanty

Contents

Foreword

The term Emotional Intelligence first came into the public consciousness in 1995 with the publication of Dr. Daniel Goleman's best-selling book *Emotional Intelligence: Why It Can Matter More Than IQ*. This book served to challenge the long-held belief that a person's IQ was the best predictor of success in life. Moreover, it served to focus our attention on how emotions, far from being irrational and incomprehensible aspects of our personality, had a critical role to play in our survival as a species and were fundamental to helping us react and behave in intelligent ways. Given that emotions make up such a fundamental aspect of what it means to be human, it is somewhat surprising that only recently has the scientific community seriously begun to focus more intensely on the topic. The critical role that emotions play in our everyday life has been highlighted by scientific investigations from a wide range of disciplines including neuropsychology, clinical psychology, organizational behavior, anthropology, sociology, sports psychology, and research from the emerging area of positive psychology. The challenges brought on by a more diverse and complex world cannot be solved by relying solely on the powers of our rational mind but will require the intelligent use of emotions as well.

Given the importance of emotional intelligence to success in our academic, professional, and personal lives, it seems natural to focus our attention on what can be done to develop our capacities and abilities as they relate to emotions. I have been fortunate to have entered the field of emotional intelligence research and practice as the field was forming in the mid-1990s. As a member of the Consortium for Research on Emotional Intelligence in Organizations, I have been able to conduct research on model programs and best practices for developing emotional intelligence in adults and have become convinced that these are abilities that can be developed. I have seen the field change and mature over the years, and I continue to draw energy from the many dedicated and talented individuals who strive to apply innovative techniques to the personal development of others.

More recently, my own research interests have led me to India, where I have had the privilege of working with the Forum for Emotional Intelligence Learning (FEIL). It is in this context that I first had the good fortune of meeting Dr. Shamira Malekar at the 1st Global Emotional Intelligence Forum in Mumbai. Her many publications, awards, and achievements speak well of her commitment and ability to advance the field of emotional intelligence through both research and implementation of best practices. As a founding member of India's first not-for-profit organization dedicated to the advancement of research and practice related to emotional intelligence, Dr. Malekar has been a positive advocate for the importance of both research and practice related to the development of emotional intelligence in both the educational system and the workplace.

Achieving Academic Success with *Emotional Intelligence* is a thoughtful and practical introduction to topic of emotional intelligence. The authors provide an excellent overview of the topic and make important links between emotional intelligence and key educational and life outcomes. By providing a coherent model of social and emotional intelligence, the authors give specific language and definition to psychological constructs that are often spoken about in more general terms. These more precise definitions allow for a more meaningful and practical approach to understanding the world of emotions and how we might go about developing our abilities to increase our understanding of ourselves and others. Our traditional education system has valued the transfer of knowledge and the development of our rational minds at the expense of the development of emotion-related skills and self-knowledge. Yet, even knowing "about" emotional intelligence is not enough to actually develop our emotional intelligence. The more "emotional" parts of our brain develop through different pathways and require that we engage in a process of self-reflection and mindful practice. The advice and exercises provided in this book give the reader a roadmap to enhancing emotion-related abilities and competencies using experiential learning techniques.

This book challenges us to take a more holistic view of ourselves and a more active and mindful approach to our emotional lives, and in so doing challenges us to be open to new experiences and new ideas. Hopefully, the publication of this book will help stimulate a greater understanding of how emotional intelligence can be utilized to help students achieve their academic objectives, while preparing them with the skills they will need to succeed in the career of their choice.

—Dr. Robert Emmerling

Acknowledgments

Soren, Simone, and Ethan require a special mention for all the unstinting support, sacrifice, and cooperation throughout the research project study and finally writing of this book.

We also express a deep sense of appreciation to Dr. Bina Niger at Haifa University Library, Israel; librarians of Bar Ilan University, Israel; ITM, Kharghar, Tata Institute of Social Sciences (TISS); and NITIE, Mumbai and ITM Group of Institutions. Thanks are due to the chairperson Dr. Mahatapa Palit, Faculty colleges and business students of the Borough of Manhattan Community College, especially Ching Hei Mok.

Sue Saad and Samantha Anne Schmidt of Kendall Hunt receive a special mention for their support and cooperation.

Thanks are also due to Mrs. Edna Charikar, Ms. Reena Solomon, Mr. Benson Samuel, Mr. Raymond, and Mr. Gershon. Kolatkar, Israel, along with Sam and Annie Malekar.

We appreciate greatly Nabnita, Madhumita, Pinaki and late Swarnalata Mohantty and they deserve a special mention.

Heartfelt thanks to Rene Caroline Balan for the edits and suggestion towards the betterment of the manuscript. The team at Kendall Hunt is acknowledged and thanked. Our gratitude to friends Shekhina Nagaonkar and Alicia Weinstein who have a significant influence in shaping many of the concepts presented in chapter 10 and 11 respectively.

Dr. Shamira Soren Malekar
Dr. Rajendra Prasad Mohanty

About the Authors

Dr. Shamira Malekar is an Assistant Professor with City University of New York—Borough of Manhattan Community College. Prior to relocating to the United States, she was an Assistant Professor at Mumbai University's Aruna Manharlal Shah's Institute of Management and Research (AMSIMR). She has several research papers to her credit published in National and International Management journals of repute. She is one of the founder members and Joint Secretary for the Forum of Emotional Intelligence and Learning (FEIL) in India.

In December 2005, she won the Best Paper Award at the National Conference at ITM Business School with a paper presentation on "Managing Human Capital." In December 2007, she won the Best Paper Award at the National Conference at ITM Business School with an empirical paper presentation on "Emotional Intelligence of school students."

She is the recipient of the 1st prize of the Best Doctoral Paper Competition at the Association of Indian Management Scholars (AIMS-7) International Conference organized at Indian Institute of Management, Bangalore, in December 2009. She also won the 1st prize of the Best Thesis Competition at the Doctoral Conclave at ICFAI Business School (IBS) in February 2010. In March 2011, she won the Best Paper Award at a Corporate Social Responsibility (CSR) National Conference organized by Babasaheb Gawde Institute of Management with an empirical paper presentation on "Social Responsibility." In January 2012, she won the Best Paper Award at the International Conference at IES Institute of Management with an empirical paper presentation on "Employee Satisfaction."

Dr. Shamira has compiled and edited the 1st book of FEIL entitled *Emotional Intelligence and Leadership: Better Work and Learning Environments* published by Excel Books, 2011 (ISBN No. 978-81-7446-902-1).

Professor R P Mohanty has 40 years' experience in Academics in India and Foreign Universities and 10 years in Indian Industry in top management positions. At present, he is engaged as the senior adviser to ICFAI group of universities and was the Vice Chancellor at Shiksha `O' Anusandhan University, Bhubaneswar, Odisha, India (2011–2014). He also undertakes research scholars pursuing Ph.D. in Engineering and Management. He is involved in leadership education, management consulting and managerial competency development programs across the country and also engaged in advising many universities to develop quality faculty resources in India and abroad.

In 2016, he was conferred with Honorary D.Sc. Degree by Sambalpur University. In 2015, International Engineering and Technology Institute (IETI), Hong Kong conferred upon him the Fellowship and Management Teachers Consortium (MTC GLOBAL) conferred the Life Time Achievement Award. In 2014, Utkal Sahitya Kala Parisad conferred upon him the Utkalshree Award.

In 2013, Prof. Mohanty found a place in Asia Pacific Who's Who (12th Edition). In 2012, he received the Excellence in Research and Innovations Award from Knowledge Resource Development and Welfare Group, IIT Delhi. In 2010, he received the exemplary leadership award in industrial engineering from (IIIE). In 2009, he has been felicitated by the "Lifetime Achievement Award" of Indian Institution of Industrial Engineering (IIIE) and also the "International Lifetime Achievement Award" from AIMS International. He received the Life Time Achievement Award from The Institution of Engineers (India) in the year 2006. VSS University of Technology, Odisha has conferred upon him the Distinguished Alumni Award in the golden jubilee year 2006. In 2004, he has been elected as a Fellow of Indian National Engineering Academy; toward outstanding contributions in "Engineering". In 2003, he received the most prestigious "Sir Visveswaraya Award" for his outstanding contribution in the field of Technical Education & Technology Management. Sambalpur University conferred upon him "Intellectual Colossus Award 2003" as an honour to his profound contributions to the field of Management Education in India and abroad. Utkal University honored him as the most distinguished HR professional in 2003. In 1997, he was chosen as the "Most Outstanding Academician" and was honored with "UNITOP" award by the Indian Institution of Materials Management. In 1995, Indian Institution of Industrial Engineering (IIIE) has honoured him by its highest award "Lilian Gilbreth Award" for his most significant and outstanding contribution to the field. In 1987, Indian Institution of Industrial Engineering has awarded him "Ramaswamy Cup" for his extraordinary services to the I.E. profession. American Biographical Institute has conferred upon him the "Distinguished Leadership Award in Academics". The Institution of Engineers (India) has also awarded him as the "Best Researcher".

He has published 17 Text Books, more than 350 research papers in reputed and scholarly International & Indian Journals and Newspapers. The total numbers of citations of most of these papers stand above 2600. He has guided 24 Ph.D. research scholars and several hundreds of master theses. He has advised more than 25 big companies in India and abroad in the areas of Engineering and Management. He is the past Chairman, Honorary Secretary, Treasurer, National Council Member, and Chairman Board of Examination, Editor-in-Chief of *Industrial Engineering Journal* and a Life Fellow of *Indian Institution of Industrial Engineering*. He has also served as Chairman and President of many Professional associations in India and also as a board member in International Professional Institutions. He represents in the Editorial Board of 17 international and national journals.

He is renowned in India as a distinguished academic leader. His innumerable value adding contributions in the field of technical education in terms of research publications, academic planning, administration, faculty development, management development, institutional development and direction of several top ranking international and national conferences, workshops, symposia, colloquium etc. are well known to the world of academia and industry professionals. Internationally, he is known as an empirical researcher, a system scientist, an organization theorist, and an organization development expert.

Preface

Our conceptualization and the research design included appraisal of factors identified by Bar-On (1997a). The following remarks are significant in our book:

- Three different perspectives of emotional intelligence (EI) such as cognitive perspective, noncognitive perspective and neurological perspective relating to emotion and intelligence were explained in the literature review. Cognitive perspective deals with individual's abilities, potentials, and intelligences; noncognitive perspective deals with individual's traits and personalities; and neurological perspective deals with the linkages with the primitive mind and the rational mind.
- Intelligence has evolved in four stages since seventeenth century till date. The four stages are termed as: development of IQ scale, expansion of theories of intelligence, development of EI, and corporate cognition.
- Self-report measures assume that nobody apart from the individual is the best judge of self and one's behavior, and therefore self-assessments provide appropriate evaluation. However, assumptions are challenged.
- Significant factors are derived from literature such as intrapersonal, interpersonal, stress management, adaptability, and general mood.
- Radar Formulation: EI radar will promote a thorough understanding of EI, as it is a structural framework for navigating and positioning the students of diverse backgrounds and classes. This EI radar aims to make each factor of EI operational and is a pragmatic methodology for creating EI maps for each and every individual student. We have created a holistic conceptual framework through construction of radar to visualize, diagnose, and improve the EI of an individual student.
- Ladder Development: EI competency ladder is constructed to give support to an individual to climb step by step so as to attain the goal of life success through EI. This ladder consists of twelve steps derived from the important factors of EI achieved by correlation.
- Curriculum Development: EI curriculum is framed based on EI radar and EI ladder. Here care is taken to observe individual scores of all factors of EI, and if one of the factors was found to be high, we do not undergo training of that step in the ladder.
- Although, these are the very essence of our contributions to the field of EI, we submit here that they are not exhaustive. In terms of finality in refinement of our postulates and propositions, further studies are necessary to advance the frontier of knowledge in the field.

This book also concludes that EI is the aggregation of the innate characteristics and the knowledge and skill that individuals acquire and develop throughout their lifetime. There is undoubtedly evidence-identifying EI as important in predicting personal and school success, and this has potential implications for students. However, educators need to be cautious in making claims until more research evidence is available from the scientific community. This book highlights to develop students in ways that are personally meaningful, as well as constructive and meaningful for society. Education, training, development, and counseling approaches aimed at developing personal excellence in individuals will provide a widely applicable model for making the world a better place as Maslow (1999) put it, by improving individual health emotionally.

In efforts to create institutional success, it seems that outstanding leaders remain mindful that healthy and successful organizations and cultures are not possible without the individual health of the people who comprise them. By focusing on excellence, emotionally intelligent students will help the country in healthy ways—raising the Human Development Index of nations and developing the human capital (HC).

A prerequisite for success in future competition and life is that students are to be engaged and motivated. The fundamentals lie in embracing all factors. It means that the ability to use student potentials becomes more evident. It means taking responsibility for the further development of the school and college curricula. It means that decisions need to be taken when it happens, at the level where it happens by navigating.

This book attempts to identify critical determinants of EI for college and school students along with corporate and general public representing the diversity of nations. Such a study will be useful in providing feedbacks about the potentials and limitations of each individual to the parents, teachers/professors, and other stakeholders.

Even though the primary attention of education is academic performance, there is simply too much convincing evidence that schools and colleges should not and cannot neglect the development of EI skills. Emerging trends necessitate new studies and applied research on the contributions of the emotional mind and the emotional domain of learning. Building healthy, strong willed, and productive students requires the active and intentional development of EI skills and competencies as normal and integral part of the process of education. To achieve this balanced perspective, the youth framework model of Bar-On (1997a) is reviewed.

The idea behind our total approach is that the students will grow into what they are capable of becoming, provided we create awareness in them about EI, and the school/college environment and parents create the proper conditions for that growth of intelligence. This book is not aimed at determining whether individual student becomes effective or ineffective. It is about exploring the linkages and relationships between EI and its constituent determinants. It is also about formulating EI radars and ladders to facilitate competency development.

Bar-On (1997b) outlined that EI scores can be measured by using five composite scales decomposed into fifteen subscale scores such as intrapersonal Emotional Quotient Inventory (EQ-i, comprising self-regard, emotional self-awareness, assertiveness, independence, and self-actualization), interpersonal EQ-i (comprising empathy, social responsibility, and interpersonal relationship), stress management EQ-i (comprising stress tolerance and impulse control), adaptability EQ-i (comprising reality testing, flexibility, and problem-solving), and general mood EQ-i (comprising optimism and happiness).

This book focuses on the factors of EI. It describes the case of Susan who tries to overcome emotional intelligence in daily living. She actually had a good life in comparison to the underprivileged and malnourished and did not realize till quite later on in her life journey. This book discusses the four clusters formed using cluster analysis that led to the formation of EI radar, which along with EI competency ladder created the basis for EI curricula. EI radar with EI ladder leads to the formation of EI curricula that is proactive in providing feedback and an effective tool in coaching and counseling. This book concludes that EI is the aggregation of the innate characteristics and the knowledge and skills that individuals acquire and develop throughout their lifetime. There is undoubtedly evidence-identifying EI as important in predicting personal and school/college success, and this has potential implications for students. However, educators need to be cautious in making claims until more research evidences are available from the EI community. The study highlighted to develop students in ways that are personally meaningful, as well as constructive and meaningful for society. Education, training, and counseling approaches aimed at developing personal excellence in individuals will provide a widely applicable model for making the world a better place. Even though the primary attention of education is academic performance, there is simply too much convincing evidence that colleges should not and cannot neglect the development of EI skills. Emerging trends necessitate new studies and applied research on the contributions of the emotional mind and the emotional domain of learning. Building healthy and productive students requires the active and intentional development of EI skills and competencies as normal and integral part of the process of education. Thus, the final purpose of this book is to create a platform that can practically be used to measure EI and its significant factors and thus provide guidance in the development of youths pursuing career-oriented studies to build the nation. Hope this book may be utilized to understand EI and will make use of the radar and the competency ladder.

SIGNIFICANCE OF THE BOOK

This book targets college students, as they are the future human capital (HC) of the nation. HC represents the knowledge, skills, and abilities that make it possible for people to do their jobs. Human capital development (HCD) is about recruiting, supporting, and investing in people, using a variety of means, including education, training, coaching, mentoring, internships, organizational development, and human resource management (LISC 2008). Students can be developed through EI—first step being testing their existing level of EQ and then building on their skills and abilities through EI. Schultz defined HC theory as "the knowledge and skills that people acquire through education and training as being a form of capital, and this capital is a product of deliberate investment that yields returns" (Nafukho et al., 2004). In 1961, Schultz wrote, "Although it is obvious that people acquire useful skills and knowledge, it is not so obvious that these skills and knowledge are a form of capital, or that this capital is in substantial part a product of deliberate investment." Schultz called the body of knowledge that sought to describe, explain, and validate this phenomenon HC theory (as cited in Baptiste, 2001). According to Becker (1993), schooling, training courses, medical care, and lectures on personal improvement are all capital too because these "improve health, raise earnings, or add to a person's appreciation of literature over his or her lifetime." Thus, Becker argued that these are investments in capital—HC. The formation of HC takes place by developing intelligent individuals in colleges, who will be capable decision makers and leaders. Thorndike (1920) divided intelligent activity into three components: social intelligence, concrete intelligence, and abstract intelligence.

Beyond social intelligence, Gardner (1983) proposed his theory of multiple intelligences, which included both interpersonal and intrapersonal intelligences. He attributed both these domains to social intelligence. Gardner defined them as follows: Interpersonal intelligence is the ability to understand other people: what motivates them, how they work, how to work cooperatively with them. Intrapersonal Intelligence is a correlative ability turned inward. It is a capacity to form an accurate, veridical model of self and to be able to use that model to operate effectively in life.

The concepts of EI are stated to be based on extensive scientific and research evidence. However, little research has been conducted in the context of educational institutions (the building blocks of HC). The corporate applications are largely case descriptions and tend to be based on derivative arguments. Therefore, it is attempted here in this book to substantiate EI applications in professional colleges of a pluralistic country like India and the United States of America. The idea that EI may lead to personal and professional success has generated a great deal of excitement among the general public, managers, academics, and business consultants alike. According to popular opinion and workplace testimonials, EI affects individual performance. EI proponents claim that increasing emotional intelligence can do everything from improving the general quality of work life to enhancing career success. Although much work has gone into the development and application of EI in people's lives, there has been a general lack of independent, systematic analysis of the claim that EI increases individual performance over and above the level expected from traditional notions of general intelligence. The idea behind our total approach is that the students will grow into what they are capable of becoming, provided we create awareness in them about EI and the school environment and parents create the proper conditions for that growth of intelligence. This study also concludes that EI is the aggregation of the innate characteristics and the knowledge and skills that individuals acquire and develop throughout their lifetime. There is undoubtedly evidence-identifying EI as important in predicting personal and school success, and this has potential implications for students. However, educators need to be cautious in making claims until more research evidences are available from the EI community. The study highlighted to develop students in ways that are personally meaningful, as well as constructive and meaningful for society. Education, training, and counseling approaches aimed at developing personal excellence in individuals will provide a widely applicable model for making the world a better place.

Even though the primary attention of education is academic performance, there is simply too much convincing evidence that schools and colleges should not and cannot neglect the development of EI skills. Emerging trends necessitate new studies and applied research on the contributions of the emotional mind and the emotional domain of learning. Building healthy and productive students requires the active and intentional development of EI skills and competencies as normal and integral part of the process of education. Thus, the final purpose of the research is to create a platform that can practically be used to measure EI and its significant factors and thus provide guidance in the development of youths pursuing career-oriented studies to build modern nations. Learnings from Lori Palatnik, Lana Milov, Sadguru Jaggi Vasudev, Late Nelson Darwin, Daniel Goleman, Reuven Bar-On, Robert Emmerling, Gary Low, and Richard Hammett are treasured and implemented.

ORGANIZATION OF THE BOOK

Chapter 1 introduces EI as an important field of study in organizational behavior and discusses concept of mood and emotions. The roles of emotion in organizational health/emotional health are presented and types of emotions are discussed. Lastly, the relationship between mood and emotion and concepts of IQ, EQ, and SQ are presented.

Chapter 2 presents the history and evolution of EI in different stages. The various definitions and chronological display of EI with emphasis on the emotional learning programs are explained.

Chapter 3 briefly reviews the models and measures of EI. A critical analysis of these models, along with various measurement tools, is also presented. A comparative evaluation of the measures of EI is carried out and discussed.

The rationale of Bar-On's model and measure is discussed in Chapter 4. The various factors that affect EI as presented in literature are also discussed in this chapter.

The applications of EI are outlined in Chapter 5. Emphasizing on the benefits of EI, applications of EI in various sectors like managerial effectiveness, child development, workplace effectiveness, social sector, parenting, and personality development are elaborated.

Chapter 6 describes the ways to enhance EI through focus on strategies for self-independence and self-regulation.

Chapter 7 presents the strategies to enhance assertiveness, various tools even if a person is shy, and then emphasizes on how to become more empathetic.

Similarly, strategies to build social skills and understand self-awareness along with strategies to enhance stress tolerance and self-esteem are discussed in Chapters 8 and 9.

Chapter 10 provides a comparative evaluation of impulse control and flexibility.

Chapter 11 introduces the concept of problem-solving ability and optimism. Anger management training, early identification and intervention are contents in this last chapter of this book.

This book presents the story of Susan whose seemingly complex life and thought process made herself miserable. Would she be able to bring herself out of such a situation?

List of Abbreviations

Abbreviations	Description
AD	Adaptability
AES	Assessment of emotional skills
AS	Assertiveness
ECI	Emotional Competence Inventory
ECI-2	Emotional Competence Inventory, Version 2
EI	Emotional intelligence
EM	Empathy
EQ	Emotional quotient
EQ-i	Emotional Quotient Inventory
EQ-i YV	Emotional Quotient Inventory: Youth Version
ES	Emotional self-awareness
FL	Flexibility
GM	General mood
HA	Happiness
HC	Human capital
HCD	Human capital development
HDI	Human development index
HRD	Human resource development
IC	Impulse control
FEIL	Forum for emotional intelligence learning
IN	Independence
IQ	Intelligence quotient
IR	Interpersonal relationship
INT	Interpersonal ability
IT	Intrapersonal ability
MEIS	Multifactor Emotional Intelligence Scale
MSCEIT	Mayer-Salovey-Caruso Emotional Intelligence Test
MSCEIT-YV Version	Mayer-Salovey-Caruso Emotional Intelligence Test: Youth
OP	Optimism
PS	Problem-solving
RE	Social responsibility
RT	Reality testing
SA	Self-actualization
SI	Social intelligence
SM	Stress management
SR	Self-regard

SSRI	Schutte Self-Report Inventory
ST	Stress tolerance
SUEIT	Swinburne University Emotional Intelligence Test
TEIQue	Trait emotional intelligence questionnaire
TMMS	Trait Meta-Mood Scale
WEIP	Workgroup emotional intelligence profile
WLEIS	Wong and Law Emotional Intelligence Scale

The Case

Susan was a Type A personality characterized by being extremely competitive, outgoing, ambitious, impatient, passive aggressive, possessive proactive, and concerned with time management.

In 2002, on a Saturday afternoon after reaching home from her workplace—a pharmaceutical, where she was a full-time employee, she couldn't focus. She found herself staring blankly on the road, nestled in the hammock of her balcony. She was trying to figure out what went wrong? How can she and her husband Solomon leave the apartment they had been for 4 years after marriage. Can the epic Ramayana reoccur considering the fact that we live in Kali Yuga. This is the era wherein parents were asked to leave and reside in an old age home for the rest of their lives. Can the vice versa happen? Can a son be asked to leave the apartment owned by parents? She was 27 years and her life started following through the memory lane.

1975–1985—THE FORMATIVE YEARS

Susan was precious baby born to her parents after years of prayers and medical aide in 1975. She did not remember distinctly first 5 years of life and her Mummy had told her that she was in a very protective environment with a full-time senior maid to take care on week days when she was working for the Bank. Her daddy was in Government service too and could work from home on some days; so Susan was supervisor by two adults. Being a Libran, born in the hot humid month of October, she was a 8.5 pound, long, healthy baby born with the C-section delivery. She had pink cheeks and exceedingly beautiful. She had seen black and white photographs of herself as a baby though they did not clearly depict the pinkness of the skin. Her mummy had told her and she believed every word. She loved the kindergarten and nursery she went to as well as the Jewish school she was admitted to. There weren't any tuition fees for Jewish students, although her parents did pay a token amount as a tuition fee. Along with being prompt in completing her homework assignments, she used to love to complete her cursive writing book. One of the pages had mentioned the rhyming lines, Monday's child is fair of face and Tuesday's child is full of grace. She had a lot of God's grace and treasured every bit of her being the apple of her parent's eye.

She was a pampered kid, though there was this philosophy of the household: "Earn your rewards." Her daddy would give her extra pocket money in case she scored great marks in Mathematics. She recited poems each night and practiced her school work daily. This resulted in her securing top slot marks and teachers adored her. She spoke well and was selected for recitation competition and quiz contests held at the school.

It was a pleasant childhood. Every gift item was treasured and played with caution. There was a stainless steel kitchen set gifted by her mummy which she played on certain occasions especially when she was alone. Her dolls given by her uncles in Israel were so pretty that she could play with them for days. She had a lot of friends in the apartment building and many cousins. So despite being the only child, she was hardly lonely. The summer vacations were spent at her grandparents' house, which was small comprising one bedroom. Yet thirteen members of the family lovingly resided together, with Susan being the fourteenth. Some of her cousins came to stay with her as well and they would attend summer camps. Susan had fond memories of the wedding of her maternal aunt. She had spent the days of the marriage ceremony with her cousins and was particularly upset when her mummy could not be seen for longer time intervals in the day. She was so attached to her mummy that she did not want to lose sight of her.

An incident she vividly remembers at school is when she was in the second grade. During the Physical Training class, students were playing together in the secured school playground. Suddenly an old woman came in from nowhere and students started throwing stones at her. Susan had not even touched a stone. The Principal was informed and there was an interrogation and Susan was identified as one of the students who threw the stone. Approximately five students were detained and Susan being one of them had to stand out of classroom and school assembly for 10 days. On the second day Susan decided to speak to her teacher and told her that she had not thrown any stones and had been wrongly accused. The teacher questioned the class and everybody supported Susan. Her punishment was annulled. Another student decided to follow suit and all students voted against her. Thus, Susan had a reputation of being truthful, conscientious, and perseverant student early on in life.

1985–1995—ADOLESCENT AND TEENAGE

Her 10th birthday was celebrated with family and friends as were her earlier ones. She had got to choose her birthday cake from "Monginis Cake shop." That was an era of an airplane- and a ship-designed cake—not the "titanic"—to be cut with family and friends. Party would last for a little over two hours. With that came a responsibility. Her daddy mentioned that one day she would be married and would need to know how to clean her apartment. Susan cleaned the floor at night (a maid did that in the mornings) and every weekend with her dad, would clean the dirt below the beds and the sofa set. She would also wash clothes if required with her mom and help with filling up the water at night as there were water timings. Every night from 8:30 p.m. to 9:45 p.m., the Municipality would send water for the residents of the building and the surrounding community and it was expected that everyone stored water. They would store water in household tanks, buckets, and tubs enough to last for twenty-four hours. Shortly after her 11th birthday, her grandparents, uncle, and aunt decided to migrate to Israel permanently. One of her uncles had a prolonged issue of his vision and was told that there could be a possibility of treatment in Israel with superior ophthalmologists. The entire family decided to leave and it was a big turning point. Her grandfather and uncles had been avid readers of services at the local synagogue and they had a big "Good Bye celebration" when they left for Israel. This created a turmoil in Susan's life. She was alone. Her neighboring friends had told her that when her cousins visited, she did not play with them and ignored them. Now came the time to give back. The neighboring friends felt that Susan needed their company and play time so started acting up. It was certain that Susan would go to her friends and continue amicably. However, with parental intervention, the friends were asked not to play with Susan and she was all by herself. She had books for company and had a big collection at home. She would borrow books from the school library. Things changed for Susan. She became more ambitious and tried to prove that she was the best in academics. She believed she could go on in life without friends. As is said once a loner, always a loner.

At school, she had a couple of friends that tagged behind only because they could borrow her note-books to complete their work. She had a set of values which she held onto despite all odds. An instance being in the 9th grade, there was a teacher who used to yell at students and on purpose gave lower grades to students who went on chattering while her class was on. Upon questioning the reason for lower grades, the teacher flared up and threw away the answer sheet. The students did not take this matter lightly and decided to complain to the principal. The principal came to class and questioned the students and asked for a vote. The vote was on two simple questions:

a. Was the teacher strict in class?
b. Did she explain the concepts correctly?

Of the forty five students, forty three students voted against the teacher. Only Susan voted for the teacher and she signaled her close friend to stand up with her to vote for the teacher. The class was angry at Susan. However, Susan had the self-confidence to stand up for her conviction. She knew that it was disrespectful and inappropriate to complain against a teacher who imparts knowledge.

In 1990, while in 10th grade she was appointed the Head Girl for the school and had received the Senior Scholar award for 9th grade. A Senior Scholar award was based on the performance in the year and students from 8th, 9th, and 10th could compete. She had to obtain the Senior Scholar award for the 10th grade as well and hope to perform well. She had joined a group tuition class which was to be attended after school. The hours of studying were extended and she used to come back late from school. She hardly got time to study during the weekdays. Some of the girls were upset with her for her noncooperation in the 9th grade and hence started playing with Susan's emotions. They did not want her to succeed. They used to talk to her on some occasions and deliberately ignore her on other. Susan was unable to fathom the reason behind the same.

The year went on in a turmoil and owing to her dedication and hard work, Susan did secure the Senior Scholar award for 10th grade. However, she did not secure the highest percentage of marks in the 10th grade board exam and stood second in her class. Every year her daddy would accompany her to collect the results and this year it was her mummy. She grew anxious and upset and blamed it on her mummy who had accompanied her just to collect her 10th grade results from the school Principal. She could not overcome her loss of the 1st rank for a long time and was extremely sad. It was as if her purpose and aim in life was not fulfilled.

She did her 11th and 12th grades in science. She did not perform well and could not get into medicine, which she had hoped for. She went to 4-year professional school specializing in pharmaceutical sciences and had a large number of friends in the 1st year. In that year, a family friend approached to ask if their daughter who was a 9th grader could be taught Mathematics and Science. She tutored well and had two more 9th graders to tutor. So her day was extremely busy with her own studies till 5:00 p.m. every day and then tutoring three 9th graders with work at home to help her mummy to fill water in the stipulated time slot of 8:30–9:45 p.m. left her with little time to revise daily. Pharmaceutical sciences educations had eight subjects to be taken over the year and the practical examination would be in April. May was the final assessment of all subjects taught in the year. Even though there was tremendous work, Susan was dedicated and perseverant. She had secured a 1st class in the 1st year, which is above 60% marks. Then things changed.

Studies seemed so complex; Courses on pharmacology and pharmaceutical chemistry were a challenge. She did not approach anyone for assistance. Her number of tuition students increased significantly. Her number of friends reduced and she just had a couple of them in the 2nd and 3rd years of pharmaceutical studies. Her school friends were getting engaged and married and she hoped to get engaged too. Her mummy and grandmother had always emphasized on marrying a Jew and she was not sure of finding a learned intelligent life partner. This was a great distraction in her life—a choice between choosing a career and a marriage. Can there be a perfect age for marriage?—She thought. Additionally, there was a grapevine communication in her community, if the girl refuses to marry at 20/21 years, there would be an assumption that she is snobbish and does not want to marry at all. Match makers would suggest many perspective grooms at that age and if the parents refused, that led to a significant reduction in proposals later on. In short, groom choices would reduce. Her grandmother would mention that it is best to marry the first prospective groom suggested by the matchmaker and not look or wait for a better one.

1995–2005—THE TWENTIES: UPS AND DOWNS OF LIFE

In the 3rd year of pharmaceutical studies, there were two prospective proposals that approached Susan's parents through a matchmaker and both of them were Engineers. Solomon's family had approached them after Susan's parents politely refused the first suitor. He was intelligent, gold and silver medalist from the University of Mumbai for Management studies and Mechanical Engineering. Susan's maternal aunt and uncle were convinced that Solomon was the best match ever possible and convinced her parents. Since she had a 4th year pharmaceutical sciences to complete, she had requested that her wedding should happen after she graduated. Everyone unanimously agreed and it was a relief. They decided to have a formal engagement ceremony and decided to wait for at least a year and half till the wedding. Susan was struggling in the 3rd year with both those courses as in 2nd year and then the dreadful happened. Typically, the results used to be announced late. A student would start the studies and classes for the next year even though the results were not announced.

Usually results were declared in August of each year. It was the second week of August 1996 and day of Tisha Be Av (9th of Av) in the Hebrew calendar. Owing to the various ill-fated occurrences on that date, it is said to be the saddest day. It is prophesized to be the happiest day some date. On that day, Susan was fasting and yet went to college to attend lectures. The results were out and she did not know. Upon reaching college, she got hold of the list and did not find her university identity number in the list of those students who has cleared 3rd year. She was distraught and shattered. She had failed in pharmacology and pharmaceutical chemistry—the subjects she was struggling on. The months of September and October were spent studying to appear for the reexamination scheduled in November. That year's Rosh ha Shanah, which is the Jewish New Year, and Yom Kippur went by praying and studying to appear for the reexamination. On Simchat Torah, a miracle happened.

Her daddy came home in the afternoon with excellent news, and told them that Susan had cleared both the courses and she was eligible to take the 4th year courses. It was such a wonderful news. She persevered day and night and when she cleared the final 4th year, she had secured a 1st class.

Susan started working in a pharmaceutical organization in June 1997 prior to her results in August and got married in November. She had a Henna Ceremony and recitation of the Eliyahu Hannavi, as with all Indian Jews, the day prior to the wedding. The marriage was a traditional ceremony including breaking of the wine glass in commemoration of the destruction of the holy temple in Jerusalem.

Susan had 10 days off from work and she being extremely ambitious convinced Solomon to have few days of vacation after the wedding. So to cut out the days of ceremonies after the wedding was a requisite. They had a short outing of 3 days to the nearby location and resumed work on Monday precisely 9 days after the wedding. The newlyweds were welcomed in the apartment at Ogden Avenue and things were fine. Solomon had decided to spend the weekdays with Susan at Ogden Avenue and have Friday night Shabbat prayers with parents in the rented apartment on Linking Street. On Saturday, they would all go to the apartment on Ogden Avenue, which an hour drive away, accompanied by Solomon's parents who Susan addressed as Mom and Dad. Now she had two sets of parents—mummy, daddy, mom, dad, and a lovely husband.

The 1st year of marriage was a dream and she was happy. She worked for a year at the pharmaceutical and upon Solomon's insistence took up a full-time management program at the well-known business school in Mumbai. That really helped Susan as she had long hours of work at the pharmaceutical and it was a long commute to the location. Almost two hours one way. She had deteriorated in her health and the break to pursue business studies was a welcome move. She could spend more time at home. She had developed a severe respiratory tract illness, which healed better when rested. She completed business studies in flying colors. She had topped her class in the 2nd year.

Susan and Solomon had planned to have a baby after the 2-year program was done and they had a baby girl in October 2000. Having a baby meant more work and Susan started taking tutoring classes for personality development and public speaking. She had some students tutored at home. She had an 8-week program, which had instruction time of three hours at the Jewish Community center. The program was conducted over the summer as well and she was able to balance time for her baby and home commitment as she had some help to manage both professional and personal life. Her parents were working and Solomon's dad continued to work after the retirement age of 60 years. His mom had retired in September 2000 upon completion of 60 years as a head of school which imparted education to students from kindergarten to 10th grade.

So, Solomon's parents stayed at the apartment on Linking Street for the weekdays and then would come over from Friday night to stay over the weekend. In May 2001, her daddy put in word for her the human resources for a pharmaceutical organization. So, Susan put a stop to the tutoring classes and started working in the export department. The working hours were long and she was away for approximately ten hours each day. They kept the baby at a day care for a couple of months and then hired a full-time maid who would cook for them and also take care of the baby.

It went smoothly for approximately 6 months, and in February 2001, they discovered that the maid was thieving cash. She would also steal bed sheets and clothes. They caught her red handed with a huge sum of money and she admitted to stealing stuff. They decided to let her go without reporting the matter to the police.

The real crux of how to manage a professional career and take care of the baby now arose, without the full-time maid. They decided to go back to the day care. The baby developed an infection and ran a high temperature. Owing to the fever, she had febrile convulsions and that needed to be addressed soon. It was decided to stay at the Linking Street apartment for the week days so that Solomon's mom could take care of the baby with the help of a maid. They also started the baby on herbal medicines so that there could be no reoccurrences of the febrile convulsion episode. From May 2001, the changes took place and all them were staying in the one-bedroom apartment for the week days and on Friday night—go to the apartment in Ogden Avenue for the weekend. As there was shortage of space with one bedroom, they began searching for another rented apartment on Linking Street. In the meantime, the current apartment owners started pestering Mom and Dad about handing over the rented apartment. It was a 35-year-old lease and there was a small rent amount to be paid each month. Now the owners wanted to utilize the extra space to further their business of day care and classes for toddlers. Seeing Susan and Solomon move in with the baby, land owners assumed that they would be moving in on a long-term basis. There was an increase in pressure for dad as the owners continuously pestered him to vacate the apartment. There were a series of meeting with the owners and finally dad decided to move out taking the money offered by the owners. It was November 2002 and the baby was 2 years old. All of them decided to move to Ogden Avenue for good. At that point in time Solomon began searching for a rented apartment on Ogden Avenue. Susan felt strange as that apartment had two bedrooms and all five of them could be accommodated easily. However, they finalized another apartment on rent, which was a ten-minute walk from the current one. So, there were two apartments on Ogden Avenue with mom and dad living in one and Susan, Solomon, and the baby in the other. It was decided that every morning mom would come to take care of the baby with a maid. It went on for 6 months and a couple of maids had changed. Every morning they share brief moments together and in the evening when Susan came back from work, they would leave immediately.

The lingering thought and fact as to why they were staying in a rented apartment was always a question for Susan. The number of confrontations and conflict between Susan and Solomon had significantly increased. Solomon, once in a fit of anger blurted out that mom and dad had asked him to rent another place when they moved from Linking Street to Ogden Avenue. They implicitly mentioned that Solomon and Susan should rent a two-bedroom apartment so that possible guests could be accommodated easily. The truth had been hidden from her for so many months. She had been surprised when they had quietly moved out of the apartment with no one coming over that weekend despite it being their wedding anniversary. Is there a repetition of the epic Ramayana? In Ramayana, to fulfill the two wishes given by his second wife Kaikeyi for saving his life in war against the demons, Ram was exiled by his father Dashratha.

The 6 months had been awkward mix of phases of not much communication, miscommunication, and silence. There was a face-to-face meeting of all the four adults and it was a means to sort out the differences if any. They came to a solution, wherein Susan decided to quit her work and care for the baby full time. There would no obligation from anyone as their daughter would be cared for by them. What could be done in this situation? Is the move appropriate? There had been so many changes in their lives and would this move be fruitful? Life had been so complex. Was there influence of relatives? Where there friends who were advising wrongly? Why did she have to quit her full-time position? Could there be a possible different approach to the problem?

PART A

Theoretical Aspects of EI

CHAPTER 1

EI: An Important Concept in Organizational Behavior

1.1 INTRODUCTION TO EI

The objective of this chapter is to introduce the importance of emotional intelligence (EI) as a field of study. There is emphasis on mood and emotions, and a comparison between intelligence quotient, (IQ), emotional quotient (EQ) and spiritual quotient (SQ) is conducted.

EI is a relatively new and rapidly evolving field in behavioral science having caught the attention of the general public, the practicing managers, and the academic researchers. The evolution of EI during the past several years has led to the publication of a variety of predominantly useful research papers and books. EI also connects with several cutting-edge areas of psychology, including the neuroscience of emotion, self-regulation theory, studies of metacognition, and the search for human cognitive abilities beyond traditional academic intelligence. Most research publications relate to the explanations, modeling, measurement, and applications of EI in the context of individuals and organizations.

Academic, sports, physical activities, environmental studies, and cognitive developments are the primary goals of schools and colleges. There are certain complex issues facing education. There needs to be a blending of academic (cognitive), behavioral (action), and affective (emotional) dimensions to address the complex issues facing education (Low et al., 2004). Too much focus on the cognitive dimension can lead to students with a set mind on academics. A proper balance of behavioral and emotional component assists in growth of the student.

In order to understand these issues and challenges of education, there is a need to develop responsible and emotionally healthy students. Emotional skills development and personal responsibilities need to be embraced and examined with academic (which is purely cognitive) and behavioral (which is action oriented) dimensions. EI has also been used in education to lay the foundations to build the culture of a school committed to learning (Parker, 2004a). Extensive studies indicate that EI skills are essential to achievement, leadership, and personal health (Goleman, 1995, 1997). Further, Goleman indicates that when high levels of leadership are required, EI is a much greater predictor of success than traditional measures of intelligence. In studying the world's best educational practices, Dryden and Vos (1994) reported that personal, behavioral, and emotional developments are at the very center of these programs. Their findings indicate that the EI skills of self-esteem, motivation, self-independence, assertiveness, and personal confidence are essential to all learning. They declare that education that fails to address these factors, which are the main focus in the personal and emotional domain, will fail in its other tasks as well.

However, there is a paucity of empirical research explaining the key determinants of EI, which need to be nurtured by the educational curricula for promoting future leadership and building future human capital. This book puts forth an effort to establish some empirical findings of factors affecting EI, as they relate to the goals of education and human development. The main implication of this study is to provide a coherent approach to human emotional behavior that students can learn and apply to stay healthy, both physically and mentally, think of career progression, and enhance individual and collective productivity, when they are young.

EI literature provides enough evidences that a number of empirical studies (Newsome et al., 2000; Petrides and Furnham, 2001, 2004; Rubin, 1999) are available to measure EI and testing its validity with business organizations. Human skill, knowledge, ability, other attributes, and ingenuity provide the essential building blocks of business success. Yet the effective management of assets so complex can prove elusive. The most commonly considered performance predictors—intelligence, education, experience, and personality—are, quite simply, not enough. How often do judgments formed on the basis of a candidate's academic achievement, skillsets documented, formal qualifications, awards/honors received, and employment record prove flawed? The key predictor missing from this list used to be regarded as an intangible something, however, has now been identified by a large and growing body of international social scientific research as EI.

Emotionally intelligent people communicate effectively, form strong relationships, are self-aware, manage self efficiently, and motivate themselves and others with creating powerful coping strategies and problem-solving ability. This is achieved through emotionally intelligent parents and teachers—the building blocks and core pillars of the education system. There are studies (Parker et al., 2004b) that demonstrate the link between EI and academic achievement in students making transition from high school to a higher education environment. A finding by Newsome et al. (2000) and Van der Zee et al. (2004) prove that EI is not correlated to cognitive ability relating to academic performance (cited in Petrides and Furnham, 2004). Organizations are allotting significant amounts of their budget to this cause of developing EI. The school/college systems are still in the beginning stages of implementing programs oriented toward emotional and social learning in many countries. These programs are still in their infancy. There could be several instances with the research base indicating the importance of EI for career success. There are some school/college system administrators still possessing the traditional view of emotion and intelligence as being the polar opposites of each other. This is problematic because research suggests that learning new skills and attributes, such as EI, is easier when one is young (Goleman, 1995). There are many governments supporting the acquisition of work-related skills when young.

This book puts forth an effort to synthesize and integrate some of the major findings of some studies on EI skills, as they relate to the goals of education and human development. The main goal of this book is to provide a coherent and practical approach to human emotional behavior that students can learn and apply to stay healthy, both physically and mentally, think of career progression, and enhance individual and collective productivity.

The use of EI to aid the student development process can address nonacademic life challenges and emotional well-being. Fostering EI can assist students in adapting to the environmental needs and demands (Sternberg, 1985) and pressures of the school environment. Investing in the emotional development of students also impacts leadership effectiveness, both on campus and in the future career. EI skills are vital to human performance and the management of successful learning organizations. Even though the primary attention of education is academic performance, there is simply too much convincing evidence that schools and colleges should not and cannot neglect the development of EI skills, other personal attributes, and social skills. Emerging trends necessitate new studies and applied research on the contributions of the emotional mind and the domain of learning noncognitive skills. Building healthy and productive students requires the active and intentional development of EI skills and competencies as normal and integral part of the process of education. To achieve this balanced perspective, the student framework model is reviewed and discussed in this book.

1.2 WHAT IS AN EMOTION?

The word "Emotion" has been derived from two different words that are defined as E-Energy in Motion. Emotion includes a range of observable behaviors, expressed feelings, and changes in the state of the body.

It is a complex psychological, physiological, and sociological experience of an individual's state of mind as interacting with internal and external environmental influences.

Emotion can be defined as a feeling that is private, objective, and subjective. Humans report an extraordinary range of states. There are some that they can feel or some they experience. Some of the reports are accompanied by obvious signs of enjoyment. Some have distress. There are any occasions when these reports have no overt indicators. In many cases, the emotions humans note in them seem to be blends of different states. There could be joy and happiness or sorrow and anger.

Emotions could have a distinct bodily expression. There could be times wherein there could not have any distinct bodily expressions. There could be feelings of pleasure and displeasure, of interest and excitement. These could be bound up with mental operations. However, there could be occasions of no obvious bodily expression for their consequence. Certain arrangements of sounds or of lines or of colors are agreeable. Sometimes it may not be agreeable. So, one's natural way of thinking about these standard emotions is that the mental perception of some fact excites the mental affection called the emotion. These latter states of mind eventually give rise to the bodily expression. Emotions are inner personal experiences and we interpret what we are feeling at any time. There are four main types of manifestations:

- Expressive behaviors seen as body language—This refers to the outward signs that a feeling is being experienced. Expressive behaviors can be intentional or unintentional. It includes facial expressions as well as body language.
- Physical reactions and body features—This involves body changes and physical transformations that occur when we experience an emotion. Physical reactions are often our awareness of the changes that makes us suddenly aware that we are experiencing an emotion.
- Adaptive functions and coping function—Emotional reactions help us cope with difficult situations. It's the stress tolerance level that occurs when we are under stress.
- Adding color to our lives through creativity—There could be expression of feelings through art, poetry, and literature. It could give us enjoyment. Along with that, the expression of emotions from day to day with people adds color to our lives and that's why there is a strong significance and impact of colors.

There are twenty hours to a day at one time or another we all experience strong feelings. These feelings are accompanied by positive or negative emotions. A day without feelings and emotions would be impossible to imagine. Each day we feel dozens of emotions—the excitement of going on holidays, the fear of flying, happiness and joy on our accomplishments, surprise celebration after a tiresome day at work, or angry due to the excessive workload. To summarize, emotions can be positive or negative and hence our interpretations could be similar. Given below are some common states of emotions:

a. Jealousy or envy: This is an emotion one feels when one wants something that someone else has. Similarly, when something good happens to someone like best friend, sister, or brother. One wishes that the good had happened to self. Instead of feeling happy for the best friend or sibling, one may be angry or upset with her or him due to envy. It could be similar feeling experienced for a relative or colleague in which one hopes that good things should happen to self.
b. Thankfulness and being grateful: This emotion about being thankful can help stay calm when the life is tough and the going gets rough. For example: Susan had a daughter, loving parents, and spouse. She could have been grateful about being able to afford a rented apartment when Solomon's parents had asked about vacating their current apartment. Instead of continuously thinking about the root cause of such an action, being grateful of having a roof over one's head

is a reason for feeling thankful. Implementing a mantra in life—this too shall pass—helps in most situations.

There are individuals who go into road rage when stuck in traffic. They allow themselves to become so upset over such trivial inconveniences, which is a one-off happening at times. When one is delayed because of traffic, just reminding self just how thankful one should be, as he or she is comfortably sitting in an air-conditioned car. This thought process helps to a great extent.

c. Unnecessary concern and worry: This emotion of being concerned unnecessarily and constant worrying involves many unrealistic fears and anxieties. It's fear of the unknown. The question to be asked is "Does worrying help solve a problem?" To a certain extent "Yes." We might get a possible solution with problem-solving ability. However, with worrying comes a series of ailments starting with interfering with a person's sleep, appetite, and food intake, concentration on a task, and inability to relax. Communication is the key first step, though, to overcome worry. To be able to speak up to a partner, confide to a close relative, maintaining a diary helps.

d. Disgust and hate: These are strong negative feelings of aversion or disapproval. Sometimes, people feel disgust for certain things that others do. Else, it could be the way they do things. There could be numerous instances wherein it's not the actual people themselves. Although, it is easy to regard someone whose actions are largely repulsive and not likeable as someone to dislike.

e. Stress: This is a feeling of holding onto the task when it is in process and much after the task is complete. When one has a feeling of being stressed out, it can trigger constant worrying, sadness, anxiety attacks, and nervous breakdowns. It could mean that there is more aggressiveness with our family and friends, or feeling that one is alone with no friends. Susan was stressed in life. She kept on carrying the burden of her family problems to work and it resulted in her being more anxious of every passing moment.

f. Sadness: These feelings are experienced by everyone. Most teenagers go through a phase of being sad about every month. It is natural to feel sad once in a while. When one feels sad, one thinks that it will last forever. However, when sadness does not go away, it is called depression. Depression implies that there is a serious problem that one is worried about.

g. Optimism: This feeling is achieving a balance of state of realism. It is hard to obtain and challenge for many individuals. People with optimistic feelings will try harder and make repeated efforts to change a difficult situation. Having an optimistic approach to life affects our health positively. Optimists generally have better health, age well, and live more. They are free of many physical problems associated with aging.

h. Stubbornness: The feeling of being stubborn indicates that one is resistant to changing our mind, opinion, or decision. Sometimes, an individual is even unreasonably obstinate to admit a mistake. If one refuses to take "no" for an answer and are determined to have our own way, then these are definitely signs showing stubborn feelings.

i. Fear: The feeling of fear describes an emotional reaction to threatening. There is an imminent danger with a strong desire to escape from the situation. Individuals who experience an abnormally high amount of fear often feel overwhelmed, immobilized, and unable to make a decision to overcome the threat of danger. There are signs of sweat and panic. Individuals could sometimes be prompted with a decision to fight resulting in conflict.

j. Kindheartedness: This is a feeling of being helpful and sensitive to others. It's a positive approach that brings the reward of kindness and a fuzzy, warm feeling inside. Kindheartedness is an emotion one feels when one is helpful and sensitive to others. Often people have no one to turn to when they are in need, watching their world get smaller each day because of all the hate they see in the world. This is happening with Susan. Her world is getting smaller each day. Could she overcome the situation by adopting positive emotions of kindness and optimism?

1.3 BRAIN AND EMOTIONS

Emotions and feelings can be overpowering at times. Despite being overpowering, they are the driving force of life. There was notion earlier that emotion and thought were separate processes. However, brain science has begun to realize that the brain is not an organ of thought. Brain is now considered as an organ that thinks. The brain comprises an amygdala, cerebrum, and cerebellum. Amygdala is a tiny, almond-shaped structure situated deep in the brain. Amygdala is the first to respond to an emotional event. It triggers a series of reactions within the brain's emotional core. Then, it sends signals and reactions throughout the body. These reactions alter and change body posture, facial expression, and heart-rate and breathing cycles. These emotions are important in our day-to-day living for social interaction and in forming social connections. The awareness of emotion is crucial for our motivation levels, effective decision-making, memory to "forgive and not forget" and forethought as well. Learning how to manage our emotions is an important skill that an individual continually develops throughout his or her life.

The reason why problems arise is when emotions persist for longer than normal periods. Two examples of negative patient disorder conditions are given below:

a. Posttraumatic stress disorder (PTSD) is one example. PTSD patients have powerful emotional memories that can trigger abnormal behavior. PTSD can and usually appears after a particular traumatic period or life event. It doesn't always appear immediately after the events but can sometimes appear several years later. It is often in the aging brain.

b. Clinical depression is another disorder that impairs the healthy function of the brain. Clinical depression is a chronic and profound disorder. Brain science has found no obvious pathology or physical abnormality for this disorder. Depression is characterized only by an assortment of clinical signs and symptoms. The core of depression is found in the activity of nerve cells in the prefrontal cortex. It's the prefrontal cortex that is employed in understanding and engaging with the world. In depression, there is impairment in the pattern of activity in this area of prefrontal cortex of the brain.

c. Stress is a state of mental or emotional strain. Certain amounts of stress are required for an individual, which is called as positive stress or eustress. However, in case of adversity or demanding situations, there could be excessive emotional and mental strain. Negative stress triggers excessive amounts of cortisol release in the brain. Cortisol is a naturally occurring hormone and excessive release can be toxic.

It is important to understand how emotions play a pivotal role in brain function. It assists in understanding the normal brain as well as the workings of the impaired brain. There are research-based findings providing insight into how sufferers of PTSD/depression/negative stress levels are unable to control emotional intrusion into their thoughts. Researchers have now discovered that the brain is able to prevent emotions from interfering with mental functioning. Similar to the workings of other organs in the body, each part of the brain works to control specific processes. Among many other tasks, our mood is probably influenced by several parts of the brain. However, there are known few areas that appear to be at the center of mood experiences. The Limbic system is the part of the brain that appears to be most directly involved in human emotion-regulation problems. There are several main parts of this system. There is a clear identification of some parts of the brain that are clearly participating in our emotional experience of the world. The brain is able to prevent emotions from interfering with mental functioning by having a specific executive processing area of the cortex inhibit activity of the emotion-processing region. To summarize, the amygdala is the brain's major center for processing emotional events.

1.4 ROLE OF EMOTIONS

Emotions play an important part in our lives. They are very important in self-improvement. There are many instances that prove that successful individuals are those who know how to take control of their emotions and use it to their benefit. On the other hand, there are many individuals who, even after achieving success or attaining an old age, remain in the grip of emotions. This is not the fault of anyone. One of the reasons could be the simple fact that individuals living in a close system of society where our previous behaviors and experiences determine our next actions. Some of the emotions like fear, sex, anger, love, and grief are so strong that they compel us to do lot of things. With an afterthought, individuals realize that those things would not have been done if one can think on them properly. Strong emotions are good; however, it is bad to be in control of them. Occasionally, individuals do not ever realize when they come in the control of these emotions. In the situations of strong emotions, a lot of hormones are secreted by our body. This makes it impossible for our brain to take any decisions. In those situations, most of the decisions are biased. They are based on previous experiences or inherent behaviors. The problem is that when individuals are in the control of emotion, then it's not only dangerous for our self and it's equally ferocious for others. Individuals sometimes never realize how our behavior hurts others mentally and physically. In psychological and intellectual terms, this state can be referred as having no control on emotions. Alternatively, it is described as a weakness of brain in controlling emotions. In order to come out of these situations, individuals need to control their emotions. They also need a strong brain, which can easily face any emotional disturbances. This is precisely why individuals need to understand emotions and their roles in our life. There needs to be a realization of the extent to which one is in control of our emotions. Precisely, it is mandatory to have knowledge about something; however, the big challenge is to correct them. This is true in many episodes where individuals hurt themselves by attempting to commit suicides. The reason is not having adequate control over their emotions. In these situations, emotions have ruined the individual. Most of these individuals never realize that they are the victims of their emotions. One action plan is to make our brain and thinking power strong enough so that no emotion can take control of us. The emotions can be expressed as follows:

a. Love and warmth
b. Appreciation and gratitude
c. Curiosity
d. Excitement and passion
e. Determination
f. Flexibility
g. Confidence—through the power of faith
h. Cheerfulness—there is a big difference in being happy inside, and showing it outside. It enhances self-esteem and self-independence, makes life more fun, and makes others happier.
i. Vitality—Take care of our body so that it's easy to take care of our emotions.

Successful individuals take control of their lives and are able to make the right decision at the right time. As emotion is the most important factor, it can make or break decision-making. Here are a few of the reasons our emotions are important in our lives:

1. Survival—Our emotions have the potential to serve us as a delicate and sophisticated internal guidance system. Our emotions alert us when natural human need is not being met. For example, when individuals feel lonely, our need for connection with other people is unmet. When individuals feel afraid, our need for safety is unmet. When they feel rejected, it is our need for acceptance, which is unmet. Emotions help in the survival of the fittest.

2. Decision-making—Our emotions are a valuable source of information and help make decisions. Studies show that when an individual's emotional connections are severed in the brain, one cannot make even simple decisions. What is the reason? It's simply because one doesn't know how he or she would feel about available choices.

3. Predicting behavior—Our feelings and emotions are also useful in helping us predict our own and others' behaviors.

4. Boundary setting—When an individual feels uncomfortable with a person's behavior, our emotions alert us. If one learns to trust emotions and feel confident expressing ourselves, then one can let individuals know when one feels uncomfortable as soon as we are aware of our feeling. This will help us set our boundaries. This is necessary to protect our physical and mental health.

5. Communication—Our emotions help us communicate with others. Our facial expressions and body language can convey a wide range of emotions. In case individuals look sad or hurt, there is a signal to others that their help is needed. In case individuals are verbally skilled, then there is more possibility to express more of our emotional needs and thereby have a better chance of filling them. If one is effective at listening to the emotional troubles of others, then he or she is better able to help them feel understood, important, and cared about.

6. Happiness—The only real way to know that one is happy is when happiness is felt. When one feels happy, then one feels content and fulfilled. This feeling comes from having our needs and demands met, particularly our emotional needs. One can be warm, dry, and full of food but could still be unhappy. Our emotions and our feelings let us know when individuals are unhappy and when something is missing or needed. The better one can identify our emotions, the easier it will be to determine what is needed to be happy.

7. Unity—Our emotions are perhaps the greatest potential source of uniting all members of the human species. Clearly, our various religious, cultural, social, economic, and political beliefs have not united us. There are many instances; in fact, they have tragically and even fatally divided us. On the other hand, emotions are universal. The emotions of empathy, assertiveness, optimism, compassion, cooperation, and forgiveness all have the potential to unite us as a species. It seems fair to say that: beliefs divide us, emotions unite us.

1.4.1 Role of Emotion in Organizational Health

Emotions in the workplace play a major role. They determine how an entire organization communicates within itself and to the outside world. There are generally two types of emotions namely as given below:

a. Positive emotions: Positive emotions in the workplace help employees obtain favorable outcomes including achievement, job enrichment, and higher quality social context. Positive emotions at work such as high achievement, success, and excitement have desirable effect independent of a person's relationships with others. This includes greater task activity, persistence perseverance, and enhanced cognitive function. Individuals, who express positive emotions and have positive mindset in the workplace, are better equipped to influence their coworkers favorably. They are more likeable. Occasionally, a halo effect may occur, when warm or satisfied employees are rated favorably on other desirable attributes. It is most likely that these people will inspire cooperation in others to carry out a task and successfully complete the assignment. It is generally observed that employees experience fewer positive emotions when interacting with their supervisors as compared with interactions with coworkers and customers. Strong positive emotions of emotionally intelligent people, such as optimism, positive mood, increased self-esteem, self-efficacy, and emotional resilience, persevere under adverse circumstances.

b. Negative emotions: Negative emotions are fear, anger, stress, hostility, sadness, and guilt. They, however, increase the predictability of deviance in the workplace and how the outside world views the organization. The outside world includes suppliers, investors, stockholders, and stakeholders. Negative emotions at work generally arise by work overload, lack of rewards, lack of benefits, and inappropriate social relations. These attributes appear to be the most negatively stressful in work-related factors. Negative emotions are caused by a range of workplace issues, including aggression, verbal abuse, sexual harassment, blogging, assertiveness training, grapevine communication, and nonverbal behavior. Negative emotions can be a cause to lead to poor leadership. People who continually inhibit negative emotions have been found to be more prone to disease than those who are emotionally expressive. Some of the effects of negative emotions on organizational health are increased risk of anxiety, stress-related depression, substance abuse, and complaints in individuals who experience job insecurity. A negative emotion also affects family life adversely. Negative emotions at work affect employee morale, turnover rate, and commitment to the organization and create a vicious cycle affecting personal lives.

Management is being cognitive and waking up to the fact that organization's success is directly related to its ability to work productively with the emotions of its employees. It is realizing the importance of how well it elicits and sustains positive emotional states in its employees who play a major role in the organization's success or failure. To summarize, it can be specified that emotions play a very important role in building up organizational health. The employee who can effectively deal with emotions can manage occupational stress and can maintain psychological well-being. This directly decreases the level of job stress and indirectly protects the employee's health.

1.4.2 Emotional Health

Emotional health can lead to success in work, relationships, and health. Earlier, researchers believed that success made people happy. Newer research reveals that it's the other way around. Happy people are more likely to work toward goals, find the resources they need, and attract others with their energy, drive, and optimism, which are the key building blocks of success. Emotional health can be defined by the degree to which one feels emotionally secure and relaxed in everyday life. An emotionally healthy person has a relaxed body, an open mind, and an open heart. The more emotional health one possesses, the more self-esteem, self-confidence, and optimism one has. This implies that one does not frequently react with knee-jerk responses, anxiety, or panic to the events that occur in our life.

Instead, one is usually calm, composed, and patient with self and others. This implies that one is an emotionally safe person. Emotionally safe people do not judge or criticize others. This is because they have not learned to judge and criticize self. Emotionally healthy people feel safe, confident, and secure with their own emotions and feelings. They feel their feelings and emotions instead of avoiding them or trying to control them. In order to be emotionally healthy, one must express our emotions in healthy, assertive ways. Emotional health is on a continuum and it fluctuates moment by moment. Emotional wellness is on the upside of this continuum. Emotional wellness is when one has such a high degree of emotional health that one radiates joy and happiness often.

Therefore, emotional wellness refers to a state where one can have so much healthy, flowing energy that one has vibrant moments, peak experiences, and top performances. Emotional wellness is the state one enjoys as one moves closer and closer to achieving high self-esteem and being self-actualized.

1.5 TYPES OF EMOTIONS

As defined earlier, an emotion is a mental state that arises spontaneously rather than through conscious effort. It is often accompanied by physiological changes; a feeling: the emotions of joy, sorrow, reverence, hate, and love. Some of the typical human emotions include love, sadness, grief, fear, anger, and joy. Each indicates a state of some kind of arousal. It is a state that can prompt some activities and interfere with others. These states are associated with characteristic feelings. They also have characteristic bodily expressions. Unlike moods they have objects. An individual grieves over some particular thing, or is angry at something. The basics of emotional arousal are that there is a goal at stake somewhere. Our emotions thus cause us to want and not want. And when one has what one wanted, then he or she has emotions about owning it. The various types of emotions are as follows:

- Emotions of wanting—They are described to be in state of anticipation, greed, hope, envy, desire, and love.
- Emotions of not wanting—They are a state of fear, shame, repulsion, contentment, and anxiety.
- Emotions of having—They are being in the state of happiness, pride, guilt, and jealousy.
- Emotions of not having—They can be anger, sadness, and distress.
- Emotions of separation—They can be individuals in the state of being contempt.
- Some of the other emotions—Surprise and arousal.

1.6 RELATIONSHIP OF MOOD AND EMOTIONS

Mood is a word that is derived from the old English word "mod," which was a representation of military courage. Mood and emotion are words that are used interchangeably. Both emotion and mood are related to each other that makes the distinction a little difficult. The following examples may help to cut out the confusion and to clear out the difference between the mood and emotion:

Susan went grocery shopping with her daughter. The young girl had a sudden craving for chocolates. Susan bought her daughter chocolates even without her daughter telling her of her desire. The daughter was really happy. In the above two instances, the first instance speaks of a desire (a mood) to eat chocolate. In the second instance, the daughter has expressed her happiness (an emotion) when her mother buys her chocolates. As clearly observed in the example, there is a thin line of difference between a mood and an emotion. That is one expresses it (emotion) and the other (mood) keeps to her. When we have desire or when we have a feeling and keep it to oneself without expressing it can lead to mood. There are moods like being sad, depressed, lonely, happy, wild with happiness, a mood to get naughty or mischievous, and a mood to tease someone.

- Mood is a state of mind and is something that cannot be expressed. It's a state in which someone generally keeps to themselves and seldom expresses it.
- Emotion on the other hand is generally expressed.

Mood can lead to an emotion when that state of mind is prolonged and the intensity is high. An emotion can last for a lesser amount of time as compared to a mood. It is imperative to note that a negative mood can have an adverse impact on one's behavior.

Moods are conceptualized with two dimensions (Russell, 1980; Larsen and Diener, 1992):

a. Hedonic tone/pleasantness
b. Arousal/activation, or positive affect and negative affect

Watson and Tellegen (1985) conceptualized moods as having a positive affect and negative affect. Weiss and Cropanzano (1996) suggested that the two dimensions were most useful for measuring mood at work. Warr (1990) believed that hedonic tone was the more important dimension. Weiss et al. (1999) found that the average hedonic tone while working was correlated with job satisfaction. Wright and Bonnett (1996) have also found that pleasantness-based measures are more predictive in organizational research.

In case of an emotion, it is mostly expressed or rather hard to hide. It is seen when one cries or is happy. It's when one lets out his or her sentiments. It's when one is carried away. Moods tend to be long-lasting; however, they are often weaker states of uncertain origin. Research shows that the prolonged mood of a person can affect the behavioral pattern of the person. In turn, it can also affect the person's emotion. In contrast, emotions are often more intense, short lived, and have a clear object or cause (Frijda, 1993). For example, in case Susan is in a low mood for long time. If this continues, she could go to a state of depression. If that happens and she does not come out of the depression, it can affect the overall outlook of her life. There will be no control over her emotion however much she tries to hide it.

There are many instances, wherein due to lack of self-control, that mood overtakes a person's emotions. In some cases, it is good. On the other hand, it has its adverse effects. In kids, it gives rise to juvenile children. At a later stage in life, this very juvenility can lead to many problems for the person. One's mood can change from time to time; however, if there is no control over it, then it can lead to relationship problems.

It is generally said that we should express our emotions. However sometimes, it is not always necessary for people to know how one feels. Our emotions and feelings can teach us something about ourselves, from which we can learn how to improve our outlook or our views on varied subjects.

For example, being happy is when one has a reason to smile. Susan has many good things happening in her life. However, joy is something that just flows within a person. One might not have a reason to be joyful. For someone to be joyful, peace and calm is not far away. But for some, it is something they feel they can never attain. Our emotions generally or mostly are expressed from our heart. Moods can be a result of intense thought process.

1.7 IQ VS. EQ

Most writers interchange the terms EQ and EI. Thus, it is useful to try to make distinction between a person's innate potential, which is EQ, and what actually happens to that potential over the person's lifetime, which is EI. Individuals are born with a certain potential for emotional sensitivity, emotional memory, emotional processing, and emotional learning ability. It is these four inborn components that form the core of one's EI. This innate intelligence can be either developed or damaged with life experiences, particularly by the emotional lessons taught by the parents, teachers, caregivers, and family during childhood and adolescence. The impact of these lessons results in one's level of EI. EI represents a relative measure of a person's healthy or unhealthy development *of* innate EI.

EQ is not a numerical test score like IQ. EQ is a distinction between inborn potential and later development and possible damage. It is possible for a child to begin life with a high level of innate EQ. However, the child could then learn unhealthy emotional habits from living in an abusive home. Such a child will grow up to have low EI. Abused, neglected, and emotionally damaged children will score much lower on the existing EI tests compared to others having the same actual original EQ at birth. It is possible for a person to start out with high EQ, however being emotionally damaged in early childhood, causing a low EI later in life. On the other hand, it is possible for a child to start out with relatively low EQ, but receive healthy emotional modeling and nurturing, which will result in moderately high EI. It is much easier to damage a high EQ child than to develop the EI of a low EI child. This follows the principle that it is generally easier to destroy than create.

EI is a measure or ability to use both emotions and cognitive skills in life. EI competencies include empathy, flexibility, stress management, problem-solving ability, social skills, intrapersonal skills, and interpersonal skills.

The concept of IQ is measured as a ratio measuring the mathematical and logical powers of an individual. In contrast, EQ measures the ability of an individual to use his or her noncognitive and EI to get success in life—personally and professionally.

Consider the example of mathematical intelligence. It is important to note that relatively few individuals start out with high innate mathematical abilities. As life progresses, these individuals have this ability damaged through misleading or false math training or modeling. There are relatively few cases. The findings are in comparison to the number of emotionally sensitive children who receive unhealthy and self-destructive emotional imprinting from any number of sources. Parents and television shows don't generally teach that $2+2=5$. However, they do often teach emotional lessons that are as equivalent in unhealthiness as this equation is in inaccuracy. Research proves that it might be as damaging to an intimate relationship as the false equation would be to the career of an accountant or mathematician. IQ is a number used to express the apparent relative intelligence of an individual, which is the ratio multiplied by 100 of the mental age as reported on a standardized test to the chronological age. IQ is the measure of cognitive abilities. For example, IQ is the ability to learn or understand or to deal with new situations. It is also the skilled use of reason, the ability to apply knowledge to manipulate one's environment or to think abstractly as measured by objective tests. It includes mental acuteness, logic skills, and analytical skills.

1.7.1 Definitions of IQ

IQ is a number that signifies the relative academic intelligence of a person. IQ is the ratio multiplied by 100 of the mental age as reported on a standardized test to the chronological age. IQ is primarily used to measure one's cognitive abilities. Cognitive abilities include the ability to learn or understand new situations, how to reason through a given problem/scenario, and the ability to apply knowledge to one's current situations. It involves primarily top portion of the brain. Given below is the interpretation of IQ scores:

- Over 140—Genius or almost genius
- 120–140—Very superior intelligence
- 110–119—Superior intelligence
- 90–109—Average or normal intelligence
- 80–89—Dullness
- 70–79—Borderline deficiency in intelligence
- Under 70—Feeblemindedness

1.7.2 The Main Components of the IQ Test

The IQ test measures different components of intelligence. Those who score high on the test are considered intellectually gifted. They fall on the right of the curve. Individuals with a score of 140 or more are considered genius. Those who fall on the left are the less intellectually gifted and the average score is 100. Individuals with a score of 90 or below are considered intellectually impaired. The various components measured on an IQ test are as follows:

- Verbal intelligence
  Verbal intelligence is one main component of the IQ test. It tests verbal abilities, our ability to use verbal skills in problem-solving, and our capacity to learn verbal material. This part of the test includes questions that involve analogies, verbal puzzles, synonyms, and antonyms.
- Mathematical ability
  Mathematical ability is measured by the IQ test. It tests ability to perform mathematical computations, manipulate problems and equations, and understand geometric shapes. Problems included in this section include math puzzles and questions where missing numbers are filled in.

- Spatial reasoning
  The testing of spatial reasoning abilities involves the visualization of objects in space. The IQ test measures ability to move 3D objects by rotating them and tossing them. The spatial reasoning part of the IQ test involves object assembly and picture completion.
- Visual intelligence
  Visual intelligence measures the ability to obtain information from visual material. If score is high for visual intelligence, it means that one can comprehend information well. He or she is also able to easily convey it to others. The visual intelligence component of the IQ test includes problems such as picking identical things from a collection of objects and putting separate pieces of information together.
- Classification skills
  The classification skills component of the IQ test measures our ability to put items together based on set criteria. It measures whether one can understand the relationships between the items. One will need to make sense of data and how it should be pieced together.
- Pattern recognition
  Pattern recognition skills on the IQ test have the highest relationship to general intelligence. This component of the test measures the ability to recognize patterns in a chaotic environment. In this section, one will need to find patterns in images, words, and symbols.
- Logical thinking
  Logical thinking measures the ability to process information and extract deductions. There are lateral thinking puzzles. Cause-and-effect relationships are easy for logical thinkers.

1.7.3 Definitions of EI

The term Emotional Intelligence was first coined by Peter Salovey of Yale University and John Mayer of the University of New Hampshire in 1990. They described Emotional Intelligence as a form of social intelligence that involves the ability to monitor one's own and others' feelings and emotions, to discriminate among them, and to use this information to guide one's thinking and action (Salovey and Mayer, 1990).

A measure of one's EI is defined by the ability to use both emotional and noncognitive thoughts.

1.7.4 How can EI Help?

In order to be successful and survive in today's society, individuals need to have the necessary communication and organizational skills. This assists in better decision-making and interacts with each other. Goleman mentions that an individual's success is 67% based on EI and only 20% based on IQ. This is because EI components are useful in assisting employees with decision-making in areas such as teamwork, inclusion, productivity, and communication. The remaining 13% for a 100% life success could be affected by boredom, fatigue, and other environmental conditions.

Furthermore, good listening habits and skills are integral components of EQ, and carry the elements of self-awareness and control, empathy, and social expertise. When a manager or higher-ups were asked to rank their top performing employees, high IQ was not the deciding factor. However, the answer would be on how the employees performed regarding the answering of e-mails, how good they were at collaborating and networking with colleagues, and their popularity with others in order to achieve the cooperation required to attain the goals. This is just one example of the benefits of high EI regarding communication skills, time management, teamwork, and leadership skills.

EI and IQ: Which is More Important in Success or Failure of a Student?

EI is more important than IQ for the success or failure of a student in this world.

IQs may be based on a student's level of knowledge. However, EI are the level of a student's ability to emotionally judge situations and/or fit into groups by managing their personal interactions.

EI is just a shadow of the actual core values, attitudes, and quest for coexistence, love, kindness, and fairness. This essentially means that the attitudes of coexistence or the attitude of learning them had already taken root in the person of high EI. It is this passion to learn the right attitudes of coexistence that is the actual core value that reflects as EI. The more of the qualities a person possesses, and the more he or she uses them, the higher EI he or she typically has. Let's take a look at EI skills as it relates specifically to managers and leaders in the real world. Managers are often appointed to the position not because of their management skills. In addition, they possess relevant knowledge and experience. Some managers go on to become great leaders. In contrast, others become only good managers.

With the changes going on within organizations today and their respective leadership ranks, it is even more important to understand the importance of EQ. It is necessary both from the volunteer and the professional staff perspective. By doing so, along with strengthening the partnership, the individual would also have a competitive advantage.

1.7.5 Comparison between IQ and EQ

a. EQ gets us through life and IQ gets us through school.
b. Appealing to reason and emotions to convince someone versus trying to convince someone by facts alone.
c. Using our emotions as well as our cognitive abilities to function more effectively versus relying solely on our cognitive skills.

Example: Susan had a high IQ. She could reason, was analytical and logical, had a steel-trap focus on tasks, and learned new things quickly. However, she ignored how she was feeling and how others were feeling. If things didn't do the way she expected them to, she would lose her temper and lash out at others. She was unable to relate to people who weren't as smart as she was and lacked empathy. This limited her ability to be effective in team situations even though her IQ was very high.

Solomon had a high EQ. He got along well with people, and managed his own emotions well. This made him highly effective in his work, even though there were others in the firm with higher IQs. Solomon was able to consider the emotional component of interactions, using both his cognitive abilities and his understanding of emotions. He was able to influence and motivate people because he understood what mattered to them and was an excellent communicator. His authenticity and integrity made him a natural leader. He was flexible and creative when faced with a challenge, and resilient in the face of temporary defeats. He was well-liked and well-respected.

Some more points of differentiation are as follows:

d. In an EQ test, the questions relate to emotions and different situations. In contrast, IQ tests have questions on logic and reasoning.
e. Suppose there is a problem at our office. We know the facts and the reason behind the failure. That is IQ. When we use these to motivate employees, it is EQ. If one knows the facts, but is unable to empathize with employees, berates, and demotivates them, then one has a low EQ. When one tries to convince someone by facts alone, it shows IQ. However, when there is an appeal to his emotions and reason together with the use of facts, that's EQ,
f. IQ utilizes the head for effective decision–making, whereas EQ utilizes a combination of the head and the heart for decision-making.

So far as the technicalities are concerned, the results of an IQ test and an EI test may be very different. For instance, children with autism tend to have a high IQ; however, they usually have a low EQ score.

EI decides how one interacts with people in our life. It, therefore, has a profound bearing in both our success and happiness. A person with a high EI will know how to make an individual work by appealing to his emotions and reason. The most important difference between the two is that while EI can be learned, IQ is something that a person is born with. One cannot alter a person's intelligence or reasoning powers. However, one can teach him or her how to handle emotions and work them for him or her. This is the greatest difference between the two and perhaps the greatest advantage of EQ.

IQ and EQ give way to SQ, the ultimate intelligence that adds value and meaning to our life.

1.7.6 SQ

Zohar and Marshall (2000) coined the term spiritual quotient derived from the Latin word—wind or breath. Literally, it is wind that is blowing through us. It's a principle that makes us alive and humane. Zohar and Marshall (2000) defined SQ as our access to and use of meaning, vision, and value in the way that we think and the decision that we make. It is this intelligence that makes us whole, and gives us our integrity. It is our soul's intelligence. It is the intelligence of deep self with which one can ask fundamental questions and reframe our answers. Zohar and Marshal (2000) quoted that while computers have IQ and animals can have EQ, it is essentially an SQ that sets human beings apart.

Spiritual intelligence motivates people to balance work schedules to spend time with the family. An executive with a high SQ might looks beyond profit margins and devotes time to volunteer with orphans. Spiritual intelligence also addresses the need to place one's life in a shared context of value.

SQ can be distinguished from IQ to EQ. IQ primarily solves logical problems. EQ allows us to judge the situation and behave appropriately. SQ allows us to ask if one wants to be in that situation in the first place. It might motivate us to create a new one. SQ has little connection to formal religion. Atheists and humanists may have high SQ, whereas someone actively religious may not.

Review Questions

1. What are the types of emotions?
2. Elaborate on the relationship between emotions and mood?
3. What are IQ, EQ, and SQ?
4. Compare IQ and EQ.

References

Dryden, G., and Vos, J. (1994), The learning revolution, Winnepeg, Canada: Skills of learning publications.
Frijda N. H. (1993), "Moods, emotion episodes, and emotions". In M. Lewis, I. M. Haviland (Eds.), *Handbook of Emotions*, New York: Guilford, 381–403.
Goleman, D. (1995), Emotional intelligence. New York: Bantam Books.
Goleman, D. (1997), "Beyond IQ: developing the leadership competencies of emotional Intelligence", Paper presented at the 2nd international competency conference, London.
Larsen R. J., and Diener E., (1992), "Promises and problems with the circumplex model of emotions", *Review of Personality and Social Psychology*, 13, 25–29.
Low, G., Lomax, A., Jackson, M., and Nelson, D. (2004), "Emotional intelligence: A new student development model", A paper presented at the 2004 national conference of the American college personnel association, Pennsylvania.
Newsome, S., Day, A. L., and Catano, V. M. (2000), "Assessing the predictive validity of emotional intelligence", *Personality and Individual Differences*, 29, 1016–1055.

Parker, J. D. A., Creque, R. E., Sr., Barnhart, D. L., Harris, J. I., Majeski, S. A., Wood, L. M., Bond, B. J., and Hogan, M. J. (2004a), "Academic achievement in high school: Does emotional intelligence matter?", *Personality and Individual Differences*, 37, 1321–1330.

Parker, J. D. A., Summerfeldr, L. J., Hogan, M. J., and Majeski, S. (2004b), "Emotional intelligence and academic success: Examining the transition from high school to university", *Personality and Individual Differences*, 36, 163–172.

Petrides, K. V., and Furnham, A. (2001), "Trait emotional intelligence: Psychometric investigation with reference to established trait taxonomies", *European Journal of Personality*, 15, 425–448.

Petrides, K. V., and Furnham, A. (2004), "The role of trait emotional intelligence in academic performance and deviant behavior at school", *Personality and Individual Differences*, 36, 277–293.

Russell, J. A., (1980). "A circumplex model of affect". *Journal of Personality and Social Psychology*, 39, 1161–1178.

Rubin, M. M. (1999), "Emotional intelligence and its role in mitigating aggression: A correlational study of the relationship between emotional intelligence and aggression in urban adolescents", *Unpublished dissertation*, Immaculata College, Pennsylvania.

Salovey, P., and Mayer, J. D. (1990), "Emotional Intelligence", *Imagination, Cognition, and Personality*, 9, 185–211.

Sternberg, R. J. (1985), Beyond IQ: A triarchic theory of human intelligence, United Kingdom: Cambridge University Press.

Van der Zee, K., Atsma, N., and Brodbeck, F. (2004), "The influence of social identity and personality on outcomes of cultural diversity in teams", *Journal of Cross-Cultural Psychology*, 35(3), 283–303.

Warr P. (1990), "The measurement of well-being and other aspects of mental health", *Journal of Occupational Psychology*, 63, 193–210.

Watson D., and Tellegen A. (1985), "Toward a consensual structure of mood," *Psychological Bulletin*", 98, 219–202.

Weiss H. M., and Cropanzano R. (1996), "Affective events theory: A Theoretical discussion of the structure, causes and consequences of affective experiences at work," *Research in Organizational Behavior*, 8, 1–74.

Weiss, C., Oppliger, W., Vergeres, G., Demel, R., Jeno, P., Horst, M., de Kruijff, B., Schatz, G., Azem, A. (1999), "Domain structure and lipid interaction of recombinant yeast", Proceedings of the National Academy of Sciences of the United States of America, 96(16), 8890–8894.

Wright T. A., and Bonett D. G., (1996), "The role of activation and pleasantness-based affect in performance prediction", Presented at the Academy of Management Annual Meeting, August, Cincinnati.

Zohar, D. and Marshall, I., (2000), SQ: Connecting with our spiritual intelligence, New York: Bloomsbury.

CHAPTER 2
Structuring the Evolution of EI

2.1 INTRODUCTION

In this chapter, different definitions of EI are presented. The history and evolution of "intelligence" and its transition to EI as a field of study is explained by review of contemporary literature. An individual's intelligence is typically described involving mental capabilities. Capability of an individual coupled with effectiveness would result in high efficiency. These capabilities usually include the ability to reason, the ability to plan, the ability to solve problems, and the ability to think abstractly. The ability to comprehend ideas and language and the ability to learn are the important aspects of capability. In the psychology field, the description of intelligence has a much broader scope. Intelligence in the area of psychology generally considers intelligence a personality trait as distinct from creativity, personality, character, or wisdom (Gardner, 1993). Many studies exist in the area of intelligences (Bar-On, 2002; Bryan, 2002; Bradberry and Greaves, 2004; Burckle, 2000; Callahan, 2008; Charbonneau and Nicol, 2002, Cherniss and Goleman, 2001; Chapman and Hayslip, 2005; Ciarrochi et al., 2000; Ciarrochi et al., 2001; Dulewicz and Higgs, 1999; Gardner, 1993; Goleman, 1995; Goleman, 1998; Mayer and Geher, 1996; McEnrue and Grove, 2006; Mayer et al., 1999; Mayer and Salovey, 1997; Mayer et al., 2000; Mayer, 2001; Pfeiffer, 2001; Salovey and Mayer, 1990; Salovey and Sluyter, 1997; Weiss, 2000). This chapter aims to understand the concept from its inception stage.

2.2 DEFINITIONS

Sociology and psychology are the two main disciplines from which the study of emotion has primarily been evolved. Each of these disciplines has been studied extensively. Both sociology and psychology models and principles have been evaluated from varied perspectives. Emotional intelligence has its roots within the discipline of psychology. For an individual, trying to know about EI means a combination of two components: emotion and intelligence. As described in the previous chapter, emotion is defined as a mental state of readiness that arises from cognitive appraisal of events or thoughts; it has a phenomenological tone. An emotion is accompanied by physiological processes; it is often expressed physically and may result in specific actions to affirm or cope with the emotion, depending on its nature and meaning for the person having it (Bagozziet et al., 1999). Emotions are evident physically and are expressed with gestures, posture, and facial features. Emotions are organized responses that include physiological, cognitive, motivational, and experiential systems (Salovey and Mayer, 1990). A few basic examples of such emotions are happiness, sadness, anxiety, apprehensiveness, fear, surprise, anger, and disgust. In this chapter discussing emotions, it not only refers to those extreme emotions, such as intense anger, but also includes

Adaptation of "Constructing an Emotional Intelligence Radar for Indian Professional College Students" by Shamira Malekar and R. P. Mohanty, which was first published in International Journal of Scientific Research in Education (IJSRE), June 11, 4(2). Adapted and reprinted by permission.

the everyday emotions of living and communicating. An organization may use selection, socialization, and rewards to encourage the display of certain emotions that it desires (Rafaeli and Sutton, 1987). For example, Susan displaying any anger toward unreasonable behavior of her mom and dad is discouraged to maintain the harmony and well-being of the household. Solomon too showed great restrain as it was a big move to shift out of the apartment they have been living for 4 years. Similarly in an organizational setting, top management may reward its members who effectively work with their customers and never show anger. Alternatively, organizations may reprimand or terminate those customer service agents who do show anger. The role of expressed emotion, then, is significant in daily living at home and at the workplace and is part of the work role.

Detterman (1986) defined intelligence as a "finite set of independent abilities operating as a complex system." He described success in understanding this system of intelligence as directly related to our ability to obtain independent measures of the various parts of the system. EI is proposed to be one of those parts of the larger construct of intelligence. Weschler (1940) defined intelligence as "the aggregate or global capacity of the individual to act purposefully, to think rationally, and to deal effectively with his environment." Intelligence, then, could be described as the umbrella, with various elements of intelligence underneath. Emotion is a psychological construct. Emotions often allow more intelligent thinking. Individuals monitor emotions and intelligently discriminate emotional choices in order to make decisions. Therefore, emotions can act as a source of information for decision-making. Epstein, instead, views emotions not as a way of thinking but as a consequence of preconscious automatic thinking. Mayer and Salovey (1993) have argued that they could have labeled the concept as "Emotional Competence" but preferred the term "Emotional Intelligence." Their use of the word "intelligence" implied that the process referred to a mental aptitude since they have conceptualized it as such. Therefore, in making such a distinction, they wished to convey that intellectual problems might either contain or require emotional information in order to make rational decisions.

It was in 1995, Goleman popularized the concept of EI through his book.

Some of the important definitions of EI as propounded by various pioneering authors are as follows:

- Goleman (1998) defined EI as the capacity for recognizing our own feelings and those of others, for motivating ourselves, and for managing emotions well in us and in our relationships. EI describes abilities distinct from, but complementary to, academic intelligence or the purely cognitive capacities measured by IQ.
- Mayer and Salovey (1997) defined EI as the ability to perceive emotions, to access and generate emotions so as to assist thought, to understand emotions and emotional knowledge, and to reflectively regulate emotions so as to promote emotional and intellectual growth.
- Bar-On (2004) defined EI as a cross-section of interrelated emotional and social competencies that determine how effectively we understand and express ourselves, understand others and relate with them, and cope with daily demands and pressures.
- Martinez (1997) stated that emotional intelligence is an array of noncognitive skills, capabilities, and competencies that influence a person's ability to cope with environmental demands and pressures.
- Freedman (1998) stated that emotional intelligence is a way of recognizing, understanding and choosing how we think, feel, and act.

The above definitions explain the same aspect of EI, which shapes our interaction with others and our understanding of self. It defines how and what is learned, and it allows us to set priorities, it determines the majority of our daily actions. However, there are some distinctions observed in these definitions. Goleman's definition denotes EI as the combination of factors that allow a person to feel, be motivated, regulate mood,

Table 2.1 Different Perspectives of EI

Perspective	Primary focus	Authors
Cognitive	* EI has been operationalized as a set of abilities. * EI is related to verbal intelligence at a low to moderate level.	Mayer and Salovey (1997) Mayer and Geher (1996) Schutte et al. (1998) Salovey et al. (1995) Jordan et al. (2002) Wong and Law (2002)
Noncognitive	* EI has been conceptualized as traits and abilities related to emotional and social knowledge.	Cooper (1998) Bar-On (1997a) Goleman (1998) Gardner and Stough (2002)
Neurological	* Research in neurobiology has divided the brain into "rational mind" and "primitive mind." * Planning, learning, and remembering are the parts of the rational mind centered in the neocortex. Primitive mind is the emotional mind associated with basic emotions such as anger, fear, and surprise. Harmony between emotional and rational mind constitutes EI.	Berry (2002) Sen (2008)

control impulse, persist in the face of frustration, and thereby succeed in day-to-day living. His definition includes a number of personality and social factors. EI is a different way of being smart. Salovey and Mayer mention EI as the ability to monitor one's own and others' feelings and emotions, to discriminate among them, and to use this information to guide one's thinking and actions. The authors consider EI as a process-oriented trait. According to the Salovey and Mayer's definition that uses the Bar-On's broader definition makes no direct reference to the acquisition, retrieval and instantiation through appropriate behaviors of emotional information (Zeidner et al., 2003). Bar-On appears to exclude cognitive skills, which might contribute to emotional management although he apparently lists cognitive abilities such as problem-solving and reality testing as components of EI. Conversely, Bar-On's definition emphasizes the need on adaptation to environmental demands. Martinez deals with EI as an array of noncognitive skills with which one can cope life's pressure with ease as a person is well equipped to face the challenges ahead. Freedman stated that EI is a way of recognizing, understanding, and choosing how we think, feel, and act, which meant one could fully recognize and choose our behavior. There is continuing controversy over how to define and measure EI, and how significant the concept of EI is in predicting various aspects of success in life.

Broadly speaking, EI is a synthesis of emotions and intelligence and is the degree to which an individual can use his or her emotions, feelings, and moods, and those of others, in a way that helps that person adapt and navigate effectively. EI is a combination of intellectual and cultural capital of an individual. It is a psychological state of mind whose core focus is to create and sustain trust, loyalty, commitment, productivity, and innovation in an individual. We make an attempt here to examine some of these definitions available in literature from three different perspectives: cognitive, noncognitive, and neurological.

As depicted in Table 2.1, different perspectives of EI (Sharma, 2008) are as follows:

a. *Cognitive perspective* considers EI as a set of abilities related to verbal intelligence.
b. *Noncognitive perspective* considers EI as a set of traits related to emotional and social knowledge.
c. *Neurological perspective* considers EI to be associated with both the primitive mind and rational mind.

2.3 EVOLUTION OF EI

EI as a field of extensive study and research emerged after Goleman's publication in 1995. But EI has its generic origin before. In the seventeenth century, Descartes discussed that a person's intelligence was responsible for creating knowledge and validating the truth (PSI Psychology tutor, 2007). He recognized that intelligence is at least partly responsible for what it is that makes each person unique. He also maintained that mind and body are separate entities. In the same century, another English philosopher Locke believed that a person was born as a blank slate and that intelligence was the ability to reason built up over time by interactions with the environment (PSI Psychology tutor, 2007).

Spinoza (1677) believed for the measurement of cognition, emotion and intellect together. He asserted that cognition comprised of emotional cognition, intellectual cognition, and some level of intuition. Despite the introduction of the concept of "intelligence," there was low empirical evidence and introduction of psychometric testing.

Section 2.4 summarizes the sequence of evolution from 1900 to 2008 chronologically.

We can classify the sequence of continuous evolution of EI in four distinct phases explained in a time frame as depicted in Fig 2.1.

2.3.1 Phase I (1900–1919) Theme: Development of IQ Measurement Scale

This phase is the nascent stage of the development of intelligences. In this phase, "intelligence" was explained.

Intelligence testing began in earnest in France, when in 1904 psychologists Binet and Simon were commissioned by the French government to find a method to differentiate between children who were intellectually normal and those who were inferior. The purpose was to put the intellectually inferior students into special schools, where they would receive more individual attention. This led to the development of the Simon-Binet Scale. In the test children are allowed to do tasks such as follow commands, copy patterns, name objects, and put things in order or arrange them properly. Binet gave the test to Paris school children and created a standard based on his data. For example, if 70% of 8-year-olds could pass a particular test, then success on the test represented the 8-year-old level of intelligence. Following Binet's work, the phrase "intelligence quotient" or "IQ" entered the vocabulary. The tests were soon available for widespread use. In 1916, Stanford and Binet modified the IQ test with the exclusion and inclusion of relevant components. Thurstone (cited in Gardner, 1983) believed the existence of a small set of primary mental factors that are relatively independent of one another and are measured by different tasks. Thurstone nominated seven such factors: verbal comprehension, word fluency, numerical fluency, spatial visualization, associative memory, perceptual speed, and reasoning. Identifying these flaws in IQ, psychologists researched further.

2.3.2 Phase II (1920–1972) Theme: Expansion of the Theories of Intelligence

This was the developmental phase of intelligences. This phase markedly showed a lot of research conducted on the development of IQ, introduction of personality parameters, and social intelligences. The roots of EI can be traced back to the concept of "social intelligence" coined by Thorndike (1920) to refer to the ability to understand, manage, and act wisely in human relations. Thorndike (1920) first identified the concept of "social intelligence" (SI). He defined SI as the ability to understand and manage men and women and boys and girls to act wisely in human relations. From 1920 through 1937 (cited in Thorndike and Stein, 1937), seven of the ten published studies discussed a measure of SI known as the George Washington SI test, developed by Moss and his colleagues at George Washington University. Thorndike and Stein (1937) criticized the test as there was no data to indicate impact of personality, interests, or academic/abstract intelligence from the social intelligence scores. Also, the test was found to be heavily loaded in verbal ability resulting in its similarity to the existing measures of academic intelligence. These 17 years were the only serious attempt to measure social intelligence, which unfortunately did not succeed.

Wechsler (1940) observed the impact of noncognitive and cognitive factors of what he referred as "Intelligent behavior." Maslow (1954) wrote about the enhancement of emotional, physical, spiritual, and mental strengths in people. His work set to life the "Human Potential Movement" and to the development of many new sciences of human capacity in the 1970s and 1980s. Cattell and Butcher (1968) tried to predict both school achievement and creativity from ability, personality, and motivation. The authors succeeded in showing the importance of personality in academic achievement. Studies to more fully assess the relative importance of both ability and personality variables in the prediction of academic achievement were also conducted. There was identification of cognitive as well as noncognitive behavior. Researchers succeeded in showing the importance of personality in academic achievement. One contribution of this stage: Ability as well as trait personality dimensions are responsible for individual's success.

2.3.3 Phase III (1973–1995) Theme: Development of EI

There is an identification of limitations of cognitive abilities in an individual in this phase. Existence of multiple intelligences in an individual is identified and concluded with the introduction of EI. McClelland (1973) launched an entirely new approach to the measure of intelligence proposing a set of specific competencies, including empathy, self-discipline, and initiative. Research in seventies focused on high academic achievement and the reasons for the same. Gardner (1983) discussed intelligence to entail a set of skills of problem-solving—enabling the individual to genuine problems or difficulties that one encounters when appropriate to create an effective product. It must also entail the potential for finding or creating problems that lays the groundwork for the acquisition of new knowledge. Gardner (1983) includes intrapersonal and interpersonal intelligences in his theory of multiple intelligences. Intrapersonal intelligence includes attributes leading to self-understanding and mastery with awareness of feelings, psychological insight, ability to manage emotions, and behave in ways that meet ones needs and goals (Gardner, 1983, 1993; Goleman, 1995). Interpersonal intelligence involves social competence with the capacity for empathy, altruism, and emotional intimacy (Gardner, 1983, 1993; Goleman, 1995).

Gardner (1983) proposed that there are seven primary types of intelligence: verbal, mathematical-logical, spatial, kinesthetic, musical, intraphysical abilities (insight, inner contentment), and personal intelligences. The personal intelligences consist of interpersonal intelligence, the ability to understand others, and intrapersonal intelligence, the ability to develop an accurate model of the self and use it effectively to operate throughout life. Gardner (1983) noted that the IQ tests have predictive power for success in schooling but relatively lesser predictive power outside the school context. This is applicable especially when more potent factors like social and economic background are considered. Gardner introduced his theory of the various frames of mind, which opened doors to other theories.

Triarchic theory as developed by Sternberg (1985) stated that in addition to academic performance, adaptation to environment, experience, and the internal world of the individual were equally important. The triarchic theory comprised the following:

a. Intelligence and the internal world of the individual
b. Intelligence and experience
c. Adaptation to the environment

Each part of the theory highlights a different aspect of intelligence that is applicable to different groups as well as individuals. Sternberg's theory also included the concept of practical intelligence (Sternberg, 1993; Sternberg et al., 1995). Practical intelligence depends on tacit knowledge that is acquired through day-to-day practical experiences and is basically about what to do in a given situation. Sternberg's theory focuses beyond the cognitive aspect of intelligence and acknowledges metacognition, including social, practical, and emotional aspects. The theories of Gardner and Sternberg were seen as expansive theories of intelligence, and with these base, researchers on EI have considered system theory account of intelligence more than the cognitive theories.

The first of the three major theories on EI to emerge was that of Bar-On (1988). In his doctoral dissertation, he coined the term emotional quotient (EQ) as an analogue to intelligence quotient (IQ). In 1990, Salovey and Meyer described that over the last few decades the beliefs about emotions and intelligence have both changed. Intelligence was once perfection, and the people soon recognized that there was more than intelligence to life. Whereas emotion was once perdition and people were recognizing that it might have substantive value. Goleman published his famous book on EI *Emotional Intelligence: Why It Can Matter More Than IQ* in 1995, which lead to mass awareness. Additionally, a paper published in Harvard Business Review vitalized the concept.

Thereafter, articles on EI began to appear with increasing frequency with empirical work on the construct along with scientific theoretical literature with academic interests.

Any science has its detractors and no science is complete without its fair share of them. EI pioneers founded their theories at different times and on a different platform. Salovey and Bar-On framed their theories as general theories of social intelligence and EI, respectively, Goleman's theory is specific to the domain of work performance. Salovey and Mayer's theory, along with Bar-On's theory, was considered for its suitability in children and adolescents.

2.3.4 Phase IV (1996–2016) Theme: Corporate Cognition

The theme of Phase IV is "corporate cognition." Cognition is a concept used in different ways by different disciplines, but is generally accepted to mean the process of thought.

Path-breaking introduction of EI marked this phase. Many accreditation programs and corporate training programs training students have been developed to enhance cognitive as well as noncognitive skills of individuals. EI is being recognized as a set of competencies to develop leaders and decision-makers. Emotionally intelligent leadership appears to be one key contributor to the development of a psychologically healthy workplace. Leaders are directly influencing morale, retention, commitment, satisfaction, and perceptions of stress. A variety of approaches are being tried by corporations to consider deploying EI in the development of a healthy workplace. Formation of a consortium for research on EI for the western countries and FEIL (Forum for emotional intelligent learning) in India concentrates on research, education, corporate training, and generating social awareness of EI. Six Seconds in USA and Javelina's A and M Texas University has programs devised for enhancing the EI of students.

Leading educators have identified and emphasized the importance of a healthy school climate for student learning and achievement (McQuary, 1983). Schools/colleges are much more than settings for producing specific learning outcomes. A healthy school/college climate is much more than an environment conducive for teaching academic content. It is also a learning environment for teaching personal and social development, successful career strategies, and healthy emotional development. Emotional intelligence skills and competencies are the important determinants to creating and maintaining a healthy and productive school climate. In recent years, low-test scores and accountability standards have been the focus of education reform and criticism directed to public education at all levels. The broader mission of education becomes clouded when effectiveness is defined solely on the basis of performance on standardized assessment models (Low et al., 2004). Test scores reflect the narrow emphasis of schooling rather than the broader mission of education. A healthy school/college climate focusing on academic, career, and leadership development requires an emphasis on affective or emotional learning as much as on academic or cognitive learning.

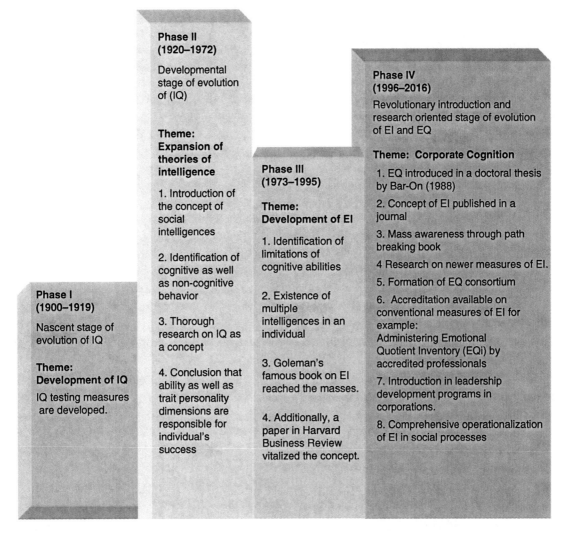

**Phase II
(1920–1972)**

Developmental
stage of evolution
of (IQ)

**Theme:
Expansion of
theories of
intelligence**

1. Introduction of
the concept of
social
intelligences

2. Identification of
cognitive as well
as non-cognitive
behavior

3. Thorough
research on IQ as
a concept

4. Conclusion that
ability as well as
trait personality
dimensions are
responsible for
individual's
success

**Phase IV
(1996–2016)**

Revolutionary introduction and
research oriented stage of evolution
of EI and EQ

Theme: Corporate Cognition

1. EQ introduced in a doctoral thesis
by Bar-On (1988)

2. Concept of EI published in a
journal

3. Mass awareness through path
breaking book

4 Research on newer measures of EI.

5. Formation of EQ consortium

6. Accreditation available on
conventional measures of EI for
example:
Administering Emotional
Quotient Inventory (EQi) by
accredited professionals

7. Introduction in leadership
development programs in
corporations.

8. Comprehensive operationalization
of EI in social processes

**Phase III
(1973–1995)**

**Theme:
Development of EI**

1. Identification of
limitations of
cognitive abilities

2. Existence of
multiple
intelligences in an
individual

3. Goleman's
famous book on EI
reached the masses.

4. Additionally, a
paper in Harvard
Business Review
vitalized the concept.

**Phase I
(1900–1919)**

Nascent stage of
evolution of IQ

**Theme:
Development of IQ**

IQ testing measures
are developed.

Figure 2.1   Stages of Development of EI

Changes in the nature of work and productivity demands of a global economy necessitate additional restructuring and reform efforts. As schools and colleges prepare students for careers and productive employment, education will continue to modify its programs and instruction. As colleges prepare students for positions of responsibility and leadership, there will be an increased interest and recognition of the importance of the contributions of the emotional mind. To adequately prepare children for future employment, we need to teach a broader range of skills and competencies than is currently addressed in schools. Schools/colleges are moving toward a preventive approach to promote student's social and emotional development. Researchers seem to agree that the best approach is comprehensive so as to develop a broad range of social and emotional skills that can be generalized to many settings (Fleming and Bay, 2004) and to integrate programs into the curriculum, not as an instructional unit but as a caring learning context that is a comprehensive, multiyear program. In short, learning and applying EI skills contribute to academic and career success.

2.4 CHRONOLOGICAL DISPLAY

The chronological evolution of IQ and EQ is seen below:

* **2000** years ago—Plato wrote about all learning's having an emotional base.
* **1677**—Spinoza held that cognition comprises emotions and intellect.
* **1872**—Charles Darwin did the early work on the importance of emotional expression for survival and adaptation.
* **1904**—A test to measure intelligence quotient is developed.
* **1920**—Thorndike described social intelligence and its importance for human performance.
* **1943**—Wechsler observed the impact of noncognitive and cognitive factors of what he referred as "Intelligent behavior."
* **1954**—Abraham Maslow wrote about the enhancement of emotional, physical, spiritual, and mental strengths in people. His work set to life the Human Potential Movement and to the development of many new sciences of human capacity in the 1970s and 1980s.
* **1968**—Cattell and Butcher tried to predict both school achievement and creativity from ability, personality, and motivation. The authors succeeded in showing the importance of personality in academic achievement.
* **1972**—Barton, Dielman, and Cattell conducted a study to more fully assess the relative importance of both ability and personality variables in the prediction of academic achievement.
* **1973**—McClelland launched an entirely new approach to the measure of intelligence, proposing a set of specific competencies including empathy, self-discipline, and initiative.
* **1983**—Gardner introduced his Theory of Multiple Intelligences, which opened doors to other theories like EI.
* **1988**—The first of the three major theories to emerge was that of Bar-On. In his doctoral dissertation, he coined the term emotional quotient (EQ), as an analogue to intelligence quotient (IQ).
* **1990**—Salovey and Meyer described that over the last few decades the beliefs about emotions and intelligence have both changed. Intelligence was once perfection and people were recognizing that there was more to life. Whereas emotion was once perdition and people were recognizing that it might have substantive value.
* **1993**—Gardner wrote about "Multiple Intelligence" and proposed that "intrapersonal" and "interpersonal" intelligences are as important as the type of intelligence measured by IQ.
* **1995**—Emotional intelligence was popularized when psychologist Daniel Goleman wrote his book, *Emotional Intelligence: Why It Can Matter More Than IQ*.
* **1998**—Goleman's second book, *Working with Emotional Intelligence*, was published and attracted the maximum attention. It brought the concept of Emotional Intelligence to the fore. Goleman's work was focused on organizations and its application in organizational life brought a different dimension to the management of human capital in organizations.
* **2002**—The consortium for research on emotional intelligence in organizations is formed and has taken the responsibility to carry out quality research on Emotional Intelligence.
* **2003**—Singh and Chadha researched on EI and found three subscales: emotional competence, emotional maturity, and emotional sensitivity.
* **2009**—Formation of FEIL is established in Mumbai, aimed at development, research, and training in EI.
* **2016**—Applications and implementation of EI in various school and college programs.

2.5 EMOTIONAL LEARNING PROGRAMS

Cohen (1999) cited that generic risk factors, for classifying a student as being at-risk, can be grouped into seven overlapping categories:

1. Constitutional handicaps include prenatal complications and biochemical imbalance.
2. Skill development delays include low intelligence, social incompetence, and learning disabilities.
3. Emotional difficulties include immaturity and low self-esteem.
4. Family circumstances include low social status, child abuse, and familial mental illness.
5. Interpersonal problems include peer rejection, alienation, and isolation.
6. School problems include suspension, expulsion, and failure.
7. Ecological context includes poverty, racial injustice, and unemployment.

These categories included very different levels of functioning and they do not distinguish symptom from cause. Hence, various programs were devised to enhance emotional learning.

2.5.1 Social and Emotional Learning Programs

Cohen suggested a three-way social and emotional learning (SEL) programs to address the specific needs of students as given below:

1. SEL can address the specific needs of at-risk students through individual efforts to diagnose and treat the problems of the student. This is traditional mental health work that includes diagnosing the problem and mapping out an individualized plan to treat the problem. Mental health professionals in collaboration with educators determine the treatment and needs of the child.
2. The second way is early detection and early secondary prevention. These programs emphasize early detection of potential or actual problems and advocate early intervention. Such programs include mental health screenings, school-based counseling, and supervised peer-counseling programs.
3. The third way is an attempt to meet the needs of at-risk students through primary prevention. Cohen suggests that advocates of primary prevention in schools can implement programs in two ways:
   a. By Implementing curriculum and noncurriculum-based programs that promote social and emotional skills and competencies.
   b. By introducing prosocial vocabulary and behaviors to affect school climate.
4. The final way to further SEL programs in schools according to Cohen (1999) is through teaching SEL to educators. Being able to recognize, understand, and learn from his or her own experiences can further an educator's capacity to, through experience, convey the process of genuine discovery and its essential value to the children with whom they work. The skill of empathy allows educators to work more effectively with students, colleagues, and parents. According to Goleman (1995), emotional literacy had an implied mandate for schools to pick up the slack for failing families in the task of socializing children. In order for this to happen, two major changes are required. First, educators and schools must go beyond their traditional mission; and second, people in the community must become more involved in schools (Goleman, 1995).

Traditional teacher training does not include teaching emotional literacy. Goleman believed that there is a self-selection process in the kind of teacher who gravitates to teaching emotional literacy courses because not every person has a temperament suitable for the subject matter that includes talking about feelings (1995). Regardless of whether there is a class specifically devoted to emotional literacy matters far less than how the lessons are taught. The quality of the teacher for this type of class especially is important because the teacher is a constant model to the class. Whenever a teacher responds to one student, twenty or thirty others learn a lesson.

Beyond teacher training, communities have a responsibility to support the lessons taught in schools. Students need opportunities both in and out of the classroom to turn moments of personal crisis into lessons in emotional competence. Consistent messages from school and home reinforce the lessons. The idea is that what children learn in emotional literacy classes will not stay behind at school, but will be tested, practiced, and sharpened in the actual challenges of life.

Salovey's research on brain development and its effects on emotional development reveal that during the maturation process, some components of emotional development occur earlier than later forms of cognition. As a result, in early development, affect is an important precursor to other modes of thinking, and therefore must be integrated with other developmental functions for optimal maturation. The manner in which behavior, emotions, and cognitions become integrated in the first decade of development has implications for psychological and emotional functioning throughout the lifespan (Salovey and Sluyter, 1997). Emotion is important to the educative process because it drives attention. It has been difficult, however, to incorporate emotions into the school curriculum because so little is truly understood about emotions, and is only relatively recently that emotional intelligence is being pursued and researched by psychologists. Salovey offers research on the development of emotions throughout three stages of childhood:

a. Infancy and toddlerhood
b. The preschool years
c. Elementary school-age years

During infancy, emotions provide infants and toddlers with their major means of communicating with others, as well as within themselves. Through the caregiver's reactions to the infant's emotional displays, the infant slowly builds expectancies regarding the nature of social interaction. So, the manner in which such emotions are socialized in early development is believed to have a major impact on the child's later ability to monitor and share emotions (Salovey and Sluyter, 1997). During the first 3 years of life, the entire repertoire of affective signals develops, and these signals are available for use throughout the rest of the individual's lifetime. By the time children begin to use language to express their feelings, most of their habitual affective responses have already been established. By the end of toddlerhood, most children have become skilled in both showing and interpreting emotional displays (Salovey and Sluyter, 1997).

According to Salovey, one of the crucial developmental tasks during the preschool years is to learn to integrate previously developed emotional signals with their newly acquired language skills (1997). Through the ability to label emotions, the child develops a new form of self-control and self-expression. Salovey and Sluyter (1997) stated that language skill serves the child's emotional control in three ways:

1. It serves the child's function of mediating between intention or desire and behavior or action.
2. It allows the child to communicate his or her emotional state to others.
3. Language allows the child to be consciously aware of how he or she is feeling (1997).

During early childhood, the role of language is particularly important in understanding the development of emotional and social competencies. Language and communication serve many important functions that are new in this preschool phase (Salovey and Sluyter, 1997). They provide a means to:

1. Symbolize one's attitudes toward others
2. Debate and act on problems both interpersonally and intrapersonally

3. Increase self-control
4. Enhance self-awareness

Finally, between the ages of five and seven, children undergo a major developmental transformation that includes increases in cognitive processing skills, a growth spurt, and changes in brain size and function. This transition and the accompanying changes allow children to undertake major changes in responsibilities, independence, and social roles (Salovey and Sluyter, 1997). The one big developmental accomplishment during this age is the child's ability to internalize much of what before was accomplished verbally, thus enhancing problem-solving skills.

When considering the development of emotional competencies as it relates to the physical development of the brain, Salovey (1997) suggested five implications for educators:

1. The nature and quality of teacher-child and peer-peer social and academic interactions impact the brain development, attention, and learning. During development, the nature of social and educational interactions plays an active role in shaping brain growth. Brain development is malleable and strongly impacted by experiences throughout childhood, which strengthen neural networks (Salovey and Sluyter, 1997).
2. Education can be considered to be a critical influence on strengthening neocortical control and self-awareness. Educators have the potential to play an important role in strengthening the pathways that lead to the integration of affect, language, and cognition. Although teaching content is important, the manner in which it is taught may be more important (Salovey and Sluyter, 1997).
3. The strengthening of frontal lobe capacities is critical to academic, social, and personal outcomes. The capacity of the frontal lobe includes maintenance of attention, social problem-solving skills, frustration tolerance, and the management of negative and positive affects (Salovey and Sluyter, 1997).
4. Helping children develop awareness of emotional processes, both in themselves and in others, applying verbal labels to emotions, and encouraging perspective taking and empathic identification with others are the first steps in developing these frontal lobe functions of interpersonal awareness and self-control. Salovey's research shows that children who show the most impulsive and aggressive behavior have the least access to verbalizing and discussing their emotions (1997).
5. Attending patiently to children's emotions and their effects as a central part of classroom processes will lead to improved personal academic outcomes. Teaching healthy strategies for coping with, communicating about, and managing emotions assists children in maintaining attention and focus during academic and interpersonal learning contexts (Salovey and Sluyter, 1997).

Childhood is a crucial window of opportunity for shaping lifelong emotional competencies. Habits acquired in childhood become set and are harder to change later in life. As developmental psychologists continue to research the growth of emotions, they are able to be more specific about just what lessons children should be learning at each point in the unfolding of emotional intelligence, what long-term deficits will exist for those who fail to master the right competencies at the appointed time, and what remedial experiences might make up for what was missed.

2.5.2 Self-Science Curriculum Programs

The developer of the Self-Science Curriculum McCown stated that learning doesn't take place in isolation from a child's feelings. Being emotionally literate is as important for learning as instruction in math and reading (Goleman, 1995; McCown, 1998). The ultimate goal of Self-Science, which was developed and implemented nearly twenty years ago, is to illuminate the child's sense of self and relationships with others. No grades are given in Self-Science; life itself is the final exam. At the end of eighth grade, as students prepare to leave the school for high school, each student is given an oral test in Self-Science, using hypothetical situations. The Self-Science Curriculum has thirteen main components:

1.	Self-awareness	8.	Insight
2.	Personal decision-making	9.	Self-acceptance
3.	Managing feelings	10.	Personal responsibility
4.	Handling stress	11.	Assertiveness
5.	Empathy	12.	Group dynamics
6.	Communications	13.	Conflict resolution
7.	Self-disclosure		

These core skills suggest a prevention strategy for the ills that plague children today. When addressing the topic of self-awareness, students aim for a sense of feeling recognition and learn to build a vocabulary for their feelings. They explore connections between thoughts, feelings, and reactions, knowing if thoughts or feelings are ruling a decision, then exploring consequences and alternative choices. Students learn to recognize their strengths and weaknesses, while learning to view themselves in a positive, but realistic light. When addressing the topic of managing emotions, students learn how to realize what triggers a feeling and learn ways to handle the feelings. Students learn responsibility by taking ownership of decisions and actions as well as following through on commitments. Empathy and relationships are a major social focus. Students learn to understand others' feelings and to respect differences. They learn how to be good listeners and question-askers.

2.5.3 K-12 Curriculum

Research and information specifically on emotional intelligence as a conceptual framework for counselors is limited. Hence, it is recommended that counselors consider existing programs as resources and individualize their program to suit the specific needs of the school. After considering the existing research, four general recommendations are made to school counselors in using emotional intelligence as a conceptual framework:

1. School counselors need to establish a developmental K-12 curriculum using emotional intelligence as a conceptual framework. The curriculum should be based on the six fundamental components of emotional intelligence: building empathy and optimism; controlling self and delaying of gratification; managing feelings; socializing effectively; motivating self; and committing to noble goals (McCown, 1998). These fundamentals lead to certain behaviors, creating new habits of mind and body. The method for assessment of learning these fundamental components is through behavior. Seven general behaviors mark the development of EQ: talking about feelings and needs; listening, sharing, and comforting; growing from conflict and adversity; prioritizing and setting goals; including others; making conscious decisions; and giving time and resources to the larger community (McCown, 1998). The K-12 curriculum should include direct instruction and specially designated and required EQ courses in the earlier K-8 grades. Emotional literacy curriculum in the later grades, 9–12, could consider a variety of possibilities including: a required course, an elective course, workshops, school counselor classroom visits, units within the required health curriculum, student-directed sessions, and integrating emotional literacy within the existing courses.

2. Recommendation to school counselors is a part of the K-12 curriculum, but it focuses on K-8 grades. Kindergarten through eighth grade should be a major focus of any developmental guidance,

emotional competency-based curriculum since the research shows that emotions are developed and shaped as early as infancy (Salovey and Sluyter, 1997). With family as the first teachers of emotional literacy, kindergarten and early elementary grades include children from a variety of emotional backgrounds. A K-8 emotional intelligence curriculum should include a weekly lesson from the counselor, followed by a daily session when the teacher reinforces the counselor's session, as well as the integration of the emotional competencies throughout the school day from the entire school staff. The program should focus on four fundamental skills: recognizing, understanding, communicating, and managing feelings; recognizing and redirecting patterns of behavior; setting goals and moving toward them; and increasing respectful communication, thinking, and behaviors (McCown, 1998).

3. Recommendation to school counselors utilizes the counselor's role as a school consultant and resource person. In order for a curriculum centered on emotional intelligence to be successful, a school counselor is responsible for teacher and school personnel training, as well as for ongoing practical support. The teachers would be trained by the counselors on the emotional intelligence curriculum, as well as practical methods of integrating aspects of the curriculum within the core content curriculum. The counselor would provide ongoing support by helping with lesson preparation, observing classes, demonstrating lessons, and conferencing with teachers.

4. Recommendation to school counselors in establishing an effective emotional literacy program addresses the counselor's role as an emotional intelligence consultant to the family. Providing workshops, newsletters, and information on the topic of nurturing emotional intelligence in the home creates a marriage between the lessons learned in school and home and also reinforces EQ messages. Topics of special importance for nurturing emotional intelligence at home include the following:
   a. Listening skills
   b. Conflict resolution
   c. Assertive feelings
   d. Expression of needs in nonjudgmental and nonattacking manners

Although the research of emotional intelligence as it relates specifically to the responsibilities of the school counselor is limited, the research and development of emotional intelligence has made great strides since the term was coined only a decade ago. It has also been in this last decade that stories of youth violence seem to headline newspapers and news programs across the country. Perhaps it is for this reason that the idea of emotional literacy, emotional intelligence, emotional competence, SEL, and EQ, whatever the term of choice, has sold itself. Continued collaboration between the researchers and the practitioners, combined with examples of successful implementation of programs and school curriculums, will promote the need for emotional literacy programs in all schools.

2.6 CONCLUDING REMARKS

In this chapter, the definitions of EI are enumerated. This chapter makes a synoptic review of emotion and intelligence and different perspectives of EI. It is noted that cognitive perspective deals with individual's abilities, potentials, and intelligences. It could be seen that noncognitive perspective has a major impact on the life of an individual and deals with individual's traits and personalities. Neurological perspective deals with linkages with the primitive mind and the rational mind. The right combination of these two minds is EI. Next, the evolutions of EI along with thematic classifications of four phases of development of intelligence as a concept are explained. Phase I discussed the development of IQ and the identification of the various flaws in its measurement. Phase II markedly showed a lot of research conducted on the development of IQ, introduction of personality parameters, social intelligences, and identification of cognitive as well as noncognitive behavior. Phase III denoted the limitations of cognitive abilities in an individual. Existence of multiple intelligences in an individual is identified and concluded with the introduction of EI. Phase IV comprised of accreditation programs, corporate training programs, and ongoing publications in journals and books. Lastly, it is concluded that benefits include positive parental influence on students who are the building blocks of the nation. The literature of studies conducted on students is also discussed. The next chapter discusses the models and measures of EI available.

Review Questions

1. Explain the three perspectives of EI.
2. Briefly describe the four stages of development of EI.
3. Describe the various types of EI curriculums.
4. Chronologically explain the evolution of EI.

References

Bagozzi, R. P., Gopinath, M., and Nyer, N. U. (1999), "The role of emotions in marketing", *Journal of the Academy of Marketing Science*, 27(2), 184–206.

Bar-On, R. (1988), *The development of a concept of psychological well-being. Doctoral dissertation*, Rhodes University, South Africa.

Bar-On, R. (1997a), Bar-On Emotional Quotient Inventory: A test of emotional intelligence, Canada: Multi-Health Systems.

Bar-On, R. (2000), "Emotional and social intelligence: Insights from the Emotional Quotient Inventory (EQ-i)", In R. Bar-On and J. D. Parker (Eds.), *Handbook of emotional Intelligence*, San Francisco, CA: Jossey-Bass.

Bar-On, R. (2004), "The bar-On Emotional Quotient Inventory (EQ-i): Rationale, description and summary of psychometric properties," In G. Geher (Ed.), *Measuring emotional intelligence: Common ground and controversy*, New York: Nova Science Publishers, Inc, 115–145.

Berry, J. W., Poortings, Y. H., Segall, M. H., and Dasen, P. R. (2002), Cross cultural psychology – research and applications, New York: Cambridge University Press.

Bradberry, T., and Greaves, J. (2004), Emotional intelligence appraisal technical manual update, San Diego: TalentSmart.

Bryan, L. L. (2002), "Just-in-time strategy for a turbulent world", *The McKinsey Quarterly, special edition*, 2, 16–28.

Burckle, M. (2000), ECI and MBTI. *Hay /McBer Research Report*, Philadelphia: HayGroup.

Callahan, J. (2008), "The 4 C's of emotion: A framework for managing emotions in organizations", *Organizational Development Journal*, 26(2), 33–38.

Cattell, R. B., and Butcher, J. (1968), The prediction of achievement and creativity. Indianapolis: BobbsMerrill, 165–166. Available from http://en.wikipedia.org/wiki/Cattell_Culture_Fair_III.

Charbonneau, D., and Nicol, A. A. M. (2002), Emotional intelligence and presocial behaviors in adolescents, *Psychological Reports*, 90, 361–370.

Cherniss, C., and Goleman, D. (2001), The emotionally intelligent workplace, San Francisco: Jossey-Bass.

Chapman, B. P., and Hayslip Jr., B. (2005), "Incremental validity of a measure of emotional intelligence", *Journal of Personality Assessment*, 85(2), 154–169.

Ciarrochi, J., Chan, A. Y. C., and Caputi, A. (2000), "A critical evaluation of the Emotional Intelligence construct", *Personality and Individual Differences*, 28, 539–561.

Ciarrochi, J., Chan, A., Caputi, P., and Robers, R. (2001), "Measuring emotional intelligence", In J. Ciarocchi, J. Forgas and D. Mayer (Eds.), *Emotional intelligence in everyday life: A scientific inquiry*, Philadelphia: Psychology Press, 3–24.

Cohen, B. (1999), "Social intelligence in the normal and autistic brain: an FMRI study", *European Journal of Neuroscience*, 13, 513–552.

Cooper, R. K. (1998), "Executive EQ: Emotional intelligence in leaders and organizations", New York: Grosset/Putnam.

Detterman, D. K. (Eds.), (1986), What is intelligence? Contemporary viewpoints on its nature and definition, Norwood: Ablex, 26–59.

Dulewicz, V., and Higgs, M. (1999),"Can emotional intelligence be measured and developed?" *Leadership and Organization Development Journal, 20*, 242–252.

Freedman, J. (1998), As seen on the 6 seconds. Available from http://www.jmfreedman.com/pdf/Six_Seconds_EQ.pdf.

Fleming, J and Bay, M. (2004), "Social and emotional learning in teacher preparation standards", In J. E. Zins, R.P. Weisberg, M.C. Wang, and H. J. Walberg (Ed.), *Building academic success on social and emotional learning: What does research say?*, Teachers college press, New York, 94–100.

Gardner, H. (1983), Frames of mind: The theory of multiple intelligences, New York: Basic Books.

Gardner, H. (1993), Multiple intelligences: The theory in practice, New York: Basic Books.

Gardner, L., and Stough, C. (2002), "Examining the relationship between leadership and emotional intelligence in senior level managers", *Leadership and Organization Development Journal*, 23(2), 68–78.

Goleman, D. (1995), Emotional intelligence. New York: Bantam Books.

Goleman, D. (1998), Working with emotional intelligence, New York: Bantam Books.

Jordan, P. J., Sashkanasy, N. M., Hartel, C. E., and Hooper, G. S. (2002), "Workgroup emotional intelligence scale development and relationship to team process effectiveness and goal focus", *Human Resource Management Review*, 12, 195–214.

Martinez, M. N. (1997), "The smarts that count", *HR magazine*, 42(11), 172–178.

Maslow, A. (1954), Motivation and Personality, New York: Harper.

Mayer, J. D., and Salovey, P. (1993), "The intelligence of emotional intelligence", *Intelligence,* 17, 432–442.

Mayer, J. D., and Geher, G. (1996), "Emotional intelligence and the identification of emotion", *Intelligence*, 22, 89–114.

Mayer, J. D., and Salovey, P. (1997), "What is emotional intelligence?" In P. Salovey and D. Sluyter (Eds.), *Emotional development and EI: Educational implications*, New York: Basic Books, 3–34.

Mayer, J. D., Salovey, P., and Caruso, D. R. (1999), "Models of emotional intelligence", In R. J. Sternberg (Ed.), *Handbook of human intelligence,* 2nd edition, New York: Cambridge, 396–420.

Mayer, J. D., Caruso, D. R., and Salovey, P. (2000), "Selecting a measure of emotional intelligence: The case for ability scales", In R. Bar-On and J. D. A. Parker (Eds.), *Handbook of emotional intelligence,* Jossey-Bass, San Fransisco, 320–342.

Mc Clelland, D. C. (1973), "Testing for competence rather than intelligence", *American Psychologist*, 28, 1–14.

McEnrue, M. P., and Grove, K. (2006), "Choosing among tests of emotional intelligence: What is the evidence?" *Human Resource Development Quarterly*, 17(1), 9–42.

McQuary, J. P.(1983), *Personal skills development in an educational setting,* A paper presented at the personal skills mapping conference, Corpus Christi, TX.

Low, G., lomax, A., Jackson, M. and Nelson, D. (2004), "Emotional Intelligence: A new student development model", A paper presented at the 2004 national conference of the American college personnel association in Pennsylvania.

Pfeiffer (2001), "Principles of Electrical grounding", National electric code and code handbook.

PSI Psychology tutor (2007), Views of descartes and locke. Available from http://Psychologytutor.wordpress.com/2007/12/30/psychology-and-the-concept-of-intelligence/htm.

Rafaeli, A., and Sutton, R. I. (1987), "The expression of emotion as part of the work role", *Academy of Management Review*, 12(1), 23–27.

Salovey, P. and Mayer, J. D. (1990), "Emotional Intelligence", *Imagination, Cognition, and Personality,* 9, 185–211.

Salovey, P., Mayer, J. D., Goldman, S. L., Turvey, C. and Palfai, T. (1995)," Emotional attention, clarity, and repair: Exploring emotional intelligence using the trait meta-mood scale", In J. W. Pennebaker (Ed.), *Emotion, Disclosure and Health,* American Psychological Association, Washington, DC.

Salovey, P., and Sluyter, D. J., (1997), Emotional development and emotional intelligence: Implications for educators, New York: Basic Books, 3–31.

Schutte, N. S., Malouff, J. M., Hall, L. E., Haggerty, D. J., Cooper, J. T., Golden, C. J., and Dornheim, L. (1998), "Development and validation of a measure of emotional intelligence", *Personality and Individual Differences,* 25, 167–177.

Sen, A., (2008), "Neurology of emotional intelligence: Interpreted for Managers", Vision, 12(1), 11–18.

Sharma, R. R. (2008), "Emotional intelligence from 17th century to 21st century: Perspectives and directions for future research", *Vision – The Journal of Business Perspective*, 12(1), 59–66.

Spinoza, B. (1677), "Ethics", In Curley (Ed.), *The collected works of Spinoza*, Princeton: Princeton University press.

Sternberg, R. J. (1985), Beyond IQ: A triarchic theory of human intelligence, United Kingdom: Cambridge University Press.

Sternberg, R. J. (1993), The psychologists comparison, 2nd edition, Cambridge: Cambridge University Press.

Sternberg, R. J., Wagner, R. K., Williams, W.M., and Horvath, J. (1995), "Testing common sense", *American Psychologist*, 50, 912–927.

Thorndike, E. L. (1920), "Intelligence and its uses" *Harper's Magazine*, 140, 227–235.

Thorndike, R. L., and Stein, S. (1937), "An evaluation of the attempts to measure social intelligence", *Psychological Bulletin*, 34, 275–285.

Wechsler, D. (1940), "Non intellective factors in general intelligence", *Psychological Bulletin*, 37, 444–445.

Weiss, T. G. (2000), "Governance, good governance and global governance: Conceptual and actual challenges," *Third World Quarterly*, 21(5), 795–814.

Wong, C., and Law, K. S. (2002), "The effects of leader and follower emotional intelligence on performance and attitude: An exploratory study", *Leadership Quarterly*, 13, 243–374.

Zeidner, M., Mattews, G., Roberts, R. D., and Mac Cann, C. (2003), "Development of emotional intelligence: Towards a multi- level investment model", *Human Development*, 46, 69–96.

CHAPTER 3

Review of Models and Measures of EI

3.1 INTRODUCTION

EI has found applications in many organizational settings and has been immensely popular as proclaimed by Petrides and Furnham (2000, 2006) and Day and Livingstone (2005). However, particularly in terms of conceptual clarity, number of models and definitions mean that vastly different constructs exist under the same label known as EI. They lead to varied and sometimes conflicting claims about what EI predicts.

Despite some recent criticisms about EI (confusion about the definition, diverse approach to measurement, overstated claims, and overlap with personality), developing highly effective leaders who are involvement oriented, relationship focused, and capable of managing their emotions appears to have strong associations with both performance and retention of high-potential talent. Despite exactly how EI is conceptualized and measured, effective leadership makes a difference to the bottom line and will continue to be important for companies to be competitive in a global market today. Because of the varied nature of models, and continuous introduction of newer models, it is observed that many human resource professionals lack a comprehensible and systemic understanding of the models and measures of EI, thus resulting in confusion about the concepts and measurement. Also there is no shortage of information regarding the validity or lack of validity of various EI tests. However, it is scattered across a host of articles, technical reports, book chapters, and unpublished articles, which makes comparison among measures a difficult task. Moreover, existing research is a piecemeal in perspective as each paper typically examines just one or two tests along one or two types of validity.

Therefore, this chapter aims at explaining the following:

- What are the different models of EI?
- How is EI measured for adults above 18 years?
- How is EI measured for children and adolescents in the age group of 7–18 years?

3.2 MODELS OF EI

As there was controversy in the definitions and conceptualization of EI, Salovey and Caruso (2000) categorized models of EI into two types:

    a. Ability model (Mayer and Salovey, 1997) and
    b. Mixed trait-ability (or personality) model (Bar-On, 2001; Goleman, 1995, 1998).

In 2001, Petrides and Furnham classified EI in two types:

    a. Ability EI (Mayer and Salovey's model 1997)
    b. Trait EI (Goleman's [1995, 1998] model and Bar-On's [1997a] model)

Three major models and their associated measures are identified as follows:

    a. Salovey and Mayer's (1990; Mayer and Salovey, 1997) four-dimensional ability model of emotional perception, appraisal, and expression, emotional facilitation of thinking, understanding emotions, and regulating emotions.

    b. Goleman's (1995, 1998) four-dimensional trait-based model of self-awareness, self-management, social awareness, and social skills.

    c. Bar-On's (1997a) five-dimensional trait-based model of intrapersonal, interpersonal, adaptability, stress management, and general mood.

To summarize, two predominant perspectives are those adopting an ability EI and a trait EI approach (Petrides and Furnham, 2000, 2001). EI is often characterized as a cognitive ability involving the cognitive processing of emotional information. This model treats EI as a traditional intelligence that is measured using ability-type tests (Mayer et al., 2000). An alternative trait approach proposes that EI involves emotion-related self-perceptions and dispositions located at the lower levels of personality hierarchies (Petrides and Furnham, 2001). Whereas the ability approach is seen as relating to the field of intelligence, this perspective relates more closely to the field of personality. A trait approach includes facets such as optimism, happiness, social competence, and self-esteem. Debates over the nature of EI continue and these include the distinctiveness of the EI construct compared with previously investigated psychological constructs and the distinctiveness of subtypes of EI (trait versus ability).

3.3 MODELS OF EI: A COMPARATIVE EVALUATION

3.3.1 Ability EI

In this model, EI is often characterized as a cognitive ability, which involves cognitive processing of emotional information (Fig 3.1). This model treats EI as a traditional intelligence. Ability EI is measured using ability-type tests (Mayer et al., 2000b).

Table 3.1 depicts the comparison of the models in terms of authors, features, potentialities, and limitations.

a) Model Elements

Mayer et al. (2000a) proposed a four-branch model of EI consisting of the following psychological processes:

    a. An awareness of one's own and others' emotions and an ability to monitor emotions and express them appropriately;

    b. An ability to use emotions to facilitate thought and to guide selective attention, for example, adopting different emotional states to enable oneself to adopt different perspectives on a painting;

    c. An ability to understand emotions, for example, why certain emotions arise in certain situations and how different emotions relate to one another; and

    d. The ability to regulate emotions, for example, knowing how to calm oneself and others down following anger or anxiety.

b) Characteristic Features

They are a conceptually related set of mental abilities with emotions and processing of emotional information. Emotional perception and expression, emotional facilitation of thinking, emotional understanding and emotional regulation are the essential elements of the ability model. It contributes to logical thought and intelligence in general. Ability EI proposes that emotions can make thinking more intelligent and one can

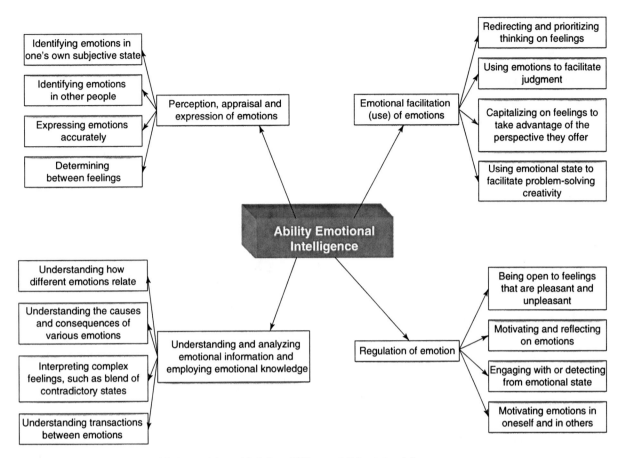

Figure 3.1   Ability EI model (adapted from Malekar, 2009 unpublished thesis)

intelligently handle emotions. According to this model, EI has a number of similarities to other types of intelligences and abilities and develops with age and experience.

c) Importance

Research supports linkage between EI and life success and finds the relationship between EI and a range of social factors. Trait EI and ability EI are strongly related to measures of social adjustment in older adolescents and adults (Schutte et al., 2001; Lopes et al., 2003; Saklofske et al., 2003; Engelberg and Sjoberg, 2004; Chapman and Hayslip, 2005), with those low on EI scoring higher on loneliness and depression than their peers.

3.3.2 Trait EI

In comparison, trait EI approach proposes that EI involves emotion-related self-perceptions and dispositions (Petrides and Furnham, 2001).

a) Model Elements

Trait EI defines EI as a mixture of emotion-related competencies and personality traits. Trait EI approach also makes references to abilities in the processing and use of emotional information but combines these abilities with other traits and characteristics such as optimism, motivation, and social relationships (Bar-On, 2000a; Goleman, 1995).

b) Characteristic Features

Trait EI approach is important as it acknowledges the importance of multiple aspects of personality that may pertain to emotion. It does not relate to the concept of emotion specifically. A trait EI approach includes facets such as optimism, happiness, social competence, and self-esteem and has EI partly or fully a personality-like trait, or behavioral disposition.

Trait models of EI are regarded as consisting of a dispositional tendency similar to personality and are measured by self-report measures. Scales such as the Emotional Quotient Inventory (EQ-i) essentially seek an assessment of individual's typical level of functioning by asking an individual to rate the extent to which a series of descriptive statements are indicative of themselves.

c) Importance

Research shows that trait EI moderates the link between stress and mental health, particularly depression, hopelessness, and suicidal ideation (Ciarrochi et al., 2002). Similarly, low trait EI has been linked to low self-esteem (Salovey et al., 2002), anxiety (Parker et al., 2006), poor impulse control (Schutte et al., 1998), and greater alcohol and drug-related problems (Riley and Schutte, 2003). Conversely, high EI has been theoretically linked to increased satisfaction with life (Palmer et al., 2002; Bastian, 2005; Livingstone and Day, 2005; Gignac, 2006).

EI has been viewed to be important in predicting academic success. Unfortunately, there are some studies that prove that EI is not a strong predictor of academic achievement regardless of whether ability or trait EI measures are used (Newsome et al., 2000; O'Connor Jr. and Little, 2003; Woitaszewski and Aalsma, 2004). It is perhaps unlikely that broadly defined EI will predict general academic success, but the specific traits and/or abilities may be important. Research supports this view, as trait EI factors—intrapersonal abilities, adaptability, and stress management—have been shown to predict academic success among university students (Lam and Kirby, 2002; Parker et al., 2004b) and younger adolescents (Parker et al., 2004a). Whereas the ability EI is seen as relating to the field of intelligence, trait EI approach relates more closely to the field of personality. Because the debate over the nature of EI continues, including the distinctiveness of the EI construct compared with previously investigated psychological constructs; the differences in the two approaches are discussed in the next section.

3.4.3 Distinctions between Trait and Ability Models

There is clear evidence indicating the importance of both ability and trait EI for success in life. Petrides and Furnham (2000, 2001) provide theoretical arguments regarding the distinction of trait and ability. Table 3.1 describes the features, potentialities, and limitations of models.

Also, there are differences between the ability and trait EI approach:

a. Because the trait EI is conceptualized as a noncognitive capability (Bar-On, 1997a; Petrides and Furnham, 2001; Saklofske et al., 2003), there are nonsignificant associations between measures of trait EI and intelligence (Newsome et al., 2000; Derksen et al., 2002; Saklofske et al., 2003; Zeng and Miller, 2003). This contrasts with findings of a positive, although still relatively weak, association between ability EI and measures of crystallized intelligence (Mayer et al., 1999; Roberts et al., 2001; Zeidner et al., 2003) and verbal IQ (Mayer et al., 1999; Barchard and Hakstian, 2004). Mayer and Salovey (1997) argue that although ability EI is correlated with other intelligences, the correlation is not so strong as to suggest that the two are measures of the same thing.

b. Trait EI has been found to portray a degree of association with various factors of personality. (Saklofske et al., 2003) This is similar in case of ability EI (Roberts et al., 2001; Lopes et al., 2003). The relationships between trait EI and personality traits ascertain the relatively lesser difference between trait EI and personality traits.

Table 3.1 Features, Potentialities, and Limitations of Models

Model	Authors	Features	Potentialities	Limitations
Ability EI	Mayer and Salovey (1997)	Four branches include ability to: a. Perceive emotions b. Utilize emotions c. Understand emotions d. Manage emotions	Social adjustment in older adolescents and adults	a. Linkages with cognitive intelligences is high

Trait EI	a. Bar-On (2000)
	b. Goleman (1995)
		a. Bar-On has identified 5 subscales:
		  i. Intrapersonal ability
		  ii. Interpersonal ability
		  iii. Stress management
		  iv. Adaptability
		  v. General mood
		b. Goleman views EI as a meta-ability and comprises 5 competencies:
		  i. Self-awareness
		  ii. Self-regulation
		  iii. Motivation
		  iv. Empathy
		  v. Social skills
			Linkages with stress and mental health, particularly depression, hopelessness, and suicidal ideation	a. Inclusion of personal factors contributing to life success
				b. Inclusion of personality and social factors
				c. Mattews et al. (2002) state that Goleman's theory represents cultural norms rather than scientific principles.

3.4 A CLASSIFICATION OF THE MEASURES OF EI

The EI measures based on ability model include the Mayer-Salovey-Caruso Emotional Intelligence Test (MSCEIT; Mayer et al., 2002), and the EI measures based on trait EI model include the Emotional Competency Inventory (ECI-2; Sala, 2002) and the Emotional Quotient Inventory (EQ-i; Bar-On, 1997a). There are a number of self-report measures based on the Mayer and Salovey (1993, 1997) model such as tests created by Schutte et al. (1998), Salovey et al. (1995), Jordan et al. (2002), and Wong and Law (2002). Similarly, there are a number of self-report measures based on the trait EI models of Goleman and Bar-On such as tests created by Gardner and Stough (2002) and Cooper (1998). A self-report measure based on the blending of Mayer and Salovey (1990, 1997) model and Bar-On (1997a) and Goleman model (1995, 1998) is the test created by Petrides and Furnham (2003). Among these measures, three tests are thoroughly reviewed and critiqued: the MSCEIT, ECI-2, and EQ-i. This study has narrowed the measures to a set to these three by using five criteria:

   a. The measure has received sufficient research attention such that there are empirical data and information on test validity available in the peer-reviewed research literature.
   b. The measure focuses on individual EI and can thus be compared to other such measures.
   c. The measure has been used for EI assessment in organizational applications and in the education field.
   d. The measure is derived from well-known, established EI theories or models.
   e. The measure has the potential application for human resource development (HRD) that can be estimated on the basis of empirical tests.

3.4.1 Validity of Tests

Test validity is an important quality. A test is valid if it measures what it is supposed to measure (Mc Enrue and Groves, 2006). Nunnally and Bernstein (1994) offer a thorough explanation of test construction, measurement, and assessment. The following discussion provides a brief summary of the evidence typically used to estimate the validity of a test: content, construct, face, predictive or concurrent, and external validity.

a. **Content validity** refers to the extent to which the items on a test are a representative sample of the content domain the test is intended to measure (Nunnally and Bernstein, 1994). The question is whether the test measures all of the dimensions of EI as defined in the model. For example, Bar-On's (1997a) model of EI incorporates five factors: intrapersonal, interpersonal, adaptability, stress management, and general mood. Assessing the test's content validity would involve identifying whether the test contained items that tapped each of these competencies.

b. **Construct validity** refers to whether the concept of interest is empirically related to other concepts theoretically similar to it and is empirically independent from those different from it (Nunnally and Bernstein, 1994). For example, Bar-On (1997a) measure is empirically related to other measures of EI and unrelated to tests of cognitive intelligence. This proves that the Bar-On's EQ-i has construct validity.

c. **Face validity** refers to whether a test and the items that comprise it are valid from the perspective of those who take it (Nunnally and Bernstein, 1994). Basically, the test should appropriately answer the following:
   • Does the test appear valid?
   • Does it challenge common sense?

   For example, MSCEIT includes items that ask respondents to identify the extent to which three emotions (challenged, isolated, and surprised) are like three sensations (cold, slow, and sharp). Some HRD professionals question whether items such as these are relevant in comparison to other questions that might have more merit when estimating the EI of an individual. Thus, the test would have little or no face validity from their perspective.

d. **Predictive validity or concurrent validity** refers to the extent one can predict some outcome such as individual behavior on the basis of test scores (Nunnally and Bernstein, 1994). For example, an empirical relationship between an individual's self-reported ability to perceive emotion and the relation to his or her performance in recognizing facial expressions of emotion is an evidence of predictive validity (Austin, 2004).

e. **External validity** refers to the extent to which it is possible to generalize beyond the characteristics of a single study or set of studies to the population at large (Nunnally and Bernstein, 1994). For example, Dulewicz and Higgs (1999) examined whether there were any differences in scores on a test of EI between managers from the United Kingdom and from non-U.K. firms. Test results obtained across sets of individuals and across sites had little difference in their scores. Thus, the measure has a high level of external validity.

It is important that a test can have a high level of face validity and a low level of construct validity. It could appear to measure emotional intelligence but actually measure something else altogether. It can have a high level of face validity but a low level of predictive validity. Scores on it do not predict important outcomes like customer satisfaction or sales performance. It can have a high level of face validity and a low level of external validity. Thus, results obtained apply only to the individuals tested under the context within which the testing occurred. In short, whether a test appears to measures EI is an insufficient basis for establishing its validity.

3.4.2 Measures of EI for the Age Group of Above 18 Years

Measures of EI for age group above 18 years similar to ability EI and trait EI models are classified as:

a. Performance-based measure of EI
b. Self-report measures of EI

Performance-based measures of EI pertain to ability models such as MSCEIT. Self-report measures are pertaining to mixed models of EI. They are determined to assess emotions within the personality framework and to assess cross-situational consistencies in behavior (Petrides and Furnham, 2000): EQ-i, ECI, the latest version ECI-2, the Schutte Self-Report Inventory (SSRI), the Workgroup Emotional Intelligence Profile (WEIP), the Swinburne University Emotional Intelligence Test (SUEIT), the Trait Meta-Mood Scale (TMMS), the Wong and Law Emotional Intelligence Scale (WLEIS), the Trait Emotional Intelligence Questionnaire (TEIQue), and the EQ-Map.

a) MSCEIT

The named authors developed the MSCEIT based on a previous test they had created, the Multifactor Emotional Intelligence Scale (MEIS).

Salient Features

The MSCEIT is a 141-item, performance-based measure, which is computer administered. This measure based on ability EI focuses on measuring responses to specific emotional tasks, rather than a self-report of emotional responding. The MSCEIT is designed to yield an overall emotional intelligence score, as well as subscale scores for perception, facilitation, understanding, and management. Each branch includes several subscales, some of which are described below.

Branch 1: Perception of Emotion

The MSCEIT contains three subtests measuring the perception of emotion: in faces, in landscapes, and in abstract designs. In this subscale, the person views the design (or face, or landscape) and must then report the amount of emotional content in it, judging, for example, how much happiness, how much sadness, how much fear, and so on.

Branch 2: Emotional Facilitation

The MSCEIT contains several subscales assessing whether people use emotion to facilitate cognitive activities. Most central to this measurement is the synesthesia subscale, which asks participants to judge the similarity between emotional feelings. For example, similarity between love and other internal experiences as temperatures and tastes is judged. The logic is that internal comparisons indicate that emotions are sensed, perceived, and processed in a meaningful way.

Branch 3: Understanding Emotions

The third group of MSCEIT tasks examines the understanding of emotion. These tasks include blends, wherein a person tries to match a set of emotions, such as joy and acceptance, to another, single, emotion that is closest to it. Responses are in a multiple-choice format. One item might ask which alternative combines "joy and acceptance, (a) guilt, (b) challenge, (c) mania, (d) love, or (e) desire."

Branch 4: Managing Emotion

The managing emotion tasks concern the best way to regulate emotions in oneself and other people. Each item of the managing emotion cluster of items describes a person with a goal of changing or maintaining a feeling, such as staying happy or feeling better. The participant must choose a given alternative that describes a course of action that might satisfy the goal. For example, if Susan wanted to cheer up, the alternatives might be "writing a journal," "involve talking to some friends," "seeing a movie," "eating a meal," or "taking a walk." Some alternatives are scored more highly according to consensus criterion as they are likely to lead to cheering the person up more than others. The managing emotion in situations subscale is similar. The scoring in this measure is difficult unlike cognitive ability tests where there is one known correct answer. There are two scoring systems available: correct answers based on experts' decisions and correct answer based on consensus of what people think is correct. The authors recommend using consensus scoring (Mayer et al., 2002a).

Reliability Assessments

The reliability for the MSCEIT ranges from $r = 0.91$ to $r = 0.93$ (Mayer et al., 2002a). Reliability for the subscales: $r = 0.81$ to $r = 0.88$ for the Emotion Perception scales, $r = 0.65$ to $r = 0.71$ for the Emotional Facilitation of Thought subscales, $r = 0.66$ to 0.70 for the Understanding Emotions subscales, and $r = 0.67$ to $r = 0.69$ for the Managing Emotions subscales. The overall reliability is good. Comparison across groups and decision with specific individuals based on their scores cannot be ascertained. Unfortunately, test-retest data on the MSCEIT is sparse, with only an overall test-retest score reported (Bracket and Mayer, 2003) as being $r = 0.86$. Although this is a good test-retest reliability, no data is presented on the subscales (MacCann et al., 2003). The MSCEIT does not correlate significantly with "Big Five" measures of personality, which suggests that it is a distinct concept. The initial research version of the MSCEIT had branch score Cronbach alpha's from 0.59 to 0.87 (based on 277 participants). The internal consistencies of the MEIS and MSCEIT are comparable to many standard tests of intelligence.

Validity Assessments

a. **Content validity:** In the Mayer and Salovey (1997) model, the test items appear to measure some skills and subskills better than others. It appears as though the test items primarily address identification of emotions in other people and objects, understanding and analyzing emotional information, employing emotional knowledge, and judging the informativeness, utility, and methods of changing a feeling. The test does not clearly tap the ability to identify one's own emotions, express emotions accurately, and discriminate between accurate and inaccurate or honest and dishonest expressions of feelings. Similarly, managing one's own emotions, redirecting and prioritizing one's thinking based on one's feelings, and encouraging different problem-solving approaches are not deeply discussed. In other words, there appears to be a gap between the model and what the test measures. If these are important competencies in a position, the MSCEIT may not provide HRD professionals with the information they need to assess and develop EI among employees.

b. **Construct validity:** Independent reviews of MSCEIT indicate that it demonstrates both discriminant and convergent validity (Daus and Ashkanasy, 2005; Brackett and Mayer, 2003; Brackett et al., 2005). The MSCEIT User's Manual (Mayer et al., 2002b) supplies information regarding the extent to which the test provides distinctive rather than redundant information relative to other tests used to measure intelligence, EI, and personality. In general, the test is distinct from others that measure different cognitive and physical phenomena. The test demonstrates a small positive relationship with IQ and is too moderately related to personality traits such as extroversion, agreeableness, and sensitivity (MacCann et al., 2004). It correlates at a low level with other tests of EI (e.g., 0.12–0.29).

c. **Face validity:** Mayer et al. (2002b) report examination of items suggests that individuals in business might have genuine concerns about the value of completing items. For example, those dealing with emotions are elicited by abstract pictures or questions concerning sensations and emotions. For example, asking respondents to identify the extent to which an emotion such as surprise represents three sensations (cold, blue, and sweet) appears unrelated to the EI of managers and employees at work.

d. **Predictive validity:** Initial studies that examined the relationship between MSCEIT scores and job performance produced contrasting results (Pusey, 2000; Bradberry and Greaves, 2004). Recently, additional predictive validity studies have demonstrated the relationships between MSCEIT scores and police officer performance (Daus et al., 2004), customer service performance (Daus et al., 2004; Daus, 2002), financial analyst and clerical performance (Lopes et al., 2005), leader emergence and transformational leadership (Daus and Harris, 2003; Rubin et al., 2005), individual performance in jobs characterized by high emotional labor (Wong and Law, 2002), and group-level performance and organizational citizenship behavior (Day and Carroll, 2004). Overall, there is growing evidence that MSCEIT scores predict a range of meaningful organizational outcomes (Daus and Ashkanasy, 2005).

e. **External validity:** The MSCEIT User's Manual (Mayer et al., 2002b) indicated that scoring of the MSCEIT is based on North American data. People from emerging or non-Western nationals taking the test, and nonnative English language speakers, should be alert to the fact that cultural variation can lower scores on the MSCEIT.

b) ECI and ECI-2

Salient Features

Goleman et al., (2002) developed an EI model based on Goleman's (1995, 1998) original EI model along with the results of research on management competencies. The measure for this EI model is the ECI-2. It contains eighteen competencies arrayed in four clusters: self-awareness, self-management, social awareness, and social skills. Sala (2002) with ECI-2 modified ECI (Boyatzis et al., 2000). The ECI is a 110–item self-report measure that assesses twenty competencies in the same four clusters. The first cluster, self-awareness, includes measures of emotional self-awareness, accurate self-assessment, and self-confidence. The second cluster, self-management, includes measures of self-control, trustworthiness, conscientiousness, adaptability, achievement orientation, and initiative. The third cluster, social awareness, consists of empathy, organizational awareness, and service orientation. The fourth cluster, social skills, includes measures of developing others, leadership, influence, communication, change catalyst, conflict management, building bonds, and teamwork and collaboration.

ECI-2 has four clusters and measures eighteen competencies. For both measures, there are also versions that can be completed by a manager, peers, and subordinates, and the use of these reports are strongly encouraged by the developers. ECI and ECI-2 can be administered through online and paper versions. Similar to the EQ-i, the ECI was developed to measure a construct distinct from personality and is a measure of behavior. The competencies share a common theoretical orientation and wordings with concepts and items on the Five-Factor model of personality (MacCann et al., 2003). Self-awareness or knowing what one feels is the first step to being able to manage our interactions with others. It is being aware of our emotions, understanding their cause and reflecting on the patterns of behavior, which we display as a consequence of that emotion (Garner, 2009; Goleman, 1995). Although self-management is more than resisting explosive or problematic behavior, it is putting your momentary needs on hold, to pursue your larger and more important goals (Garner, 2009). To elaborate, it is the ability to regulate distressing effects like anxiety and anger and to inhibit emotional impulsivity (Goleman, 1995).

On the other hand, social awareness that encompasses the competency of empathy is the ability to read nonverbal cues for negative emotions, particularly anger and fear, and to judge the trustworthiness of others. It is about understanding other's feelings, not experiencing them (Garner, 2009). Relationship management is how the effectiveness of our relationship skills hinges on our ability to attune ourselves to or influences the emotions of another person. It is the specific skills of influencing and persuading others, managing and improving the performance of others, utilizing and managing the diverse strengths of a team, and negotiation as well as conflict handling skills (Garner, 2009). It is useful and interesting to consider how significant emotional intelligence is for effective performance at work because a person's ability to perceive, identify, and manage his or her emotions is the origin of social and emotional competencies that are important for success in almost anything in life.

Reliability Assessments

For the self-assessment, internal consistency ranges from poor to adequate for the cluster scores $(r = 0.61$ to $r = 0.85$; Sala, 2002). Individual subscales for the self-assessment are generally poor $(r = 0.47$ to $r = 0.76)$ and should not be used for analysis. For assessments completed by others, such as supervisors and associates, the internal consistency for the cluster scores ranges from adequate to good $(r = 0.76$ to $r = 0.96)$. The self-assessment ratings do not correlate strongly with the ratings of others and causes a problem in establishing an overall rating.

Test-retest reliability for the self-assessment is poor (average $r = 0.36$). Test-retest for the other assessments is better $(r = 0.59)$. There are substantially fewer items in the ECI-2 (72 versus the original 110). Boyatzis and Sala (2004) report that a key reason the test was shortened was to increase ease of use and utilization.

Validity Assessments

a. **Content validity:** The definition and measurement of EI captured in the ECI-2 and its precursor (ECI-1) use a broad conception of EI, including competencies like initiative, achievement, maintaining standards of honesty and integrity, customer service orientation, change catalyst, and flexibility in handling change. Several appear to be the product of EI rather than dimensions of it. Furthermore, the measure appears to assess competencies that are not necessarily emotional, such as serving as a change catalyst or flexibility in handling change. The ECI-2 does not measure some competencies that emotionally intelligent people probably demonstrate. For example, it does not appear to measure whether, how, or when to neither express emotions, nor does it measures the ability to express emotions. It does not deal with deciding whether to recognize or not recognize emotions expressed by others such as calming a frightened group of employees or ignoring feigned anger. In addition, the test does not discriminate between accurate and inaccurate or honest and dishonest expressions of feelings; redirect and prioritize one's thinking based on one's feelings; or generate emotions to facilitate one's own and others' decision-making. In short, the test does not appear to directly measure the effect of emotions on perceptions of issues and people, how individuals think about issues, choices a manager makes including allocation of his or her time and attention, and the actions managers take.

b. **Construct validity:** The technical manual for the ECI-2 provides no information regarding the extent to which the test provides distinctive rather than redundant information relative to other tests for measuring cognitive intelligence, emotional intelligence, personality traits, or other phenomena. Boyatzis and Sala (2004) provide some evidence regarding the issue of construct validity. They recently described a series of studies that assessed the ECI-2's construct validity relative to several measures of personality (Diamantopoulu, 2001; Burckle, 2000; Murensky, 2000). The cumulative results of these studies revealed that the ECI-2 competencies are significantly related to many existing personality tests. This suggests that the ECI-2 offers little incremental value over existing tests already available on the market.

c. **Face validity:** The technical manual does not offer any information concerning the face validity of the ECI-2. However, the results of study state that the tool is face valid.

d. **Predictive validity:** Sala (2002) describes researchers reporting a strong relationship between self-reported ECI-2 scores and the performance of thirty-three area development managers and correlations of small to moderate size between ECI-2 scores received from others for sixty-seven firefighters and officers and several job performance ratings (Stagg and Gunter, 2002). More recently, Gowing et al. (2005) described a series of field studies in which ECI-2 scores differentiated high-performing employees in government and private sectors according to supervisor, peer, and direct report ratings. Overall, there is somewhat limited evidence of the measure's predictive validity.

e. **External validity:** The technical manual for ECI-2 does not include normative data for the test (Sala, 2002). Moreover, it does not identify the age, gender, ethnicity, cultural background, or other demographics, such as occupation, of respondents. Therefore, it may or may not be appropriate to use with individuals operating in different cultures where, for example, the concept of "face" or the value of maintaining smooth, pleasant interpersonal relationships are foremost concerns.

c) EQ-i
Salient Features

The first measure of emotional intelligence created was the Emotional Quotient Inventory, created by Bar-On (1997a), which is a 133-item self-report measure that takes approximately 30 minutes to complete. It consists of fifteen subscales, each containing between seven and eleven items. The measure produces an overall score as well as five composite scores. It can be administered online or through a paper-and-pencil format. The five composite areas include intrapersonal ability, interpersonal ability, stress management, adaptability, and general mood. Although Bar-On (2004) indicates that the measure is designed to be distinct from personality, MacCann and colleagues (2003) have documented the theoretical similarity and even item wording similarity between the EQ-i and the Five-Factor model.

Reliability Assessments

The internal consistency of the overall EQ-i ranges from 0.76 to 0.97 (Bar-On 1997a; Bar-On 2000; Petrides and Furnham, 2001). Test-retest reliability is adequate, being 0.85 after 1 month and 0.75 after 4 months (Bar-On, 1997a). Reliability measures for the subscales are poor and suggest that these should not be examined on an individual level. They should not be used for hiring/acceptance decisions (Bar-On, 1997a).

The EQ-i reports strong correlations with the Five-Factor model of personality. This strong correlation has caused many to question whether the whole concept of emotional intelligence is just studying personality characteristics by a new name (Davies et al., 1998). The EQ-i correlates most strongly with Neuroticism, with correlations ranging from -0.29 to -0.77 (Dawda and Hart, 2000; MacCann et al., 2003). Correlations with the conscientiousness, extraversion, and agreeableness scales were also high (ranging from $r = 0.30$ to $r = 0.56$). Given these high correlations, it would be difficult to justify the use of this measure in place of the personality measures.

Validity Assessments

a. **Content validity:** The content of the items in the EQ-i appears to match the concepts included in Bar-On's model. Logically, however, why Bar-On defines problem-solving, flexibility, or reality testing as social and emotional competencies and there is no theoretical justification for including or excluding these. Furthermore, several competencies that emotionally intelligent people likely demonstrate are missing from Bar-On's model. For example, the test does not appear to measure whether, how, or when to express emotions. In addition, the test does not appear to clearly tap the ability to discriminate between accurate and inaccurate or honest and dishonest expressions of feelings, to redirect and prioritize one's thinking based on one's feelings, or to generate emotions to facilitate one's own and others' decision-making. Many of the scales in the EQ-i appear to measure products of EI such as establishing satisfying relationships and working cooperatively with others, not emotional intelligence per se. Finally, the scales appear biased toward positive affect, as there is no room for grief, guilt, rage, or any other painful emotions that may be perfectly intelligent and natural feelings to experience or acknowledge.

b. **Construct validity:** Bar-On has examined the extent to which the EQ-i provides information that is distinctive from or duplicates that generated by other measures of personality characteristics, emotional competence, and cognitive intelligence. Others have done so as well. Some research suggests considerable overlap between what the EQ-i measures and that which can be obtained from existing personality tests, including the Big Five and 16PF (Dawda and Hart, 2000; Newsome et al., 2000; Brackett and Mayer, 2003). In fact, O'Connor and Little (2003) contend that EQ-i essentially measures personality traits. Bar-On cited results of a meta-analysis conducted by Van Rooy and Viswesvaran (2003) to support his claim. However, their analysis does not break out the EQ-i. Consequently, it is not a good test of the potential incremental value of the EQ-i in predicting work phenomena above and beyond the contribution of personality factors. Many studies have examined the relationship of EQ-i scores, measures of cognitive intelligence, and other EI measures. According to a wealth of research described in Bar-On (2004), only minimal overlap exists between the EQ-i and a wide range of cognitive intelligence measures. The technical manual for the MSCEIT indicates that correlations between it and the EQ-i range from 0.13 to 0.18. Correlations with other tests are considerably higher.

c. **Face validity:** The EQ-i appears to have adequate face validity. Dulewicz et al. (2003) suggest that face validity is of paramount importance to staff and managers operating in the world of work.

d. **Predictive validity:** Bar-On (2004) and other researchers report a series of studies that examined the ability of the EQ-i to identify and predict occupational performance in the workplace. The study looked at the power of EQ-i scores to predict the performance of military recruiters in the U.S. Air Force in achieving their annual recruitment quotas. Researchers found a significant difference in EQ-i scores between high and low performers. Further analysis indicated that the following seven factors of fifteen were significant predictors of performance: assertiveness, interpersonal relationship, happiness, empathy, stress tolerance, social responsibility, and problem-solving. Second study by Bachman et al. (2000) examined the connection between EI and successful collection of debt by account officers. They found that successful account officers scored significantly higher than less successful account officers on all dimensions of the EQ-i except impulse control and empathy. In addition, Slaski and Cartwright (2002) reported that managers in a large retail organization with higher scores on the EQ-i received higher performance ratings by their immediate managers.

e. **External validity:** Bar-On (2004) reports no differences between males and females on overall scores. However, significant gender differences were reported on twelve of the scales. Females scored higher than males in some scales. In contrast, males scored higher than females in some scales. Older groups generally scored significantly higher than younger groups, but no significant differences in EI appeared between the various ethnic groups that were compared. Overall, research evidence has demonstrated a moderate level of external validity for the EQ-i.

3.4.3 Relationship between Ability and Trait EI

Comparing the MSCEIT scores with those of the Bar-On's EQ-i, a self-report measure of emotional intelligence (Bar-On, 1997a), the overall test-to-test correlation in 137 respondents was $r = -0.36$, which indicates the two tests share about 10% of their variance in common.

3.4.4 Other Measures of EI

Several other measures of EI exist. MacCann et al. (2003) have already researched and reviewed the three major measures of EI. In this section, a brief overview and summary of the available information on measures of EI is discussed. This summary will cover each measure separately, referring to the reliability, validity, and cost of each measure. Though minimal research is available on these measures, a few of them are reviewed here with comparison displayed in Table 3.2:

a. SSRI (Schutte et al., 1998) is a 33-item self-report measure based on the Salovey and Mayer (1990) theory of Emotional Intelligence. Schutte et al. (1998) report an internal consistency of 0.90 for the overall scale. There is no test-retest data presented. Significant correlations between the SSRI and the Five-Factor model have also been reported, wherein $r = 0.21$ to $r = 0.51$ (MacCann et al., 2003).

b. SUEIT is a 65-item self-report measure with five subscales. The coefficient alpha for the total scale is good $(r = 0.88$ to $r = 0.91)$. Coefficient alphas for the subscales vary from fair to good $(r = 0.70$ to $r = 0.91)$. Gardner and Stough (2002) have found a significant relationship between self-reported leadership style and emotional intelligence.

c. TMMS (Salovey et al., 1995) is a 48-item self-report measure with three subscales, based on the Mayer and Salovey model of EI. The overall scale coefficient alpha is adequate $(r = 0.82)$ with the subscales ranging from fair to adequate $(r = 0.66$ to $r = 0.83)$.

d. WLEIS (Wong and Law, 2002) is a 16-item self-report measure with four subscales based on the Mayer and Salovey model of EI. The internal consistency is adequate $(r = 0.78$ to $0.89)$ with similar consistency for the subscales.

e. WEIP (Jordan et al., 2002) is a 27-item self-report measure with adequate internal consistency $(r = 0.86)$. It is based on the Mayer and Salovey model of EI.

f. TEIQue (Petrides and Furnham, 2003) is a 144-item self-report measure based on a blending of the Bar-On, Goleman, and Mayer and Salovey models of EI. It has fifteen subscales. Internal consistency for the overall scales is adequate $(r = 0.86)$, with subscales ranging from poor to good $(r = 0.61$ to $r = 0.91)$.

g. Another self-report scale, the EQ-Map (Cooper, 1997, 1998), also divides emotional intelligence into five factors. The first, current environment, measures life pressures and life satisfactions. The second, emotional literacy, includes measures of emotional self-awareness, emotional expression, and emotional awareness of other. The third, EQ competencies, includes internationality, creativity, resilience, interpersonal connections, and constructive discontent. The fourth, EQ values and attitudes, includes outlook, compassion, intuition, trust radius, personal power, and integrated self. Finally, the outcomes area of the EQ-Map measures explicit outcomes of emotional intelligence: general health, quality of life, relationship quotient, and optimal performance.

h. In 2000, Dulewicz and Higgs designed a questionnaire to measure the emotional intelligence—the EIQ. They found that on a sample of general managers, an EI scale-based sixteen relevant competencies showed promising reliability and predictive validity over a seven-year period. The EIQ was designed to specifically assess seven elements of an individual's emotional intelligence through self-report (Dulewicz and Higgs 1999–2000):

1. Self-awareness—being aware of one's feeling and managing it.
2. Emotional resilience—being able to maintain one's performance when under pressure.
3. Motivation—having the drive and energy to attain challenging goals or targets.
4. Interpersonal sensitivity—showing sensitivity and empathy toward others.
5. Influence—influencing and persuading others to accept one's views.
6. Intuitiveness—making decisions using reason and intuition when appropriate.
7. Conscientiousness—being consistent in one's words and actions, behaving according to prevailing ethical standards.

3.4.5 Major Findings

A comparison between measures leads us to the following important remarks:

a. It is encouraging that the majority of the measures demonstrate adequate to good reliability for the overall scores. Most of the subscales do not demonstrate adequate reliability for use in any individual manner.

b. Another difficulty in using EI measures is that very little research with these EI measures has been done in an educational context. It is doubted whether results found within a business context would translate easily to an educational context.

c. The available reviews (MacCann et al., 2003; Conte, 2005) suggest that the MSCEIT does not overlap as much with personality factors. It is a clearly defined theory and has a relationship to accepted definitions of intelligence.

d. The MSCEIT is expensive, and the most distinct measure of EI and the prediction of success in academics and other areas could be done with other EI measures.

e. All self-report measures are susceptible to underreporting of low skill scores based on social desirability and defensive responding (Weber, 2004).

Table 3.2 Comparison of the Various Measures of EI

Measure	Format of administration	No. of items	Time taken to complete test (minute)	Reliability of scales	Reliability of subscales	No. of scales and subscales
Emotional Quotient Inventory (EQ-i)	Online or paper and pencil	133	30	Test-retest reliability = 0.85	Poor reliability of subscales	5 scales 15 subscales
Emotional Competence Inventory (ECI-2)	Paper and online	72	40	No test-retest data available	No test-retest data available	5 scales 18 subscales
Mayer-Salovey-Caruso Emotional Intelligence Test (MSCEIT)	Online only	141	45	0.91–0.93	0.86	4 subscales
The Schutte Self-Report Inventory (SSRI)	Paper and pencil	33	20	No test-retest data available	No test-retest data available	No subscales
The Swinburne University Emotional Intelligence Test (SUEIT)	Paper and pencil	65	30	0.88–0.91	0.70–0.91	5 subscales
The Trait Meta-Mood Scale (TMMS)	Paper and pencil	48	30	0.82	0.66–0.83	3 subscales
The Wong and Law Emotional Intelligence Scale (WLEIS)	Paper and pencil	16	20	0.78–0.89	0.78–0.89	3 subscales
The Workgroup Emotional Intelligence Profile (WEIP)	Paper and pencil	27	20	0.86	No test-retest data available	4 subscales
The Trait Emotional Intelligence Questionnaire (TEIQue)	Paper and pencil	144	45s	0.86	0.61–0.91	Combination of the model of the 3 pioneers. 15 subscales

3.4.6 Measures of EI for the Age Group of 7–18 Years

A number of assessment devices purporting to measure EI have been developed. The devises differ in two significant ways: they are based on different conceptual frameworks and they use different measurement approaches including performance tests, self-report inventories, or observer ratings.

Thus, there has been a lot of debate concerning the most suitable method to be used for measuring EI. Some have argued that measurement approach rather than the theoretical approach ultimately determines the nature of EI model being assessed (MacCann et al., 2004; Petrides and Furnham, 2000). It is argued that performance measures are more valid if EI is a type of ability, whereas self-report instruments can be used if EI is viewed of comprising a number of non–ability-related traits or attributes (Goldenberg et al., 2006). Thus, the measures of EI similar to ability EI and trait EI models are classified as:

   a. **Performance-based measure of EI** pertain to ability models such as Mayer-Salovey-Caruso Emotional Intelligence Test (MSCEIT YV) by Mayer et al. (2005), which is available to academic researchers only.

   b. **Self-report measures of EI** pertain to mixed models of EI. They are determined to assess emotions within the personality framework and to assess cross-situational consistencies in behavior (Petrides and Furnham, 2000)—Emotional Quotient Inventory: Youth Version (EQ-i YV) by Bar-On and Parker (2000a).

3.5 CONCLUDING REMARKS

This chapter discusses the models and measures of EI. Five types of validity are discussed for every measure of EI. The commonalities and differences between various models and measures are explained. The next chapter discusses the model and measures selected for experimentation with the various factors of EI.

Review Questions

   1. What are the different models of EI?
   2. How is EI measured for adults above 18 years?
   3. How is EI measured for children and adolescents in the age group of 7–18 years?
   4. Explain the various tests for validity conducted on the measures?

References

Austin, E. (2004), "An investigation of the relationship between trait emotional intelligence and emotional task performance", *Personality and Individual Differences,* 36, 1855–1864.

Bachman, J., Stein, S., Campbell, K., & Sitarenios, G. (2000). Emotional intelligence in the collection of debt. *International Journal of Selection and Assessment,* 8(3), 176–182.

Barchard, K., and Hakstian, A. R. (2004), "The nature and measurement of emotional intelligence abilities: Basic dimensions and their relationships with other cognitive ability and personality variables", *Educational and Psychological Measurement*, 64, 437–462.

Bar-On, R. (1997a), Bar-On Emotional Quotient Inventory: A test of emotional intelligence, Canada: Multi-Health Systems.

Bar-On, R. (2000), "Emotional and social intelligence: Insights from the Emotional Quotient Inventory (EQ-i)", In R. Bar-On and J. D. Parker (Eds.), *Handbook of emotional Intelligence*, San Francisco: Jossey-Bass.

Bar-On, R. (2001), "Emotional intelligence and self-actualization", In J. Ciarrochi, J. Forgas, and J. D. Mayer (Eds.), *Emotional intelligence in everyday life: A scientific inquiry,* Philadelphia: Psychology Press.

Bar-On, R. (2004), The Bar-On Emotional Quotient Inventory (EQ-i): Rationale, description and summary of psychometric properties. In G. Geher (Ed.), *Measuring emotional intelligence: Common ground and controversy,* New York: Nova Science Publishers, Inc, 115–145.

Bar-On, R. and Parker, J. D. A. (2000a), The Bar-On EQ-i: YV': Technical manual, Canada: Multi-Health Systems.

Bastian, V. (2005), Are the claims for emotional intelligence justified? Emotional intelligence predicts life skills but not as well as personality and cognitive abilities, *Unpublished Thesis*, University of Adelaide.

Bastian, V. A., Burns, N. R., and Nettelbeck, T. (2005), "Emotional Intelligence predicts life skills, but not as well as personality and cognitive abilities", *Personality and Individual Differences*, 39, 1135–1145.

Boyatzis, R. E., Goleman, D., and Rhee, K. S. (2000), "Clustering competence in emotional intelligence: Insights from the emotional competence inventory", In R. Bar-On and J. D. A. Parker (Eds.), *Handbook of emotional intelligence*, San Fransisco: Jossey-Bass, 343–362.

Boyatzis, R., and Sala, F. (2004), Assessing emotional intelligence competencies. Unpublished manuscript, Cleveland, Ohio: Case Western Reserve University.

Brackett, M. A., and Mayer, J. D. (2003), "Convergent, discriminant, and incremental validity of competing measures of emotional intelligence", *Personality and Social Psychology Bulletin*, 29, 1147–1158.

Brackett, M. A., Warner, R. N., and Bosco, J. S. (2005), "Emotional Intelligence and relationship quoting among couples", *Personal Relationships*, 12, 197–212.

Bradberry, T., and Greaves, J. (2004), Emotional intelligence appraisal technical manual update, San Diego: TalentSmart.

Burckle, M. (2000), ECI and MBTI. Hay /McBer Research Report. Philadelphia: HayGroup.

Chapman, B. P., and Hayslip Jr., B. (2005), "Incremental validity of a measure of emotional intelligence", *Journal of Personality Assessment*, 85(2), 154–169.

Ciarrochi, J. V., Deane, F. P., and Anderson, S. (2002), "Emotional intelligence moderates the relationship between stress and mental health", *Personality and Individual Differences*, 32, 197–209.

Conte, J. M. (2005), "A review and critique of emotional intelligence measures", *Journal of Organizational Behavior*, 26, 433–440.

Cooper, R. K. (1998), "Executive EQ: Emotional intelligence in leaders and organizations", New York: Grosset/Putnam.

Daus, C. (2002), "Dissatisfaction as a function of emotional labor", Paper presented at the Seventeenth Annual Meeting of the Society for Industrial and Organizational Psychology, Toronto, Canada.

Daus, C., and Harris, A. (2003), "Emotional intelligence and transformational leadership in groups", Paper presented at the Eighteenth Annual Meeting of the Society of Industrial and Organizational Psychology, Orlando, FL.

Daus, C., Rubin, R., Smith, R., and Cage, T. (2004), *Police performance: Do emotional skills matter?* Paper presented at the Nineteenth Annual Society for Industrial and Organizational Psychology, Chicago.

Daus, C., and Ashkanasy, N. (2005), "The case for an ability-based model of emotional intelligence in organizational behavior", *Journal of Organizational Behavior*, 26, 453–466.

Davies, M., Stankov, L., and Roberts, R.D. (1998), "Clustering competence in emotional intelligence: Insights from the Emotional Competence Inventory (ECI)s".

Dawda, D., and Hart, S. D. (2000), "Assessing emotional intelligence: Reliability and validity of the Bar-On Emotional Quotient Inventory (EQ-i) in university students", *Personality and Individual Differences*, 28, 797–812.

Day, A., and Carroll, S. (2004), "Using an ability-based measure of emotional intelligence to predict individual performance, group performance, and group citizenship behaviors", *Personality and Individual Differences*, 36, 1443–1458.

Day, A. L., and Livingstone, H. A. (2005), "Comparing the construct and criterion-related validity of ability-based and mixed-model measures of emotional intelligence", *Educational and Psychological Measurement*, 65, 757–763.

Derksen, J., Kramer, R. I., and Katzo, M. (2002), "Does a Self- report measure of emotional intelligence assess something different from general intelligence?" *Personality and Individual Differences*, 32, 37–48.

Diamantopoulu, M. (2001), *An investigation of type A and type B behavior patterns in relation with the emotional intelligence of bank employees in their working environment.* Unpublished doctoral dissertation, Middlesex University of London.

Dulewicz, V., and Higgs, M. (1999), "Can emotional intelligence be measured and developed?" *Leadership and Organization Development Journal*, 20, 242–252.

Dulewicz, V., Higgs, M., and Slaski, M. (2003), "Measuring emotional intelligence: Content, construct and criterion-related validity", *Journal of Managerial Psychology*, 18, 405–420.

Engelberg, E., and Sjoberg, L. (2004), "Emotional intelligence, affect intensity, and social adjustment", *Personality and Individual Differences*, 37, 533–542.

Garner, P. (2009), Special educational needs: The Key concepts, Abingdon: Routledge.

Gardner, L., and Stough, C. (2002), "Examining the relationship between leadership and emotional intelligence in senior level managers", *Leadership and Organization Development Journal*, 23(2), 68–78.

Gignac, G. E. (2006), "Self-reported emotional intelligence and life satisfaction: Testing incremental predictive validity hypotheses via Structural Equation Modeling (SEM) in a small sample", *Personality and Individual Differences*, 40, 1569–1577.

Goldenberg, I., Matheson, K., & Mantler, J. (2006). The Assessment of Emotional Intelligence: A Comparison of Performance-Based and Self-Report Methodologies. [Article]. *Journal of Personality Assessment, 86*(1), 33–45.

Goleman, D. (1995), Emotional intelligence. New York: Bantam Books.

Goleman, D. (1998), Working with emotional intelligence, New York: Bantam Books.

Goleman, D., Boyatzis, R., and McKee, A. (2002), Primal leadership: Realizing the power of emotional intelligence. Boston: Harvard Business School Press.

Gowing, M., O'Leary, B., Brienza, D., Cavallo, K., and Crain, R. (2005), "A practitioner's research agenda: Exploring real-world applications and issues", In V. Druskat, F. Sala, and G. Mount (Eds.), *Linking emotional intelligence and performance at work*, New Jersey: Erlbaum.

Jordan, P. J., Sashkanasy, N. M., Hartel, C. E., and Hooper, G. S. (2002), "Workgroup emotional intelligence scale development and relationship to team process effectiveness and goal focus", *Human Resource Management Review*, 12, 195–214.

Lam, L. T., and Kirby, S. (2002), "Is emotional intelligence an advantage? An exploration of the impact of emotional and general intelligence on individual performance", *The Journal of Social Psychology*, 142, 33–143.

Livingstone, H. A., and Day, A. L. (2005), "Comparing the construct and criterion-related validity of ability-based and mixed-model measures of emotional intelligence", *Educational and Psychological Measurement*, 65, 757–779.

Lopes, P. N., Salovey, P., and Straus, R. (2003), "Emotional intelligence, personality, and the perceived quality of social relationships", *Personality and Individual Differences, 35*, 641–658.

Lopes, P. N., Salovey, P., Côté, S., & Beers, M. (2005). "Emotion regulation ability and the quality of social interaction." *Emotion, 5,* 113–118.

MacCann, C., Mattews, G., Zeidner, M., and Roberts, R. D. (2003), "Psychological assessment of emotional intelligence: A review of self-report and performance-based testing", The International Journal of Organisational Analysis, 11, 247 –74.

MacCann, C., Roberts, R. D., Matthews, G., and Zeidner, M. (2004), "Consensus scoring and empirical option weighting of performance-based Emotional Intelligence (EI) tests", *Personality and Individual Differences*, 36(3), 645–662.

Matthews, G., Zeidner, M., and Roberts, R. D. (2002), *Emotional intelligence: Science and myth,* Cambridge: MIT Press.

Mayer, J. D., and Salovey, P. (1993), "The intelligence of emotional intelligence", *Intelligence*, 17, 432–442.

Mayer, J. D., and Salovey, P. (1997), "What is emotional intelligence?", In P. Salovey and D. Sluyter (Eds.), *Emotional development and EI: Educational implications,* Basic Books, New York, 3–34.

Mayer, J. D., Salovey, P. and Caruso, D. R. (1999), "Models of Emotional Intelligence", in R. J. Sternberg (ed.), *Handbook of Human Intelligence,* New York: Cambridge, 2nd edn, 396–420.

Mayer, J. D., Caruso, D. R., and Salovey, P. (2000a), "Selecting a measure of emotional intelligence: The case for ability scales", In R. Bar-On and J. D. A. Parker (Eds.), *Handbook of emotional intelligence.* San Fransisco: Jossey-Bass, 320–342.

Mayer, J. D., Caruso, D. and Salovey, P. (2000b), "Emotional intelligence meets traditional standards for an intelligence", *Intelligence*, 27(4), 267–298.

Mayer, J. D., Salovey, P., and Caruso, D. R. (2002a), Mayer-Salovey-Caruso emotional intelligence test (MSCEIT) item booklet, Canada: MHS Publishers.

Mayer, J. D., Salovey, P., and Caruso, D. R. (2002b), Mayer-Salovey-Caruso emotional intelligence test (MSCEIT) user's manual, Canada: MHS Publishers.

Mayer, J. D., Salovey, P., and Caruso, D. (2005), The Mayer-Salovey-Caruso emotional intelligence test–youth Version (MSCEIT-YV), Research Version 1.0, Canada: Multi Health Systems.

Murensky, C. (2000), The relationship between emotional intelligence, personality, critical thinking ability, and organizational leadership performance at upper levels of management. *Unpublished doctoral dissertation*, George Mason University.

Nunnally, J., and Bernstein, I. (1994), *Psychometric theory*, New York: McGraw-Hill.

O'Connor, R. Jr., and Little, I. S. (2003), "Revisiting the predictive validity of emotional intelligence: Self-Report versus ability-based measures", *Personality and Individual Differences*, 34, 1893–1902.

Palmer, B. R., Donaldson, C. & Stough, C. (2002). Emotional intelligence and life satisfaction. *Personality and Individual Differences*, 33, 1091–1100.

Parker, J. D. A., Creque, R. E. Sr., Barnhart, D. L., Harris, J. I., Majeski, S. A., Wood, L. M., Bond, B. J., and Hogan, M. J. (2004a), "Academic achievement in high school: Does emotional intelligence matter?", *Personality and Individual Differences*, 37, 1321–1330.

Parker, J. D. A., Summerfeldr, L. J., Hogan, M. J., and Majeski, S. (2004b), "Emotional intelligence and academic success: Examining the transition from high school to university", *Personality and Individual Differences*, 36, 163–172.

Parker, J. D. A., Hogan, M. J., Eastabrook, J. M., Oke, A., and Wood, L. M. (2006), "Emotional intelligence and student retention: Predicting the successful transition from high school to university", *Personality and Individual Differences*, 41, 1329–1336.

Petrides, K. V., and Furnham, A. (2000), "On the dimensional structure of emotional intelligence", *Personality and Individual Differences*, 33, 1091–1100.

Petrides, K. V., and Furnham, A. (2001), "Trait emotional intelligence: Psychometric investigation with reference to established trait taxonomies", *European Journal of Personality*, 15, 425–448.

Petrides, K. V., and Furnham, A. (2003), "Trait emotional intelligence: Behavioral validation in two studies of emotion recognition and reactivity to mood induction", *European Journal of Personality*, 17, 39–57.

Petrides, K. V., and Furnham, A. (2006), "The role of trait emotional intelligence in a gender-specific model of organizational variables", *Journal of Applied Social Psychology*, 36, 552–569.

Pusey, F. (2000), Emotional intelligence and success in the workplace: Relationship to job performance. *Unpublished master's thesis*, Guildhall University, London.

Riley, H., and Schutte, N. S. (2003), "Low emotional intelligence as a predictor of substance-use problems", *Journal of Drug Education*, 33, 391–398.

Roberts, R. D., Zeidner, M., and Mattews, G. (2001), "Does emotional intelligence meet traditional standards for an intelligence? Some new data and conclusions", *Emotion*, 1, 196–231.

Rubin, R., Munz, D., and Bommer, W. (2005), "Leading from within: The effects of emotion recognition and personality on transformational leadership behavior", *Academy of Management Journal*, 48(5), 845–858.

Sala, F. (2002), "Emotional competence inventory: Technical manual", Philadelphia: McClelland Center for research, Hay Group.

Saklofske, D. H., Austin, E. J., and Minski, P. (2003), "Factor structure and validity of a trait emotional intelligence measure", *Personality and Individual Differences*, 34, 707–721.

Salovey, P., and Mayer, J. D. (1990), "Emotional Intelligence", *Imagination, Cognition, and Personality*, 9, 185–211.

Salovey, P., Mayer, J. D., Goldman, S. L., Turvey, C. and Palfai, T. (1995)," Emotional attention, clarity, and repair: Exploring emotional intelligence using the trait meta-mood scale", In J. W. Pennebaker (Ed.), Emotion, *Disclosure and Health*, American Psychological Association, Washington, DC.

Salovey, P., Stroud, L. R., Woolery, A. and Epel, E. S. (2002), "Perceived Emotional Intelligence, Stress Reactivity, and Symptom Reports: Further Explorations Using the Trait Meta-Mood Scale", *Psychology and Health*, 17, 611–27.

Schutte, N. S., Malouff, J. M., Hall, L. E., Haggerty, D. J., Cooper, J. T., Golden, C. J., and Dornheim, L. (1998), "Development and validation of a measure of emotional intelligence", *Personality and Individual Differences,* 25, 167–177.

Schutte, N. S., Malouff, J. M., Bobik, C., Coston, T. D., Greeson, C., Jedlicka, C., (2001), "Emotional intelligence and interpersonal relations", *The Journal of Social Psychology,* 141(4), 523–536.

Slaski, M., and Cartwright, S. (2002). "Health, performance and emotional intelligence: an exploratory study of retail managers", *Stress and Health,* 18, 63–68.

Stagg, G., and Gunter, D. (2002), Emotional intelligence in the fire service, Working paper, London Fire Brigade.

Van Rooy, D., and Viswesvaran, C. (2003). Emotional intelligence: A meta-analytic investigation of predictive validity and nomological net. *Unpublished paper,* International University, Florida.

Vygolsky, L. S. (1978), Mind in society. Cambridge: Harvard University Press.

Warwick, J., and Nettelbeck, T. (2004), "Emotional intelligence is . . . ?", *Personality and Individual Differences,* 37, 1091–1100.

Woitaszewski, S. A., and Aalsma, M. C. (2004), "The contribution of emotional intelligence to the social and academic success of gifted adolescents as measured by the multifactor emotional intelligence scale – Adolescent version", *Roeper Review,* 27(1), 25–30.

Wong, C., and Law, K. S. (2002), "The effects of leader and follower emotional intelligence on performance and attitude: An exploratory study", *Leadership Quarterly,* 13, 243–374.

Woodruffe, C. (1992), What is meant by competency? In P. R. Sparrow, R. Boam (Eds.), *Designing and achieving competency,* United Kingdom: Mcgraw Hill International.

Zeidner, M., Roberts, R. D., and Mattews, G. (2002), "Can emotional intelligence be schooled? A critical review", *Educational Psychologist,* 37(4), 215–231.

Zeidner, M., Roberts, R. D., and Matthews, G. (2004), "Emotional intelligence in the work place: A critical review", *Applied Psychology: An International Review,* 53(3), 371–399.

Zeidner, M., Mattews, G., Roberts, R. D., and Mac Cann, C. (2003), "Development of emotional intelligence: Towards a multi- level investment model", *Human Development,* 46, 69–96.

Zeng, X., and Miller, C. E. (2003), "Examinations of measurements of emotional intelligence", *Ergometrika,* 3, 38–49.

Zikmund, W. (2005), Business research methods, *Thomson Asia,* 29–75.

CHAPTER 4

Factors Affecting EI

4.1 INTRODUCTION

There is currently an upsurge of interest in all matters emotional and affective in education. Goleman (1995) suggested that EI could predict academic success better than the traditional measures of intelligences. Zeidner et al. (2004) correctly pointed out that there hasn't been sufficient research to fully understand the impact EI has on academic success. On further research, it has been proved that there is conflicting evidence regarding the relationships between EI and academic success measured as grade point average (GPA). Possibility of greater variability in the measures of EI could have resulted in conflicting evidences. Using the Mayer-Salovey-Caruso emotional intelligence test (MSCEIT) has not observed any correlations between EI and academic achievement (O'Connor and Little, 2003; Bastian et al., 2005). In case of associations between EI and GPA, the results have been found to be inconsistent. In a study made by Parker et al. (2004a) with the Emotional Quotient Inventory: Youth Version (EQ-i YV), significant associations were found between three subscales—stress management, adaptability, and intrapersonal EQ-i. However, overall EI scores did not correlate with GPA. Newsome et al. (2000) used the EQ-i measure and found no correlations between academic achievement and EI. Similarly, Petrides and Furnham (2004) examined the role of trait EI on academic performance. They tested in individuals with low intelligence quotient (IQ) relative to individuals with high IQ. The results suggested that trait EI was related to academic performance only in individuals with low IQ scores. Specifically, the study concluded that high trait EI was more important for academic success in individuals with low IQ. Similarly, numerous studies were conducted examining the relationship between emotional intelligence and cognition (Barchard, 2003; Brackett and Mayer, 2003) personality (Bastian et al., 2005; Van der Zee et al., 2002) and academic transitions (Parker et al., 2006) for students.

The pioneers of EI also claim that family socialization practices determine the development of EI in children (Rubin, 1999; Schutte et al., 2001; Salovey, and Sluter, 1997). Parental socializations have been found to directly impact child's social and emotional competencies as well as work indirectly on the understanding of emotions and gaining social knowledge (Zeidner et al., 2002). Parental socializations take effect through explicit lessons or informal conversations about regulation of emotion. Parental influences also occur through the child's observational capacity. The basic assumption is that a child whose parent displays constructive EI-related behavior in everyday life is most likely to implement it as a part of its own behavior. In addition to parents, school setting is one of the most important contexts for learning emotional skills and competencies (Mayer and Salovey, 1997). In the process of emotional learning, the individual develops the aptitudes, skills, attitudes, values attributes, and characteristics necessary to acquire higher emotional intelligence. Mayer and Geher (1996) hypothesized that those who are low in emotional intelligence could be educated to recognize, express, and regulate their feelings better. It can be specified that EI is the aggregation of the innate abilities and the knowledge and skill that individuals acquire and develop throughout their lifetime. EI includes physical, intellectual, and psychological capacities. EI is nontradable and intrinsically possessed by an individual. Individuals do not always control the channels and pace by which they acquire EI either formally or informally (Goleman, 1997).

An attempt is to identify factors, which could be implemented for directing students to attain higher EI.

4.2 EI SKILL SET

A specified set of skills (Low et al., 2004) that students need to be successful in the workplace are listed below:

   a. Career and job search skills
   b. Appropriate personal competence skills
   c. Appropriate social competence skills

The first set of skills that students need is career and job search skills, which helps in developing career management skills. Counselors often begin by administering and interpreting a variety of career assessments, exploring irrational thinking students are engaged in, matching personal characteristics with similar occupations, teaching decision-making skills, and helping in the decision-making process. They also teach job search skills and help students adjust to the workplace and develop an appropriate lifestyle consisting of a balance between work, leisure, family, and education.

The second set of skills that students need is appropriate personal competence skills. In helping students develop these skills, the counselor can administer assessments to make students more aware of their personal competence strengths and weaknesses, increase their self-esteem by focusing on strengths they possess, and enhance their personal responsibility for their career development. They discuss the importance of being trustworthy and dependable in the workplace.

The third set of skills that students need is appropriate social competence. In helping students develop these skills, the counselor can help students learn to be more cooperative, be supportive of coworkers, take the initiative to lead when called upon, be a good follower of leadership, communicate effectively, value diversity, and relate well to individuals.

The EI construct has important clinical and therapeutic implications because it has emerged from an amalgamation of research findings on how individuals appraise, communicate, and use emotion (Salovey and Mayer, 1990). The ability to identify and describe internal mental states and the ability to link specific mental events with particular behaviors and situations are core dimensions in most models of emotional intelligence. Bar-On's model of emotional intelligence relates to the potential for performance and success, rather than performance or success itself, and is considered process oriented rather than outcome oriented (Bar-On, 2002). It focuses on an array of emotional and social abilities, including the ability to be aware of, understand, and express oneself, the ability to be aware of, understand, and relate to others, the ability to deal with strong emotions, and the ability to adapt to change and solve problems of a social or personal nature (Bar-On, 1997a). In his model (Fig. 4.1), Bar-On outlines five components of emotional intelligence: intrapersonal, interpersonal, adaptability, stress management, and general mood.

Within these components are subcomponents; Bar-On posits that emotional intelligence develops over time and that it can be improved through training, programming, and therapy (Bar-On, 2002). Bar-On hypothesizes that those individuals with higher than average EI are generally more successful in meeting environmental demands and pressures. He also notes that a deficiency in emotional intelligence can mean a lack of success and the existence of emotional problems. Problems in coping with one's environment is thought, by Bar-On, to be especially common among those individuals lacking in the subscales of reality testing, problem-solving, stress tolerance, and impulse control. In general, Bar-On considers emotional intelligence and cognitive intelligence contribute equally to a person's general intelligence, which then offers an indication of one's potential to succeed in life (Bar-On, 2002).

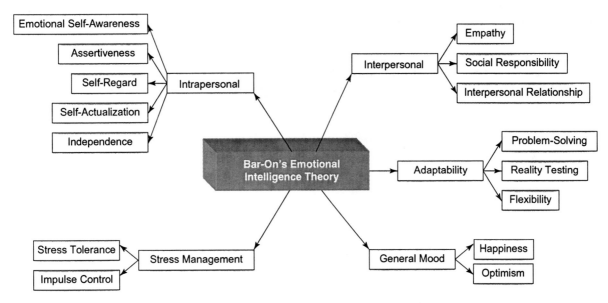

Figure 4.1   Bar-On's EI Model (adapted from Malekar, 2009 unpublished thesis)

4.3 BAR-ON'S EQ-I MEASURE

The first consideration in evaluating a measure of emotional intelligence is the aspect of mental life it measures (Bar-On, 1997b). The content of emotional intelligence tests varies greatly due to the fact that interpretations of the meaning of the term emotional intelligence vary widely.

The EQ-i has a total EQ score and the following five EQ composite scale scores comprising fifteen subscale scores: (1) Intrapersonal EQ-i (comprising self-regard, emotional self-awareness, assertiveness, independence, and self-actualization), (2) Interpersonal EQ-i (comprising empathy, social responsibility, and interpersonal relationship), (3) Stress Management EQ-i (comprising stress tolerance and impulse control), (4) Adaptability EQ-i (comprising reality testing, flexibility, and problem-solving), and (5) General Mood EQ-i (comprising optimism and happiness). The inventory includes the following four validity indicators: omission rate (the number of omitted responses), inconsistency index (the degree of inconsistency between similar types of items), positive impression (the tendency to give an exaggerated positive response), and negative impression (the tendency to give an exaggerated negative response.

The fifteen subscales on the EQ-i are defined by Bar-On (1997b) as follows:

1. Self-regard (SR) is the ability to be aware of, understand, accept, and respect oneself.
2. Emotional self-awareness (ES) is the ability to recognize and understand one's emotions.
3. Assertiveness (AS) is the ability to express feelings, beliefs, and thoughts, and to defend one's rights in a nondestructive manner.
4. Independence (IN) is the ability to be self-directed and self-controlled in one's thinking and actions and to be free of emotional dependency.
5. Self-actualization (SA) is the ability to realize one's potential and to do what to do, enjoys doing, and can do.
6. Empathy (EM) is the ability to be aware of, understand, and appreciate the feelings of others.
7. Social responsibility (RE) is the ability to demonstrate oneself as a cooperative, contributing, and constructive member of one's social group.

8. Interpersonal relationship (IR) is the ability to establish and maintain mutually satisfying relationships that are characterized by emotional closeness, intimacy, and by giving and receiving affection.
9. Stress tolerance (ST) is the ability to withstand adverse events, stressful situations, and strong emotions without "falling apart" by actively and positively coping with stress.
10. Impulse control (IC) is the ability to resist or delay an impulse, drive, or temptation to act, and to control one's emotions.
11. Reality testing (RT) is the ability to assess the correspondence between what is internally and subjectively experienced and what externally and objectively exists.
12. Flexibility (FL) is the ability to adjust one's feeling, thoughts, and behavior to changing situations and conditions.
13. Problem-solving (PS) is the ability to identify and define personal and social problems as well as to generate and implement potentially effective solutions.
14. Optimism (OP) is the ability "to look at the brighter side of the life" and to maintain a positive attitude, even in the face of adversity.
15. Happiness (HA) is the ability to feel satisfied and with one's life, to enjoy oneself and others, and to have fun and express positive emotions.

4.3.1 InterScale Correlations

The EQ-i subscales were examined for the degree of correlation. This was done to examine the level of correlation between the Positive Impression Scale and the other inventory subscales in order to assess the level of social desirability response bias, as well as to examine the intercorrelations among the subscales themselves. The overall correlation among the subscales and the Positive Impression Scale proved to be 0.19, indicating that the subscales is not strongly socially biased. It can, thus, be concluded that the subscales and the inventory as a whole are relatively independent from a social desirability factor. It means that they are contributing unique information.

The average intercorrelation of the fifteen subscales is 0.50; this indicates a fairly high intercorrelation among factors, which was expected. The optimism subscale demonstrated the highest degree of intercorrelation with the other factors (an average of 0.61). Other interesting high correlations among the subscales are worthy of comment. For example, the highest intercorrelation was observed between the social responsibility and the empathy subscales (0.80). This may mean that responsible behavior is highly dependent on one's ability to be aware of and appreciate the feelings of others; and a lack of empathy may help to better explain psychopathic behavior. Especially, high intercorrelations also appeared between assertiveness and independence (0.60) and between self-regard and self-actualization (0.67), optimism (0.75) and happiness (0.71). Finally, the high correlation between optimism and stress tolerance (0.76) suggests that optimism most likely is a significant factor in one's ability to cope with stress and could very well be an important facilitator of this important component of emotional intelligence.

4.3.2 Internal Consistency

The internal consistency of the EQ-i scales was examined on several population samples around the world. The average Cronbach alpha coefficients are high for all of the subscales, ranging from a low of 0.69 (social responsibility) to a high of 0.86 (self-regard), with an overall average internal consistency coefficient of 0.76 for the seven countries examined in the EQ-i technical manual (Bar-On, 1997b). Additional studies have produced similar internal consistency results on large population samples (e.g., approximately 9,500 children and adolescents in the United states and Canada, 5,000 late adolescents and young adults in Israel, and 1,700 adults in the Netherlands). Average to above average scores on the EQ-i suggest that individual who is potentially effective in emotional and social functioning (i.e., one who is most likely emotionally and socially intelligent), the higher the scores, the more positive the prediction for effective functioning in meeting environmental demands and pressures. On the other hand, inability to succeed in life and possible existence of emotional social or behavioral problems are suggested by low scores. Low scores on the following subscales are considered more problematic for coping with one's environment: stress tolerance, impulse control, reality testing, and problem-solving (Bar-On, 1997b).

4.4 FACTORS OF EI

Goleman (1995) identified five factors that affect EI. They are self-awareness, self-regulation, motivation, empathy, and social skills. These factors continue to be analyzed extensively by many researchers. These are also the core dimensions measured by the Emotional Competencies Inventory.

Goleman's study (1995) stated that EI accounts for more than 85% of exceptional achievement. It is universally accepted that even though technical skills are necessary for productivity, these are insufficient to explain the difference between high and mediocre performers. As the complexity of tasks increases, high performance individuals show higher emotional intelligence. Goleman's (1995, 1998) study agreed that individuals with high emotional intelligence are aware of self, motivated, self-disciplined, and strong socially, aspire to excel, and continually seek re-skilling, learning, and adding value. This helps in long-term business development and builds a high morale organizational culture.

Self-aware individuals have a deep understanding of their own emotions, strengths, weaknesses, needs, and drives. They are neither overly critical nor unrealistically optimistic; instead they are honest with themselves and with others. McLagan's study (2002) stated that self-awareness extends to an understanding of values, goals, and other drivers of behavior and performance and are able to reduce cognitive dissonance by operating in agreement with their values, and influence others through demonstration of these values. In this drive for self-improvement, a culture of constructive feedback is created that fosters personal growth.

Goleman (1995, 1998) described self-regulation as the ability to choose to respond to an event rather than reacting; reasonable individuals create an environment of trust and fairness, effectively managing politics and infighting by example. Such organizations attract and retain talent, leading to competitive advantage in addition to coping well in ambiguous business environments. Bryan (2002) stated that as they operate from a place of authenticity and integrity, they are able to model solid corporate citizenship and governance in changing conditions. Self-regulators think strategically and delay gratification in short-term results, which results in more sustainable alternative of investment in long-term growth.

Empathy along with social skills is important in appreciation of teams, group dynamics, diversity, and diversity management. The fundamentals of this component of EI are rapid globalization, increase in competitive requirements for specialized talents, and relevance of flexible, temporary project teams. Social skills enhance coaching and mentoring relationships, improve performance, increase job satisfaction, and reduce employee turnover. Social skill also helps in gaining agreement on a new policy or system and building enthusiasm for a new product launch. The essential characteristics of managerial competence are visible when an individual building broad networks, knows intuitively how to persuade, understand the importance of collaboration and are adept at managing teams.

However, many managers use four clusters of emotional competency. They are as follows:

- Self-Awareness—defined by emotional self-awareness, accurate self-assessment, and self-confidence.
- Self-Management—defined by self-control, transparency, achievement, initiative, and optimism.
- Social Awareness—defined by empathy, organizational awareness, and service orientation.
- Relationship Management—defined by inspiration, influence, developing others, change catalyst, conflict management, teamwork, and collaboration.

Similarly, Bar-On (2000) has identified five factors, such as intrapersonal EQ-i, interpersonal EQ-i, stress management EQ-i, adaptability EQ-i, and general mood EQ-i. These five factors are further divided into fifteen subscales as discussed in section 3.3. Thus, placing all competencies such as achievement orientation, impulse control, and adaptability EQ-i that are components of self-regulation, we can conclude that such concepts confuse rather than clarify the role of emotional competencies in the workplace. Because the field of EI remains relatively new, many of these factors, which have been studied in organizational psychology for some time, now are much better understood than the concept of EI.

Mayer et al. (2000b) described EI as a component of emotional perception, emotional facilitation of thought, emotional understanding, and emotional management. Their concept has gained popularity because the theory is performance oriented and empirically based. They have alternative scoring procedures in order to discriminate right from wrong answers on performance-based measures of EI.

To summarize, Goleman (1995) identified five factors that affect EI. They are: self-awareness, self-regulation, motivation, empathy, and social skills. He has also mentioned the influence of communication on all these factors. Similarly, Bar-On (2000) has identified five factors, such as intrapersonal EQ-i, interpersonal EQ-i, stress management EQ-i, adaptability EQ-i, and general mood EQ-i along with the subscales discussed in section below.

4.4.1 Intrapersonal EQ-i

According to Bar-On (1997b), intrapersonal EQ-i includes emotional awareness and the ability to identify it correctly. Individuals scoring high on intrapersonal EQ-i tend to understand their emotions and are able to express and communicate their feeling and needs. Shearer (2006) defined intrapersonal EQ-i as an ability to think about and understand one's self, to be aware of one's strengths and weaknesses, and to plan effectively to achieve personal goals, reflecting on and monitoring one's thoughts and feelings and regulating them effectively. It's the ability to monitor one's self in interpersonal relationships, be aware of and understand one's emotions, feelings, and ideas, and to act with personal efficacy. It consists of related abilities like recognizing and labeling one's feelings. Intrapersonal EQ-i consists of five subscales described below:

a. **Self-regard (Measured by the EQ-i SR subscale)**
   Self-regard is an important resource for managing averse affect (Parke and Ladd, 1992). Self-regard is related to our self-worth and our value. Building esteem is a first step toward our happiness and a better life. Self-regard increases confidence. If one has confidence, one will respect self. If one respects self, then others would be respected, improve relationships, achievements, and happiness. Self-esteem is the experience of being competent to cope with the basic challenges of life and of being worthy of happiness.

b. **Emotional self-awareness (Measured by the EQ-i ES subscale)**
   Goleman (1998) defined self-awareness as the ability to recognize and understand personal moods and emotions. It drives their effect on others. Hallmarks of self-awareness include self-confidence, realistic self-assessment, and a self-deprecating sense of humor. Basically, it is being aware of our moods as we are having them. Self-aware individuals have higher degree of sophistication about their emotional lives. They are extremely sure of their own boundaries and are as a result in good health. They have a positive attitude toward life. Self-aware individuals get into a bad mood at times; however, they don't ruminate neither are obsessed with it and they are able to get out of it sooner. It's the ability to recognize and understand moods, emotions, and drives as well as their effect on others. This means that one is realistic when assessing self. One is able to recognize weaknesses and strengths and find humor in areas where one may fall short. Self-aware individuals have a deep understanding of one's emotions, strengths, weaknesses, needs,

and drives. Individuals with strong self-awareness are neither overly critical nor unrealistically hopeful. Rather, they are honest with themselves and with others.

c. **Assertiveness (Measured by the EQ-i AS subscale)**

According to Bar-On (1997b) assertiveness is the ability to express oneself and one's emotions. It is a very important component required in conceptual models that attempt to describe emotional intelligence and closely related concepts. It is, therefore, encouraging noting a fairly high correlation (+0.60) between the EQ-i AS subscale and the 16PF Factor (Bar-On, 1997b), confirming that AS subscale is tapping the ability to be assertive and express one in general. Motivation is an inner desire or drive to achieve and is passion to work for reasons beyond money or status. This implies that an individual who is self-motivated is able to tackle steps to accomplish an objective with determination, persistence while maintaining a consistent level of high energy.

d. **Independence (Measured by the EQ-i IN subscale)**

Tapping the various aspects of self-directive thinking and behavior, the ability to be independent is apparently dependent on one's degree of self-confidence, as well as desire to meet expectations and obligations without becoming a slave to them. Tap the feeling that one is in control and one can influence difficult situations. It is important to reiterate that independence and self-directive in one's thinking and ability to relate with others correlates with emotionally and socially intelligent behavior.

e. **Self-actualization (Measured by the EQ-i SA subscale)**

Self-actualization, defined within the Bar-On model, is apparently tapping what has been referred to as achievement drive. This is one of the key cognitive factors considered by Wechsler to play an important role in facilitating intelligent behavior, probably by supplying emotional energy, which helps motivate the individual to do his or her best. The ability to actualize oneself requires drive and emotional energy.

4.4.2 Interpersonal EQ-i

According to Bar-On (1997b), interpersonal EQ-i deals with the relationship with peers, subordinates, and superiors. Those high on the interpersonal EQ are likely to have satisfying interpersonal relationships, are good listeners, and are able to understand and appreciate the feelings of others. It is defined by Shearer (2006) as the ability to recognize the feelings of other individuals that are facilitated by linguistic skill. It's the ability to be aware of and understand others' emotions and feelings. Skill in managing relationships with other individuals is also a factor in one's overall mood and emotional well-being. It consists of related abilities like identifying emotions in others and having empathy toward others. In order to build great interpersonal EQ-i, one needs to have the ability to control or redirect disruptive impulses and moods as having self-regulation. Having self-regulation is to think before making judgment or taking action.

Interpersonal EQ-i comprises of three subscales described below:

a. **Empathy (Measured by the EQ-i EM subscale)**

Another extremely important component that has surfaced in most conceptual models that have attempted to describe emotional and social intelligence (ESI) over the years is empathy (the ability to be aware of and understand the feelings and needs of others). These correlations are moderate in magnitude. They help to define the EM subscale and match fairly closely with the way the underlying construct (empathy) was conceptualized within an ESI framework. The lack of empathy may be an important factor in aggressive antisocial behavior, which may prove to have both diagnostic and remedial applicability. Researchers have known for years that it contributes to occupational success. Rosenthal and his colleagues at Harvard discovered over two decades ago that individuals who were best at identifying others' emotions were more successful in their work as well as in their social lives. More recently, a survey of retail sales buyers found that apparel sales reps were valued primarily for their empathy. The buyers reported that they wanted reps who could listen well and really understand what they wanted and what their concerns were.

b. **Social responsibility (Measured by the EQ-i RE subscale)**
Social responsibility subscale is related to identifying and understanding feelings in addition to being considerate and concerned about others and their feelings (Dawda and Hart, 2000). Demonstrating responsibility (Bar-On, 1997b) and being cooperative and willingness to contribute to the group orientation and social responsibility component are described as respect and consideration for others and are responsible for both the success and failure of the organization.

c. **Interpersonal relationship (Measured by the EQ-i IR subscale)**
The EQ-i IR subscale tap a wide area often referred to as social skills, considered by many to represent an important component of ESI defined as the ability in form and maintain relations characterized by the capacity for giving and receiving emotional closeness. The ability to give and receive emotional closeness in relations is not only dependent on the ability to be aware of emotions, but also on the ability to understand feelings and emotions within those relations. The IR subscale also correlates well with a number of other scales that measure various aspects of interpersonal relationships.

4.4.3 Stress Management EQ-i

It is defined as the ability to be flexible and alter one's feelings with changing situations (Livingstone and Day, 2005). It consists of abilities like delaying or resisting an impulse. Those with high stress management are generally calm and work well under pressure; they are rarely impulsive and can usually respond to a stressful event without an emotional outburst. Stress management EQ-i comprises of two subscales described below:

a. **Stress tolerance (Measured by the EQ-i ST subscale)**
The results from a number of studies clearly indicate that the EQ-i ST subscale assesses one's ability to effectively manage stress and anxiety-provoking conditions. The importance of stress management for emotional intelligence can be seen in the way it is related to identifying feelings (Bar-On, 1997b). This factor has to do with the ability to deal with environmental demands; to influence stressful events and to actively do something to improve the immediate situation and the inability to cope with stress will most likely lead to anxiety.

b. **Impulse control (Measured by the EQ-i IC subscale)**
The impulse control subscale according to Bar-On (1997b) measures acceptance of one's aggression. It is also the ability to be composed and to control aggression, hostile, aggressive, and irresponsible behavior. These scales measure a tendency toward impulsiveness, low frustration tolerance, abusiveness, unpredictable behavior, anger control problems, loss of self-control, and explosive behavior. The component of EI that frees us from the being prisoners of our feelings. An individual engaged in such conversation feels bad moods and emotional impulses just as everyone else does. However, he or she finds ways to control them and even to channel them in useful ways.

4.4.4 Adaptability EQ-i

Adaptability according to Bar-On (1997b) involves skills related to management of change. Managing change involves the ability to manage stressful situations in a relatively calm and proactive manner. Individuals who score high on this dimension are impulsive rarely and work well under pressure (Bar-On, 1997b, 2000, 2002). Livingstone and Day (2005) defined adaptability as the ability to be flexible and alter one's feelings with changing situations. It consists of abilities like being to adjust one's emotions and behavior to changing situations or conditions. Individuals with high adaptability scores are flexible, realistic, and effective in managing change and good at finding positive ways of dealing with everyday problems.

    a. **Reality testing (Measured by the EQ-i RT subscale)**
    The reality testing subscale (Bar-On 1997b) shares a common domain with these particular measures that tap disturbances in perception, affect, and cognition characterized by an impaired ability to validate that which one perceives, feeling, or thinking. This suggests that the ability to accurately identify and understand feelings is dependent on accurate reality testing. This could also mean that reality testing plays an important role in the cognitive processing of emotions, a point that has not yet been fully addressed in the emotional intelligence literature. Reality testing possibly acts as a "rudder" in keeping the cognitive processing of emotions on track; this also might explain what happens in psychotic behavior.

    b. **Flexibility (Measured by the EQ-i FL subscale)**
    Bar-On (1997b) suggests that individuals who score low on the flexibility subscale most likely exhibit rigidity in their thinking and behavior, which is characteristic of both disturbances (American Psychiatric Association, 1994). In addition to thinking and behaving in rigid patterns, those with neurosis exhibit rigidity in the way they emotionally react to certain events. Individuals who receive a low score on the FL subscale resist change in general and in their own self in particular.

    c. **Problem-solving (Measured by the EQ-i PS subscale)**
    Bar-On (1997b) implied that it is important to understand emotions in order to solve problems or, at least, problems of a more emotional nature (e.g., problem-solving with specific emotional or affective content is most likely facilitated by possessing knowledge of one's and others' feelings). Impairment in problem-solving is also observed in anxiety and depression.

4.4.5 General Mood EQ-i

It is defined as the ability to feel and express positive emotions and remains optimistic (Bar-On, 1997b). It represents the ability to enjoy life and maintain a positive disposition. Higher levels on general mood feel satisfied with their lives and maintain a positive outlook. Happiness and optimism are two aspects of general mood including maintenance of positive aspects and brighter side of life.

    a. **Optimism (Measured by the EQ-i OP subscale)**
    Wechsler considered optimism (together with drive and positive mood) to be part of the cognitive factors that he thought facilitated intelligent behavior. These factors were considered to be motivational in nature rather an integral part of intelligence itself (Wechsler, 1940).

    b. **Happiness (Measured by the EQ-i HA subscale)**
    Happiness is "barometric in nature"—it both monitors one's overall well-being and interjects positive mood into the way one copes with daily demands. In a way, it helps us to do what we want to do and then tells us how well we are doing. It is this positive mood that fuels the emotional energy required to increase one's motivational level to get things done. Markedly low score on the HA subscale may possess typical symptoms of depression, such as a tendency to worry, sadness, uncertainty about the future, withdrawal from one's immediate environment, lack of drive, depressive thoughts, guilt, dissatisfaction with one's life, and possible suicidal thoughts.

4.5 THE RELIABILITY AND FACTORIAL STRUCTURE OF THE BAR-ON MODEL

The reliability of the EQ-i has been examined by a number of researchers over the past 20 years. A consensus of findings reveals that the Bar-On conceptual and assessment model is consistent, stable, and reliable (Bar-On, 2004). More specifically, the overall internal consistency coefficient of the EQ-i is 0.97 based on the North American normative sample (Bar-On, 1997b). This well exceeds the 0.90 minimum for total scores suggested by Nunnally (1978). Internal consistency was recently reexamined on 51,623 adults in North America, revealing nearly identical results with a slight mean increase of 0.025 in consistency coefficients (Bar-On, 2004). An overall retest reliability examination of the EQ-i is 0.72 for males (n=73) and 0.80 for females (n=279) at 6 months (Bar-On, 2004). Other researchers around the world have reported similar findings regarding the reliability of the EQ-i (e.g., Matthews et al., 2002; Newsome et al., 2000; Petrides and Furnham, 2000). These findings compare favorably with those of other measures of this construct.

Factor analysis was applied to study the 15-factor structure of the EQ-i to empirically evaluate the extent to which it is theoretically valid. Moreover, this statistical procedure was used to examine the factorial structure of the Bar-On model (to examine the extent to which the factorial components of this model structurally exist). This analysis was first performed on the normative sample, progressing from exploratory to confirmatory factor analysis (Bar-On, 1997b).

Based on a varimax rotation, a 13-factor solution afforded the most theoretically meaningful interpretation. These results provided a reasonable match with the subscale structure of the EQ-i. Nonetheless, the 13-factor empirical structure that emerged raised an important question that had to be addressed: Can the 15-factor model used in the Bar-On model and measure of ESI still be justified in light of the findings which suggested a 13-factor structure? The essential differences that were identified between the theoretical structure and the one that surfaced as a result of exploratory factor analysis were as follows: (a) two factors emerged from the impulse control items; (b) although self-regard, self-actualization, optimism, and happiness represent four separate scales, most of their items are loaded on two factors; (c) although assertiveness and independence are considered to be two separate subscales, items from both subscales loaded on one factor; and (d) although two separate experimental factors emerged from the empathy and social responsibility items, they are the two highest correlating factors.

The results of this analysis clearly suggested a 10-factor structure, which is both empirically feasible and theoretically acceptable as an alternative to the above-mentioned 15-factor structure. In the order of their extraction, the ten factors that emerged are as follows: (1) self-regard, (2) interpersonal relationship, (3) impulse control, (4) problem-solving, (5) emotional self-awareness, (6) flexibility, (7) reality testing, (8) stress tolerance, (9) assertiveness, and (10) empathy. These ten factors appear to be the key components of ESI, while the five factors that were excluded from the second confirmatory factor analysis (optimism, self-actualization, happiness, independence, and social responsibility) appear to be important correlates and facilitators of this construct. The ten key components and the five facilitators together describe and predict emotionally and socially intelligent behavior.

4.6 CONCLUDING REMARKS

In this chapter, the various factors affecting EI and the subscales are described and understood. These factors tend to facilitate one's overall ability to effectively cope with daily demands and pressures. The next chapter describes design of experiment used in this research.

Review Questions

1. What are the various factors affecting EI?

References

American Psychological Association. (2001), *Publication Manual of the American psychological Association.* Washington, D.C.

Barchard, K. (2003), "Does emotional intelligence assist in the prediction of academic success?" *Educational and Psychological Measurement,* 63, 840–858.

Bar-On, R. (1997a), Bar-On Emotional Quotient Inventory: A test of emotional intelligence, Canada: Multi-Health Systems.

Bar-On, R. (1997b), Bar-On Emotional Quotient Inventory: Technical manual, Canada: Multi-Health Systems.

Bar-On, R. (2000), "Emotional and social intelligence: Insights from the Emotional Quotient Inventory (EQ-i)", In R. Bar-On and J. D. Parker (Eds.), *Handbook of emotional Intelligence,* San Francisco: Jossey-Bass.

Bar-On, R. (2002), Bar-On emotional quotient short form (EQ-i: Short) Technical manual, Canada: Multi-Health Systems.

Bar-On, R. (2004), "The Bar-On Emotional Quotient Inventory (EQ-i): Rationale, description and summary of psychometric properties", In G. Geher (Ed.), *Measuring emotional intelligence: common ground and controversy,* New York: Nova Science Publishers, Inc, 115–145.

Bar-On, R. and Parker, J. D. A. (2000a), The Bar-On EQ-i: YV': Technical manual, Canada: Multi-Health Systems.

Bastian, V. (2005), Are the claims for emotional intelligence justified? Emotional intelligence predicts life skills but not as well as personality and cognitive abilities. *Unpublished Thesis,* University of Adelaide.

Bastian, V. A., Burns, N. R., and Nettelbeck, T. (2005), "Emotional intelligence predicts life skills, but not as well as personality and cognitive abilities", *Personality and Individual Differences,* 39, 1135–1145.

Brackett, M. A., and Mayer, J. D. (2003), "Convergent, discriminant, and incremental validity of competing measures of emotional intelligence", *Personality and Social Psychology Bulletin,* 29, 1147–1158.

Bryan, L. L. (2002), "Just-In-Time strategy for a turbulent world", *The McKinsey Quarterly,* special edition, 2, 16–28.

Dawda, D., and Hart, S. D. (2000), "Assessing emotional intelligence: Reliability and validity of the Bar-On Emotional Quotient Inventory (EQ-i) in university students", *Personality and Individual Differences,* 28, 797–812.

Goleman, D. (1995), Emotional intelligence. New York: Bantam Books.

Goleman, D. (1997), "Beyond IQ: developing the leadership competencies of emotional Intelligence", Paper presented at the 2nd international competency conference, London.

Goleman, D. (1998), Working with emotional intelligence, New York: Bantam Books.

Livingstone, H. A., and Day, A. L. (2005), "Comparing the construct and criterion-related validity of ability-based and mixed-model measures of emotional intelligence", *Educational and Psychological Measurement,* 65, 757–779.

Low, G., Lomax, A., Jackson, M., and Nelson, D. (2004), "Emotional intelligence: A new student development model", A paper presented at the 2004 national conference of the American college personnel association in Pennsylvania.

Matthews, G., Zeidner, M., and Roberts, R. D. (2002), *Emotional intelligence: Science and myth,* Cambridge: MIT Press.

Mayer, J. D., and Salovey, P. (1997), "What is emotional intelligence?", In P. Salovey and D. Sluyter (Eds.), *Emotional development and EI: Educational implications,* Basic Books, New York, 3–34.

Mayer, J. D., Caruso, D., and Salovey, P. (2000b), "Emotional intelligence meets traditional standards for an intelligence", *Intelligence,* 27(4), 267–298.

Mayer, J. D., and Geher, G. (1996), "Emotional intelligence and the identification of emotion. Intelligence", 22, 89–114.

Newsome, S., Day, A. L., and Catano, V. M. (2000), "Assessing the predictive validity of emotional intelligence", *Personality and Individual Differences,* 29, 1016–1055.

Nunnally, J. C. (1978). *Psychometric theory (2nd ed.).* New York: McGraw-Hill.

O'Connor, R. Jr., and Little, I. S. (2003), "Revisiting the predictive validity of emotional intelligence: Self-Report versus ability-based measures", *Personality and Individual Differences,* 34, 1893–1902.

Parker, J. D. A., Hogan, M. J., Eastabrook, J. M., Oke, A., and Wood, L. M. (2006), "Emotional intelligence and student retention: Predicting the successful transition from high school to university", *Personality and Individual Differences,* 41, 1329–1336.

Parke, R. D., and Ladd, G. W. (1992), Family-Peer relationships: Modes of linkage, Hillsdale: University of Illinois.

Petrides, K. V., and Furnham, A. (2000), On the dimensional structure of emotional intelligence, *Personality and Individual Differences*, 33, 1091–1100.

Petrides, K. V., and Furnham, A. (2004), "The role of trait emotional intelligence in academic performance and deviant behavior at school", *Personality and Individual Differences*, 36, 277–293.

Rubin, M. M. (1999), "Emotional intelligence and its role in mitigating aggression: A correlational study of the relationship between emotional intelligence and aggression in urban adolescents", *Unpublished dissertation*, Pennsylvania, Immaculata College.

Salovey, P., and Mayer, J. D. (1990), "Emotional intelligence", *Imagination, Cognition, and Personality*, 9, 185–211.

Salovey, P., and Sluyter, D. J. (1997), Emotional development and emotional intelligence: Implications for educators, New York: Basic Books, 3–31.

Schutte, N. S., Malouff J. M., Bobik C., Coston T. D., Greeson, C., Jedlicka, C. (2001), "Emotional intelligence and interpersonal relations", *The Journal of Social Psychology*, 141(4), 523–536.

Shearer, B. C. (2006), Exploring the relationship among the multiple intelligences and emotional intelligence, Ohio: MI Research and Consulting, Inc.

Van der Zee, K., Thijs, M., and Schakel, L. (2002), "The relationship of emotional intelligence with academic intelligence and the big five", *European Journal of Personality*, 16, 103–125.

Zeidner, M., Roberts, R. D., and Mattews, G. (2002), "Can emotional intelligence be schooled? A critical review", *Educational Psychologist*, 37(4), 215–231.

Zeidner, M., Roberts, R. D., and Matthews, G. (2004), "Emotional intelligence in the work place: A critical review", *Applied Psychology: An international review*, 53(3), 371–399.

CHAPTER 5

Applications of EI

5.1 BENEFITS OF EI APPLICATIONS

EI has been used as a developmental tool in many human activities. Usage of EI as a human resource development tool has benefited many business corporations. EI has also found applications in social sector, education sector, and healthcare sector. We present only a few of these applications in the subsequent sections.

5.1.1 Literature on EI and Age

Age-related differences in EI have been found in a number of studies. In relation to ability EI measures, Mayer et al. (1999) have found adults (N = 503; aged 17–70 years) to have significantly higher scores on the Multifactor Emotional Intelligence Scale (MEIS) for all scoring methods than did an adolescent sample (N = 229; aged 12–26 years). Kafetsio (2004) has also found significant age differences favoring older adults on three out four subscales of the Mayer-Salovey-Caruso emotional intelligence test (MSCEIT), in a sample of 239 community members aged 19 to 66 years. However, contrary to these results, Day and Carroll (2004) in a sample of 246 university students aged 17 to 54 years found only one significant, but weak, age-related difference, which actually favored younger individuals (r = −0.14). Significant age-related differences in EI favoring older adults have also been found with Emotional Quotient Inventory (EQ-i). For example, Bar-On (1997b) has reported significant increases in EI with age from early adulthood to middle age; with individual's ages 40 to 49 years having significantly higher total scores than individuals aged 20 to 29 years. Derksen et al. (2002) have also found EQ-i scores to increase with age in a community sample of 873 individuals aged 19 to 84 years. Scores were found to generally peak at 35 to 44 years of age and to decline thereafter, although the rate of increase and decline with age varied somewhat according to the component scale. Derksen et al. (2002) have, therefore, concluded that different psychological factors must underlie EI and general intelligence. Based on these studies, it is possible that EI increases with age during middle adulthood. It should, however, be noted that these studies have been cross-sectional, not longitudinal, and, therefore, it is possible that differences in EI in these instances may have been due to cohort, rather than age-related effects. Having EI increase in this way, however, suggests that EI reflects a set of acquired skills rather than intrinsically innate abilities and thus it may be possible for at least some aspects of EI to be "taught" and "learned" in some way.

5.1.2 Literature on EI and Gender

It is a point of contention as to whether EI has a correlation with the gender of a child (Table 5.1). Contrary to popular belief, some studies show that girls are not more emotionally intelligent as compared to boys (Hein, 1996). They are emotionally intelligent in a variety of ways that boys are not due to a specific combination of the key components of EI. Girls on an average are more aware of their emotions, show more empathy, and are adept interpersonally. Boys on the other hand are self-confident, optimistic, adaptable, and handle stress better (Segal, 1997).

Table 5.1   Literature on EI and Gender

Sr. No	Author	Population	Sample size (N)	Assessment
1.	Mayer, Caruso and Salovey (1999)	Adult community sample	503	MEIS
2.	Ciarrochi et al. (2000)	College students	120	MEIS
3.	Kafetsios (2004)	College students	239	MSCEIT
4.	Brackett et al. (2003)	College students	330	MSCEIT
5.	Brackett et al. (2005)	College students	86	MSCEIT
6.	Reiff et al. (2001)	College students	128	EQ-i
7.	Dawda and Hart (2000)	College students	243	EQ-i
8.	Parkar et al. (2001)	College students	734	EQ-i
9.	Schutte et al. (1998)	College students	329	AES
10.	Charbonneau and Nicol (2002)	School children	134	AES
11.	Ciarrochi et al. (2001)	School children	131	Modified AES
12.	Saklofske et al. (2003)	College students	354	Modified AES

In a study by Barret et al. (2000), it was observed that females were emotionally responsive and by experiencing and expressing emotions more intensely were more "emotional" than men. Gender differences indicated that females tend to experience and express higher levels of fear, anxiety, depression, guilt, and happiness. Males were found to be high on anger (Barret et al., 2000).

Mayer et al. (1999) observed that females scored higher than men when tested with MEIS (the earlier version of MSCEIT). Ciarrochi et al. (2000) have found that females scored higher than males on all scales of the MEIS. Kafetsios (2004) noted that females scored higher than males on the perception branch of the MSCEIT. The other subscales scores were not statistically significant. Similarly females scored significantly higher than males on the total MSCEIT score in a study by Brackett et al. (2003) and Brackett et al. (2005).

On the self-report measure testing, females were found to be significantly high on the interpersonal ability as studied on the EQ-i by Reiff et al. (2001) and Parkar et al. (2001). Other factor studies were nonsignificant. Similarly on a population of college students, Dawda and Hart (2000) have reported no significant differences on the scores of EQ-i. In addition, Schutte et al.'s (1998) study on a university student's sample and Charbonneau and Nicol (2002) on a sample of school students have reported significant differences favoring females with the American Education services (AES). Ciarrochi et al. (2001a) have reported females scoring significantly higher than males on three subscales: perception, utilization, and regulation of other's emotions. The scores of the fourth scale, regulation of one's own emotions, were not found to be significant. In other study, Saklofske et al. (2003) on the modified AES reported females scoring higher than males on the subscales: appraisal of emotions and social skills. Surprisingly, males scored higher than females on the subscale: utilization of emotions. To summarize, we can claim that on some aspects of EI, gender differences favor females. Based on previous research males are less sensitive to emotional considerations than females and females have a high measure of EI than males. A person with high EI can better perceive emotions, use them in thought, understand their meanings, and manage emotions better than others. Solving emotional problems requires less cognitive effort for this individual. The person also tends to be somewhat higher in verbal, social, and other intelligences, particularly if the individual scored higher in the understanding emotions portion of EI (Goleman, 1998). The individual tends to be more open and agreeable than others. The high-EI person is drawn to occupations involving social interactions such as teaching and counseling more so than to occupations involving clerical or administrative tasks.

So, perhaps even more important than scoring high on an emotional intelligence test, knows one's level at this group of skills. Discovering one's level means that you can know whether and how much to be self-reliant in emotional areas and when to seek others' help in reading the emotional information that is going on around oneself. Whether one is high or low in emotional intelligence is perhaps not as important as knowing that emotional information exists and that some individuals can understand it. Knowing just that (Goleman et al., 2002), one can use emotional information by finding those who are able to understand and reason with it.

5.1.3 EI in Organizations

Individuals at all organizational levels—from executives to administrative staff—experience the same emotions even though the challenges, pressures, and demands they face at various organizational levels are quite different. Individuals become internally self-managed and capable of making their greatest contributions when they develop their EI skills. And as they work in that zone of peak performance, so does the organization. The examples below detail how the development of EI skills can benefit various business professionals such as sales individuals, customer service representatives, and technical professionals (e.g., analysts, engineers, information technologists, and scientists):

1. Sales—Individuals in sales frequently work with difficult prospects and customers. They often find themselves in adversarial situations over price, features, delivery schedules, etc. These situations can generate anxiety, fear, frustration, or even outright anger on the part of both the sales person and the customer. This can lead to a vicious negative emotional cycle where sales decline, they are unmotivated, and customers are unsatisfied and leave. When sales force enhance their EI skills, they become more capable of controlling or managing themselves and thus the situation. They are not as apt to let the customer to push their buttons. They are more able stay focused on the key issues and not give away the store. Research shows that the more optimistic a sales person is, the higher his or her volume and sales dollars. Optimism leads to persistence that leads to more sales. Being able to empathize with the customer allows for faster, more effective problem-solving, and better communication. Consequently, the strong positive customer relationships that are developed ensure better cooperation and higher sales when problems do arise.

2. Customer service representatives—customer service representatives (CSRs) deal with angry, frustrated customers continuously throughout their day. Through no fault of their own, they can find themselves being verbally abused. The customer's anger, frustration, and rage can cause representatives to become nervous, mad, disgusted, and angry themselves. If the representative does not have a high level of EI skills, the discussion may escalate and require the intervention of the CS Supervisor. Or worse, inadequate skills may cause the company to lose that customer. An upset customer will typically tell 10 to 15 friends about the poor treatment he or she received. With enhanced EI skills, CSRs can easily manage their emotional reactivates to angry customers, maintaining a polite, calm, and sincere attitude and conversation with customers. Loyal customers tell their friends. Higher customer loyalty leads to higher profitability.

3. Technical professionals—On a daily basis, technical professionals are required to do more with less faster, better, and cheaper. To complete their projects, they must work long, hard hours. They are challenged to work with many individuals from different functions to create, innovate, and do tasks, in many cases, they would like to avoid. These situations can cause technical professionals to be agitated, resentful, anxious, frustrated, and stressed-out much of the day. These negative emotions cause what is known as "emotional hijacking," which is a physiological response in the brain that literally keeps individuals from thinking clearly. Creativity is blocked, communication is hampered, and more mistakes and errors are made. Enhancing the technical professionals' EI skills provides them with what they never were taught in school. They build interpersonal skills that allow them to get other technical colleagues to help them when they need it through learning

how to manage their own emotional reactivates to individuals and situations. Enhancing EI skills increases the likelihood that projects are completed on schedule, using the best, innovative thinking available.

5.2 EI AND WORKPLACE EFFECTIVENESS

Application of EI has been most frequently documented in the professional workplaces. Organizations have traditionally had better human resource management systems as compared to those at the individual level because of a far more evolved research base on organizational behavior. (Bastian et al., 2005) Organizations manage HC through recruitment, training, performance review, and recognition/reward mechanisms. With EI, organizations have become far more alive to the emotional engagement that they offer their employees. From assigning tasks to engaging individuals is a journey that most organizations have embarked upon, after understanding EI. Human resource managers strive to attract good employees by measuring EI, and retain them by developing EI. Beinhocker (2000) and Rijamampianina and Maxwell's (2002) mention that EI of a company is an aggregate of EI of individuals. Beinhocker (1997) in a study mentioned that effective and continuously appropriate decision-making leads to long-term superior performance. Firm needs innovation acquired by development and adaptation of competitive advantage. This is achieved by focusing on flexibility, adaptability, and creativity—the three innate characteristics of the individuals in an organization—to gain competitive advantage (Beinhocker, 2000; Eisenhardt, 1999).

The following is a brief introduction to the many workplace applications of emotional intelligence:

a. Selection and succession: Used in conjunction with existing evaluation criteria (experience, qualifications, and interview results), properly interpreted emotional intelligence test scores provide unprecedented predictability. One would better know whom to hire and whom to promote, have better success aligning the right individuals with the right jobs, and achieve greater clarity in planning for the succession of senior leadership.

b. Development: Emotional intelligence is elastic. Those who lack it can acquire it; those who have it can enhance it. Emotional intelligence tests identify areas of strength and weakness that training and coaching can be designed around. Individuals at every level of the organization, from new hires to senior managers, can develop their emotional intelligence skills and see their job performance improve significantly.

c. Team and organization building: The emotional intelligence tools go beyond the success of the individual. Tools are also available for assessing the emotional intelligence of teams, departments, and the organization as a whole. With the implementation of appropriate programs, entire organizational cultures can be reengineered to deliver higher productivity and better bottom-line results.

d. Global versatility: Ethical tests are used in a variety of cultures and languages and they don't discriminate on the basis of race, gender, or age, meaning that results can be used without fear of bias. Results for each test are compared to a large normative sample that carefully represents the population's demographics.

5.3 EI AND MANAGERIAL EFFECTIVENESS

Organizations have traditionally had better human resource management systems as compared to those at the individual level because of a far more evolved research base on organizational behavior. (Bastian et al., 2005) Organizations manage HC through recruitment, training, performance review, and recognition/reward mechanisms. With the evolution of the theory of EI, organizations have become far more alive to the emotional engagement that they offer their employees. From assigning tasks to engaging individuals is a journey that most organizations have embarked upon, after understanding the impact of the emotional context. Assessments of EI dimensions have facilitated training and development modules for customer service skills, conflict management strategies, and stress management programs (Parker et al., 2004a; Cherniss, 2000). Similarly, HRD professionals have used EI measures as components in individual development plans (Cummings and Worley, 2005; Kunnanatt, 2004), organization wide competency models (Gowing et al., 2005), and executive coaching interventions (Peterson, 1996).

5.4 EI AND LEADERSHIP DEVELOPMENT

High levels of EI create a climate of trust where healthy risk taking and learning flourish; on the contrary, low EI creates a climate of fear and anxiety. EI is carried through the organizations like electricity through the wires. Also, EI is sine qua non of leadership without which a leader would not be effective. With this in view, identification and enhancement of EI competencies among managers/marketing professionals have been receiving considerable attention during recent times (Stein, 2007). Positive association is noted between leadership and EI. Hence, with EI intervention, leadership abilities of an individual can be enhanced (Gardner and Stough, 2002; Sivanathan and Fekken, 2002). Joseph (2006) studied the relationship between EI and leadership in the corporate sector, which is applicable to students. As most experienced leaders are acutely aware, social and emotional competencies are critical to managerial success. Specialized offerings like the EQ-i leadership report have helped organizations formulate clear profiles and development plans for future leaders.

5.5 EI AND DECISION-MAKING

Emotional intelligence is an extremely important factor in decision-making. As emotional intelligence deals with the ability to be aware of one's own emotions and recognize others as well, one should also be able to anticipate the impact of such an element on decision-making. One must possess the quality of recognizing others and one's own emotional capacities to be able to become a good leader. Developing one's emotional intelligence will help the person in tackling his or her emotions. Also, an emotionally intelligent person will never lose track of his or her thoughts and will not crumble under pressure since he or she will be capable of handling them in a better way. In our work places, we come across such individuals every day and we wonder how they can manage such stressful situations masterfully. The reason behind being a successful decision-maker is to be aware of one's own self and also be aware of the feelings of others. Thus, the better one is able to respond to the emotional needs, the better decision-maker he or she is.

Knowledge of the salient features of emotional intelligence will help in the making of a good leader. The features include self-awareness, self-regulation, social skills, motivation, and empathy. Only when one will be able to gauge the needs of others will there be power to manage employees. The capability of decision-making is indispensable in a leader. EI is of immense help in such a circumstance.

Not many of us are born with this kind of ability. Mostly one needs to hone our skill. In order to improve our emotional intelligence, start by being a good observer. Study our reactions to different incidents. Try to find out whether one is judgmental or whether one is capable of thinking out of the box. Emotional intelligence not only takes into consideration self-awareness, but also considers how much receptive one is. A very important part of decision-making is to be more open to others perspectives.

Evaluate self from time to time and see if we are able to empathize with others. This is extremely important in decision-making. This is an art and with practice one will be able to master the art of decision-making through emotional intelligence.

5.6 EI AND ENTREPRENEURSHIP DEVELOPMENT

Entrepreneurs are those who excel themselves, shine, and succeed beyond the set standards. Cross and Travaglione (2003) had proved in an Australian sample that entrepreneurs had high scores on all the scales of the Mayer and Salovey model (1990) as well as Goleman's model (1998) of EI. To summarize, there are other applications in organizational settings like recruitment, succession planning, and performance management among other things. Martin Seligman had developed a construct that he termed learned optimism. It refers to the causal attributions individuals make when confronted with failure or setbacks. Optimists tend to make specific, temporary, and external causal attributions, whereas pessimists make global, permanent, and internal attributions. In research at Met Life, Seligman and his colleagues found that new entrepreneurs who were optimists had 37% more insurance business in their first 2 years than did pessimists. When these entrepreneurs hired a special group of individuals who scored high on optimism but failed the normal screening, they outsold the pessimists by 21% in their first year and 57% in the second. They even outsold the average agent by 27%.

5.7 APPLICATIONS IN THE SOCIAL SECTOR

The high-EI individual (Merlevede et al., 2001), relative to others, is less apt to engage in problem behaviors, and avoids self-destructive, negative behaviors such as smoking, excessive drinking, drug abuse, or violent episodes with others. The high-EI person is more likely to have possessions of sentimental attachment around the home and to have more positive social interactions, particularly if the individual scored highly on emotional management. Such individuals may also be more adept at describing motivational goals, aims, and missions.

They're particularly good at establishing positive social relationships with others, and avoiding conflicts, fights, and other social altercations. They're particularly good at understanding psychologically healthy living and avoiding such problems as drugs and drug abuse (Stein and Lebeau-Craven, 2002). It seems likely that such individuals, by providing coaching advice to others, and by directly involving themselves in certain situations, assist other individuals and groups of individuals to live together with greater harmony and satisfaction. EI is also useful in etiology as well as mood disorders in social relationships. Studies reveal that there could be recurrence of mood disorders in social relationships. Many interpersonal factors such as lack of social skills, excessive criticism by peers could be the reason for the development, maintenance, and relapse of depression. In many cases, it has been observed that social support from others reduces the risk of depression. Similarly, Schutte et al. (2001) observed positive associations between the factors of interpersonal functioning and self-reported trait EI. Results indicate that high-EI depressed individuals would reduce their chances of being more depressed and the tendency to relapse would also be minimal.

5.8 EI AND CHILD DEVELOPMENT

Freedman (1998) shows that emotion is not just important, but absolutely necessary for us to make good decisions, take action to solve problems, cope with change, and succeed. Children are unaware of how they are feeling and what it's called. So, if a person doesn't have these skills, he or she can get into trouble, especially as a child transitions into adulthood. If a person does have these abilities or EI, they can help one throughout life. These abilities affect everything from success in marriage to how well one does on the job.

Emotional skills also help students academically (Roberts et al., 2001). Such skills as delaying satisfaction or enjoyment when searching for long-term goals are helpful to children academically. Children who can stick with tasks and finish homework or assignments do much better later in life than those children who are easily distracted and go off to do something else. Rubin (1999) proved that their peers rate school students, who are high on EI, as less aggressive and more social. They are also less likely to engage in tobacco and alcohol consumption (Trinidad and Johnson, 2002). A study by Ciarrochi et al. (2002) proves that EI moderates the link between stress and mental health, particularly depression, hopelessness, and suicidal ideas. To summarize, research shows that through EI screening and coaching, one can ensure student success and curtail dropout rate.

5.9 EI AND PARENTING

Parenting is one of the most challenging tasks of all human purpose. Children can be difficult and frustratingly stubborn at times to parents. Children often think the same of parents. A different context of EI is at work. Children behave and conform to norms that they imbibe from their social systems. It is important for parents and teachers to understand what these social norms are, how they affect the minds of children, and hence influence their behavior. Although children are born with different temperaments, EQ helps parents and teachers work with these qualities so that children can better cope in the world. For example, instead of protecting shy children from the world and catering to them, parents encouraged their young children to participate in challenging situations (meeting new kids and going to new places). EI has been used as a predictor of ability by parents as it has been found to be a predictor of life satisfaction, healthy psychological adaptation, positive interactions with peers and family, and higher parental warmth (Warwick and Nettelbeck, 2004).

5.10 APPLICATIONS IN EDUCATION SECTOR

Pediatric psychologists have started using measuring tools that now have a platform built on their EI. There is an evolving understanding of how the emotional context is probably an even more significant impact-creating driver. Reactions to children's failures and successes at home and at school are being shaped by these assessments, and there is a far lesser categorization of children into the standard straitjackets of good or bad, intelligent or slow, and sharp or obtuse. It is clearer now that the same child can be both in different emotional circumstances, and the key to that child's success is in the right emotional environment that accepts the child's capabilities. To summarize, EI has been used in education to lay the foundations to build the culture of a school/college committed to learning (Parker, 2004a). This is achieved through emotionally intelligent parents and teachers—the building blocks of a school.

In this section, the myriad applications of EI are discussed, which enhance the effectiveness of an individual's life as well as organizational processes—public sector or private sector. From American Express to Johnson and Johnson to Zydus Cadila, businesses have begun to embrace the concepts of EI. Schools, hospitals, and government agencies worldwide are adopting EQ practices.

There is currently a tendency to consider schools as organic wholes that grow and develop, and within which all the stakeholders, their actions, and their knowledge are interrelated and interact with the surrounding environment. This organic metaphor for institutions is taken up by those who seek to increase the efficiency of schools as places of learning. Among other things, in drawing a parallel with the functioning of living organisms, they stress internal communication and, in particular, the impact of daily negotiations between the actors concerning ways and means of running the school. They argue that only a far greater collaboration between all the actors can lead to real improvement of school performances. They also see the school as a place where pupils can learn something of their future social behavior from these exchanges. Yet they stop short of pointing to the need for a more systematic approach to certain skills related to understanding emotions in oneself and in one's relationships with others. Every child enters the world with a unique combination of components of EI such as emotional sensitivity, emotional memory, emotional processing, problem-solving ability, and emotional learning ability (Mayer et al., 2000a). The way a child is raised can dramatically affect what happens to the potential in each of these components. For example, if a child is born with a high potential for the arts, but is never given a chance to develop that potential, the world may miss out on this person's special gift. Children raised in an emotionally abusive home or from a lower economic strata home may use their emotional potential in destructive ways later in their lives (Parker et al., 2004a). Hopfl and Linstead (1997) highlighted the importance of how children learn and demonstrate that children learn value of emotions. They specified that children learn to value work, relate to peers, and feel toward their teachers. The way a child is raised can dramatically affect what happens to the potential in each area. For example, if a child is born with a high potential for the arts, but is never given a chance to develop that potential, the world may miss out on this person's special gift.

On the basis of this research on school students in the western context, EI has been found, among other things, to be positively correlated with relations with others, perceived parental support, and fewer negative interactions with close friends (Lopes et al., 2003); prosocial behavior, parental warmth, and positive peer and family relations (Mayer et al., 2002); more optimism (Schutte et al., 1998); and higher empathic perspective taking, self-monitoring in social situations, and higher social skills (Schutte et al., 2001). Rozell (2002) studied the impact of EI on the undergraduate business management students of U.S. Universities and reported lower EI scores of students representing developing countries. Mclin (2006) studied the EI of school students and the findings could be instrumental in designing interventions for those students who need to either reduce socially inappropriate emotion or induce socially appropriate emotions in themselves for social success. Opengart (2007) reviewed the content of existing social-emotional learning programs in the American K-12 curriculum and the relationship between the school-based programs and the needs of the American workplace. There was a comparison done also with critical emotional intelligence skills for the workplace on the basis of which areas for training programs in emotional intelligence could be considered.

Goleman presented EI as a main factor of success. He rejected the conventional concepts of intelligence, IQ scoring reliability, and alertness of mind as elements of success. He argued that self-control, zeal, and persistence are the main features of every successful story.

5.11 CONCLUDING REMARKS FOR APPLICATIONS OF EI

Our emotions also help us communicate with others. Our facial expressions, for example, can convey a wide range of emotions. If Susan looks sad or hurt, then she is signaling to others that she needs their help. If she is verbally skilled, then she will be able to express more of our emotional needs and thereby have a better chance of filling them. If she is effective at listening to the emotional troubles of others, she is better able to help them feel understood, important, and cared about. The only real way to know that she is happy is when she feels happy. When Susan would feel happy, she would feel content and fulfilled. This feeling comes from having our needs met, particularly our emotional needs. We can be warm, dry, and full of food, but still unhappy. Our emotions and our feelings let us know when we are unhappy and when something is missing or needed. The better we can identify our emotions, the easier it will be to determine what is needed to be happy. Our emotions are perhaps the greatest potential source of uniting all members of the human species. Clearly, our various religious, cultural, and political beliefs have not united us. Far too often, in fact, they have tragically and even fatally divided us. Emotions, on the other hand, are universal. The emotions of empathy, compassion, cooperation, and forgiveness all have the potential to unite us as a species. It seems fair to say that beliefs divide us and EI unites us.

The benefits of EI applications are discussed and include gaining competitive advantage for a firm and lower incidences of depression and suicide cases. To conclude, EI helps in survival, decision-making, boundary setting, communications, happiness, and unity. Nature developed our emotions over millions of years of evolution. As a result, our emotions have the potential to serve us today as a delicate and sophisticated internal guidance system. Our emotions alert us when natural human need is not being met. For example, when Susan felt lonely, her need for connection with other individuals is unmet. When she feels afraid, her need for safety is unmet. When she feels rejected, it is her need for acceptance that is unmet. Our emotions are also a valuable source of information. Our emotions help us make decisions. Studies show that when a person's emotional connections are severed in the brain, one cannot make even simple decisions. This is simply because one doesn't know how he or she will feel about the choices. When one feels uncomfortable with a person's behavior, our emotions alert us. If one learns to trust our emotions and feel confident expressing ourselves, then the person knows about the feeling of uncomfortableness as soon as one is aware of our feeling. This will help us set our boundaries which are necessary to protect our physical and mental health.

Review Questions

1. What are the various applications of EI?

References

Bar-On, R. (1997a), *Bar-On Emotional Quotient Inventory: A test of emotional intelligence,* Canada: Multi-Health Systems.

Bar-On, R. (1997b), *Bar-On Emotional Quotient Inventory: Technical manual,* Canada: Multi-Health Systems.

Barret, L. F., Lane, R. D., Sechrest, L., and Schwartz, G. E. (2000), "Sex differences in emotional awareness". *Personality and Social Psychology*, 26, 927–1035.

Bastian, V. A., Burns, N. R., and Nettelbeck, T. (2005), "Emotional intelligence predicts life skills, but not as well as personality and cognitive abilities", *Personality and Individual Differences*, 39, 1135–1145.

Beinhocker, E. D. (1997), "Strategy at the edge of chaos", *The McKinsey Quarterly*, 1, 24–40.

Beinhocker, E. D. (2000), "Robust adaptive strategies", *Sloan Management Review,* 40(3), 95–106.

Brackett, M. A., and Mayer, J. D. (2003), "Convergent, discriminant, and incremental validity of competing measures of emotional intelligence", *Personality and Social Psychology Bulletin*, 29, 1147–1158.

Brackett, M. A., Warner, R. N., and Bosco, J. S. (2005), "Emotional Intelligence and relationship quoting among couples", *Personal Relationships,* 12, 197–212.

Charbonneau, D., and Nicol, A. A. M. (2002), Emotional intelligence and presocial behaviors in adolescents, *Psychological Reports*, 90, 361–370.

Cherniss, C., & Deegan, G. (2000). The creation of alternative settings. In J. Rappaport & E. Seidman (Eds.), *Handbook of community psychology* (pp. 359–378). New York: Plenum.

Ciarrochi, J., Chan, A. Y. C., and Caputi, A. (2000), "A critical evaluation of the Emotional Intelligence construct", *Personality and Individual Differences*, 28, 539–561.

Ciarrochi, J., Chan, A., Caputi, P., and Robers, R. (2001), "Measuring emotional intelligence", In J. Ciarocchi, J. Forgas and D. Mayer (Eds.), *Emotional intelligence in everyday life: A scientific inquiry*, Philadelphia: Psychology Press, 3–24.

Ciarrochi, J. V., Deane, F. P., and Anderson, S. (2002), "Emotional intelligence moderates the relationship between stress and mental health", *Personality and Individual Differences*, 32, 197–209.

Cross, B., and Travaglione, A. (2003), "The untold story: Is the entrepreneur of the 21st century defined by emotional intelligence?" *International Journal of Organisational Analysis*, 11(3), 221–228.

Cummings, T., and Worley, C. (2005), Organization development and change Mason, 8th edition, Ohio: Thompson-Southwestern College.

Day, A., and Carroll, S. (2004), "Using an ability-based measure of emotional intelligence to predict individual performance, group performance, and group citizenship behaviors", *Personality and Individual Differences*, 36, 1443–1458.

Dawda, D., and Hart, S. D. (2000), "Assessing emotional intelligence: Reliability and validity of the Bar-On Emotional Quotient Inventory (EQ-i) in university students", *Personality and Individual Differences*, 28, 797–812.

Derksen, J., Kramer, R. I., and Katzo, M. (2002), "Does a self- report measure of emotional intelligence assess something different from general intelligence?" *Personality and Individual Differences*, 32, 37–48.

Eisenhardt, K. M. (1999), "Strategy as strategic decision-making", *Sloan Management Review*, 40(3), 65–72.

Freedman, J. (1998), As seen on the 6 seconds. Available from http://www.jmfreedman.com/pdf/Six_Seconds_EQ.pdf.

Gardner, L., and Stough, C. (2002), "Examining the relationship between leadership and emotional intelligence in senior level managers", *Leadership and Organization Development Journal*, 23(2), 68–78.

Goleman, D. (1998), Working with emotional intelligence, New York: Bantam Books.

Goleman, D., Boyatzis, R., and McKee, A. (2002), Primal leadership: Realizing the power of emotional intelligence, Boston: Harvard Business School Press.

Gowing, M., O'Leary, B., Brienza, D., Cavallo, K., and Crain, R. (2005), "A practitioner's research agenda: Exploring real-world applications and issues", In V. Druskat, F. Sala, and G. Mount (Eds.), *Linking emotional intelligence and performance at work*, New Jersey: Erlbaum.

Hein, S. (1996), Emotional quotient for everybody: a practical guide to emotional intelligence, New York: Äristotle Press.

Hopfl, H., and Linstead, S. (1997), "Learning to feel and feeling to learn: emotion and learning in organizations", *Management Learning*, 28(1), 5–12.

Joseph, P. T. (2006), EQ and Leadership, New Delhi: Tata McGraw Hill, 11–28.

Kafetsios, D. (2004), "Attachment and emotional intelligence abilities like course", *Personality and Individual Differences*, 37, 1, 129–146.

Kunnanatt, J. (2004), "Emotional intelligence: The new science of interpersonal effectiveness", *Human Resources Development Quarterly*, 15, 489–495.

Lopes, P. N., Salovey, P., and Straus, R. (2003), "Emotional intelligence, personality, and the perceived quality of social relationships", *Personality and Individual Differences*, 35, 641–658.

Mayer, J. D., Salovey, P. and Caruso, D. R. (1999), "Models of Emotional Intelligence", in R. J. Sternberg (ed.), *Handbook of Human Intelligence,* New York: Cambridge, 2nd edn, 396–420.

Mayer, J. D., Salovey, P., and Caruso, D. R. (2002a), Mayer-Salovey-Caruso emotional intelligence test (MSCEIT) item booklet, Canada: MHS Publishers.

Merlevede, P. E., Bridoux, D., and Vandamme, R. (2001), 7 Steps to emotional intelligence, United Kingdom: Crown Publishing house, 17–21.

Opengart, R., (2007), "Emotional intelligence and emotion work: Examining constructs from an interdisciplinary framework", *Human Resource Development Review*, 4(1), 49–62.

Parker, J. D. A, Taylor, G. J., and Bagby, R. M. (2001), "The relationship between emotional intelligence and alexithymia", *Personality and Individual Differences*, 30, 107–115.

Parker, J. D. A., Creque, R. E. Sr, Barnhart, D. L., Harris, J. I., Majeski, S. A., Wood, L. M., Bond, B. J., and Hogan, M. J. (2004a), "Academic achievement in high school: Does emotional intelligence matter?", *Personality and Individual Differences*, 37, 1321–1330.

Peterson, D. B. (1996). *Executive coaching at work: The art of one-on-one change.* Consulting Psychology Journal, 48(2), 78–86.

Reiff H. B., Hatzes N. M., Bramel M. H., and Gibbon, T. (2001), "The relation of LD and gender with emotional intelligence in college students", *Journal of Learning Disabilities*, 34, 66–78.

Rijamampianina, R., and Maxwell, T. (2002), "The sharing principle: a way of managing multicultural organisations", *South African Journal of Business Management*, 33(2), 1–11.

Roberts, R. D., Zeidner, M., and Mattews, G. (2001), "Does emotional intelligence meet traditional standards for an intelligence? Some new data and conclusions", *Emotion*, 1, 196–231.

Rozell, E. J., Pettijohn, C. E., and Parker, R. S. (2002), "An empirical evaluation of emotional intelligence: The impact on management development", *Journal of Management Development*, 21(1), 272–289.

Rubin, M. M. (1999), "Emotional intelligence and its role in mitigating aggression: A correlational study of the relationship between emotional intelligence and aggression in urban adolescents", *Unpublished dissertation*, Immaculata College, Pennsylvania.

Saklofske, D. H., Austin, E. J., and Minski, P. (2003), "Factor structure and validity of a trait emotional intelligence measure", *Personality and Individual Differences*, 34, 707–721.

Schutte, N. S., Malouff, J. M., Hall, L. E., Haggerty, D. J., Cooper, J. T., Golden, C. J., and Dornheim, L. (1998), "Development and validation of a measure of emotional intelligence", *Personality and Individual Differences,* 25, 167–177.

Schutte, N. S., Malouff J. M., Bobik C., Coston T. D., Greeson, C., and Jedlicka, C. (2001), "Emotional intelligence and interpersonal relations", *The Journal of Social Psychology,* 141(4), 523–536.

Segal, J. (1997), Raising your emotional intelligence, New York: Henry holt.

Sivanathan, N., and Fekken, G. C. (2002), "Emotional intelligence and transformational leadership", *Leadership and Organization Development Journal,* 23, 198–204.

Stein, S. J. (2007), The EQ edge: Emotional intelligence and your success, Canada: Jossey-Bass.

Stein, L. A. R., and Lebeau-Craven, R. (2002). "Motivational interviews & relapse prevention for DWI: A pilot study", *Journal of Drug Issues,* 32(4), 1051–1070.

Trinidad, D. R., and Johnson, C. A. (2002), "The Association between Emotional Intelligence and Early Adolescent Tobacco and Alcohol Use", *Personality and Individual Differences,* 32, 95–105.

Warwick, J and Nettelbeck, T. (2004), "Emotional intelligence is . . . ?", *Personality and Individual Differences,* 37, 1091–1100.

CHAPTER 6
Caselets on EI

6.1 SELECTING A HEAD OF RESEARCH DIVISION IN A FOOD COMPANY

Dr. Thomas Schultz is the Vice President for research and development at Salim Foods Company, which is a large snack food company that has approximately 1,500 employees across the city of Berlin. As a result of a recent reorganization, Dr. Thomas Schultz must choose the new Head of research division. The Head will report directly to vice president and will be responsible for developing and testing new products. The research division of Salim employs about 300 individuals. The choice of Head is important because vice president is receiving pressure from the Managing Director and board of directors to improve the company's overall productivity and profitability.

Dr. Thomas Schultz has identified three candidates for the position. Each candidate is at the same managerial level in the company. He is having difficulty choosing one of them because each of them has very strong academic credentials. Peter Wilson is a longtime employee of Salim who started part-time in the mailroom while in high school and after finishing his master's degree in commerce worked in as many as ten different positions throughout the company to become manager of new product marketing. Performance reviews of Peter Wilson's work have repeatedly described him as being very creative and insightful. In his tenure at Salim, Peter Wilson has developed and brought to market four new product lines. Peter Wilson is also known throughout the company as being very persistent about his work; when he starts a project, he brings it to a successful conclusion. It is this quality that probably accounts for the success of the two new products with which he has been involved.

A second candidate for the new position is Pablo Basic, who has been with Salim Foods for 5 years and is manager of quality control for established products. Pablo Basic has a reputation of being very bright. Before joining Salim Foods, he received his MBA from a reputed institute, graduating at the top of his class. Employees talk about Pablo Basic as the kind of person who will become Managing Director of his own company someday (in case he does develop his own company). He is also very personable. On all his performance reviews, he received extra-high scores on sociability and human relations. There isn't a single supervisor in the company who doesn't have positive things to say about how comfortable it is to work with Pablo Basic. Since joining Salim Foods Company, he has been instrumental in bringing two new product lines to market.

Thomas John, the third candidate, has been with Salim for 10 years and is often consulted by upper management regarding strategic planning and corporate direction setting. Thomas has been very involved in establishing the vision for Salim and is a company person all the way. He believes in the values of Salim Foods Company, and he actively promotes its mission. The two qualities that stand out above the rest in Thomas's performance reviews are his honesty and integrity. Employees who have worked under his supervision consistently report that they feel they can trust Thomas to be fair and consistent with them. Thomas is highly respected at Salim. In his tenure at the company, Thomas has been involved in some capacity with the development of three new product lines.

The challenge confronting the Vice President is to choose the best person for the newly established Head's position. Because of the pressures from upper management, Vice President knows he must select the best emotionally intelligent person as the head of research division.

Questions

1. Which candidate should the Vice President select based upon the attributes of emotional intelligence that you have learned?
2. Outline a comparative guideline for future use by the company for the purpose of recruitment.

6.2 AN EMOTIONALLY INTELLIGENT CEO

Mrs. Sandra Rodrigues was married for 30 years to the owner of the XYZ Company until he died in a tragic air crash. After his death, Sandra decided not to sell the business but to try to run it herself. Before the tragic accident, her only involvement in the business was in informal discussions with her husband over dinner, although she had a master's degree in commerce, with a major in accounting.

XYZ Company has ten office supply stores in a city with a population of 30,000 employees. The company had not grown for a number of years and was beginning to feel the pressure of the advertising and lower prices of the departmental retail chains.

For the first 6 months, Sandra spent her time familiarizing herself with the employees and the operations of the company. Next, she did a citywide analysis of companies that had reason to purchase office supplies. Based on her understanding of company's capabilities and her assessment of the potential market for their products and services, she developed a specific set of short-term and long-range goals for the company. Behind all of her planning, she had a vision that XYZ could be a viable, healthy, and competitive company. She wanted to carry on the business that her husband had started, but more than that, she wanted it to grow.

Over the first 5 years, Sandra invested significant amounts of money in advertising, sales, and services. These efforts were well spent because the company began to show rapid growth immediately. Because of the growth, the company hired another 200 employees. The company has opened new stores in other cities also.

The expansion at XYZ was particularly remarkable because of another major hardship Sandra had to confront. Sandra was diagnosed with uterus cancer a year after her husband died. The treatment for her cancer included 2 months of radiation therapy and 6 months of strong chemotherapy. Although the side effects included hair loss and fatigue, Sandra continued to manage the company throughout the ordeal. Despite her difficulties, Sandra was successful. Under the strength of her leadership, the growth at XYZ continued for 10 consecutive years.

Interviews with new and old employees at XYZ revealed much about Sandra's capabilities. Employees said that Sandra is a very emotionally intelligent lady.

She cared deeply about others and was fair and considerate. They said she created a family-like atmosphere at XYZ. Few employees had quit XYZ since Sandra took over. She was devoted to all the employees, and she supported their interests. For example, the company sponsors a hockey team in the summer and a basketball team in the winter. Others described Sandra as a regulated person. Even though she had cancer, she continued to be positive and interested in them. She did not get depressed with the cancer and its side effects, even though it was difficult. Employees said she was a model of strength, goodness, and quality.

At age 55, Sandra turned the business over to her two sons. She continues to act as the Chairperson but does not supervise the day-to-day operations. The company is doing more than $1,500 million in sales, and it outpaces the other chain stores in the city.

Questions

1. How would you describe Sandra's abilities and traits?
2. How big a part did Sandra's EI traits play in the expansion of the company and growth of the employees?

6.3 SELECTION AND RECRUITMENT CRITERIA

Mr. K. Raymond is the Head of Human Resources in charge of recruitment of a private bank. The bank is considerably a large, full-service banking institution. One of the major responsibilities of the head of recruitment is to visit as many college campuses as he can to interview graduating seniors for credit analyst positions in the commercial lending area at the bank. Although the number varies, he usually ends up hiring about twenty new employees, most of who come from the different colleges year after year.

Raymond has been doing recruitment for the bank for more than 10 years, and he enjoys the job very well. However, for the upcoming year, he is feeling increased pressure from the management to be particularly discriminating about whom he recommends hiring. Management is concerned about the retention rate at the bank because in recent years as many as 35% of the new hires have left. Departures after the first year have meant lost training cost, overtime cost, and strain on the staff that remain. Although management understands that some new hires always leave, the executives are not comfortable with the present compensation and they have begun to question the recruitment and training procedures.

The bank wants to recruit employees who can be groomed for higher level leadership positions. Although certain competencies are required of entry-level credit analysts, the bank is equally interested in skills that will allow individuals to advance to upper management positions as their careers progress.

In the recruitment process, banks in general always look for several characteristics. First, applicants need to have strong interpersonal skills, they need to be confident, and they need to show poise and initiative. Next, because banking involves fiduciary responsibilities, applicants need to have proper ethics, including a strong sense of the importance of confidentiality. In addition, to do the work in the bank, they need to have strong analytical and technical skills and experience in working with computers. Lastly, applicants need to exhibit a good work ethic, and they need to show commitment and a willingness to do their job even in difficult circumstances. Ability to develop social networks is also important.

Raymond is fairly certain that he has been selecting the right employees to be leaders at the bank, yet upper management is telling him to reassess his hiring criteria. Although he feels that he has been doing the right thing, he is starting to question himself and his recruitment practices.

Questions

1. Do you think the bank is looking for the right characteristics in the employees it hires?
2. Could it be that the retention problem raised by upper management is unrelated to recruitment criteria?
3. If you were recruitment manager of a bank, would you change your approach to recruiting? What criteria would be needed to recruit emotionally intelligent bank officers?

6.4 EFFECTIVENESS OF TRAINING PROGRAM

R.C. Nicholas is a training specialist in the human resource department of a large pharmaceutical company. In response to a recent companywide survey, Nicholas specifically designed a 6-week training program on listening and communication skills for effective management in the company. Nicholas' goals for the seminar are twofold: for participants to learn new communication behaviors and for participants to enjoy the seminar so that they will be motivated to attend future seminars.

The first group to be offered the program was middle-level managers in research and development. This group consisted of about twenty-five individuals, nearly all of whom had advanced degrees. Most of this group had attended several in-house training programs in the past, and so they had a sense of how the seminar would be designed and run. Because the previous seminars had not always been very productive, many of the managers felt a little disillusioned about coming to the seminar. As one of the managers said, "Here we go again: a fancy in-house training program from which we will gain nothing." Because Nicholas recognized that the managers were very experienced, he did not put many restrictions on attendance and participation. He used a variety of presentation methods and actively solicited involvement from the managers in the seminar. Throughout the first two sessions, he went out of his way to be friendly with the group. He gave them frequent coffee breaks during the sessions, and during these breaks he promoted socializing and networking.

During the third session, Nicholas became aware of some difficulties with the seminar. Rather than the full complement of twenty-five managers, attendance had dropped to only about fifteen managers. Although the starting time was established at 8:30 a.m., attendees had been arriving as late as 10:00 a.m. During the afternoon session, some of the managers were leaving the sessions to return to their offices at the company.

As he approached the fourth session, Nicholas was apprehensive about why things had been going poorly. He had become quite uncertain about how he should approach the group. Many questions were running through his mind. Had he treated the managers in the wrong way? Had he been too easy regarding attendance at the sessions? Should he have said something about the managers skipping out in the afternoon? Weren't the participants taking the seminar seriously? Nicholas was certain that the content of the seminars was innovative and substantive, but he could not figure out what he could change to make the program more successful. He sensed that his style was not working for his group, but he didn't have a clue as to how he should change what he was doing to make the sessions better.

Questions

1. What style is Nicholas using to run the seminars?
2. How to assess the participant's ability to attend a training program from an EI stand point?
3. From the EI stand point, what is Nicholas doing, wrong or right?
4. What specific changes could Nicholas implement to improve the effectiveness of seminars?

6.5 GETTING THE MESSAGE ACROSS

Mr. Rusi Palitnik is the program director of campus radio station that is supported by the university. The station has a long history and is seen favorably by students, faculty, the board of management, and the individuals in the community.

Palitnik does not have a problem getting students to work at the station. In fact, it is one of the most sought-after university-related activities. The few students who are accepted to work at the station are always highly motivated because they value the opportunity to get hands-on media experience. In addition, those who are accepted tend to be highly confident (sometimes naively so) of their own radio ability. Despite their eagerness, most of them lack a full understanding of the legal responsibilities of being on the air.

One of the biggest problems that confronts Palitnik every semester is how to train new students to follow the rules and procedures of the radio station when they are doing on—air announcing for news, sports, music, and other radio programs. It seems as if every semester numerous incidents arise in which an announcer violates in no small way the rules for appropriate airtime communication. Sometimes some announcers out of fun do illegal communication.

Palitnik is frustrated with his predicament but cannot seem to figure out why it keeps occurring. He puts a lot of time and effort into helping new students, but they just do not seem to get the message that working at station is a serious job and obeying the rules is an absolute necessity. Palitnik is wondering whether his skills are missing the mark.

Each year, Palitnik gives the students a very complete handout on policies and procedures. In addition, he tries to get to know each of the new students personally. Because he wants everybody to be happy, he tries very hard to build a relational climate at the station. Repeatedly, students say that Palitnik is the nicest manager on campus. Because he recognizes the quality of students, Palitnik lets them do mostly what they want at the station.

Question

1. If you are in Palitnik's position, what should have been your approach to manage the campus radio station?

6.6 A CASE OF UNIVERSITY TASK FORCE

A senior faculty member, Dr. Brockington, from the management faculty, was asked to chair a major university committee to plan the mission of the university for the next 20 years. Three other senior faculty and seven administrators from across the campus were also asked to serve on this committee. The Vice Chancellor of the university, Dr. A. Salsburghe, gave the committee its charge. What should XYZ University be like in the year 2035? Dr. Salsburghe told the committee that the work of this task force was of utmost importance to the future of the university and the charge of this committee should take precedence over all other matters. The task force was allowed to meet in the University conference room and use the Vice Chancellor's secretary. The report of the committee was due in 2 months.

The task force members felt very good about being selected for such an important team. The team met on a weekly basis for about 2 hours. At first, the members were very interested in the task and participated enthusiastically. They were required to do a great deal of outside research. They came back to the meetings proud to share their research and knowledge. However, after a while the meetings did not go well. The members could not seem to agree on what the charge to the group meant. They argued about what they were supposed to accomplish and resented the time the committee was taking from their regular jobs. Week after week the team met but accomplished nothing. Attendance became a problem, with individuals skipping several meetings, showing up late, or leaving early. Group members stopped working on their committee assignments. Dr. Brockington didn't want to admit to the university. Vice Chancellor didn't know what they were doing. He just got more and more frustrated. Meetings became sporadic and eventually stopped altogether. The Vice Chancellor was involved in a crisis in the university and seemed to lose interest in the committee. The Vice Chancellor never called for the report from the committee, and the report was never completed.

Questions

1. Which characteristics of excellence were lacking in this task force?
2. Which characteristics of competence were evident in this task force?
3. How would you assess Dr. Brockington as an academic leader?
4. What actions would you take (internally or externally) if you were the leader of this task force?

6.7 UNEXPECTED REACTIONS

Andrea is a manager with more than 20 years of experience. She has come up through the ranks and obtained her MBA degree 10 years ago. Her approach to supervising is to lay out in the most direct and simple terms what she sees as an issue or problem. She always seeks to get the best answer she can and is willing to delay a decision if there appears to be a need for it.

Andy is a recent transfer into the group, Andrea manages. He is an extremely competent person in his specialty, one that is crucial to the operation of the group. He came into the group with high evaluations from his previous manager, who was a somewhat authoritarian person. Andy is used to being told what the problem is, what to do, when it is to be completed, and, in some cases, how to work out a solution. He was comfortable with that kind of situation because it allowed him to apply his skills directly to many fascinating problems.

Since he joined the group, Andy's reactions to Andrea's way of managing have been unpredictable. His most common response is to argue with Andrea about how she has defined the problem or even whether it really represents a problem. Andy does not seem to enjoy this kind of confrontation but appears to be unable to react differently except on a few occasions. In those situations, Andy becomes very obedient and asks Andrea for more direction. That bothers Andrea who feels she does not have the time to mentor Andy.

Questions

1. Should Andrea just adapt to Andy's way of interacting?
2. Should she try to figure out why his reactions are so unpredictable?
3. Should she contact Andy's previous manager to find out whether his reactions were unpredictable in that setting?
4. From an emotional analysis perspective, what do you think is going on?

CHAPTER 7

Formulation of EI Radar and Competency Ladder

This chapter discusses the formation of EI radar and EI competency ladder, which in conjunction form the EI curriculum that is student specific.

7.1 INTRODUCTION

There are important issues and challenges facing education at the public school level. While academic achievement and scholastic performance have been the primary thrust of recent reform efforts, other equally important issues have taken center stage in education. Physical safety, healthy emotional development, standards of excellence and equalitarianism, a global economy and world perspective, changing workforce demands and the nature of work, multicultural and diversity issues, retention through graduation, and personal/career needs of students and educators are just a few examples. These important issues require a different and more balanced perspective of accountability and quality standards, to include emotional learning and affective domain. Our study is concerned with school and college students, who are academically being developed to contribute to the human capital inventory. Our postulate is that human capital inventory of a nation comprises many items, but the most important item is EI. We presume that EI can be nurtured in the students at an early age. Our basic proposition is that in knowledge-based, globally interconnected society we require individuals and teams who will demonstrate personal and professional competencies in the workplace. One of the primary objectives of this study is to establish a pioneering direction for the education sector to prepare youths to be outstanding professionals.

This study is a diagnostic research. In such a diagnostic research, self-report instrument is administered personally. It is a cross-sectional, field-setting study. Cross-sectional studies are carried out once and represent a snapshot at one point in time. Our research has been conducted in real-life situations. Hence, it is field-setting statistical study, covering 5,464 school students (9–14 years) and 752 college students (21–27 years) representing the pluralistic diversity of the socio-economic conditions, parental backgrounds, institutional administrative structure and processes, academic instruction and examination pattern, ethnicity, religious beliefs, and gender. These samples statistically explain the relevance, significance, magnitude, and dimensions of the study undertaken here.

The statistical analysis for students in the age group of 9–14 years was performed. The category of EI of students was determined by discriminant analysis. Lastly, cluster analysis was carried out, which lead to grouping of students based on homogeneity. Similarly, statistical analysis was conducted for students in the age group of 21–27 in a similar manner starting with descriptive statistics, discriminant analysis, cluster analysis, and validation.

A comparative analysis of statistical results obtained for students in the age group of 9–14 years and 21–27 years was carried out.

Adaptation of "Constructing an Emotional Intelligence Radar for Indian School Students," by Shamira Malekar and R.P. Mohanty, which was published in Educational Research, January 2011. Adapted and reprinted by permission.

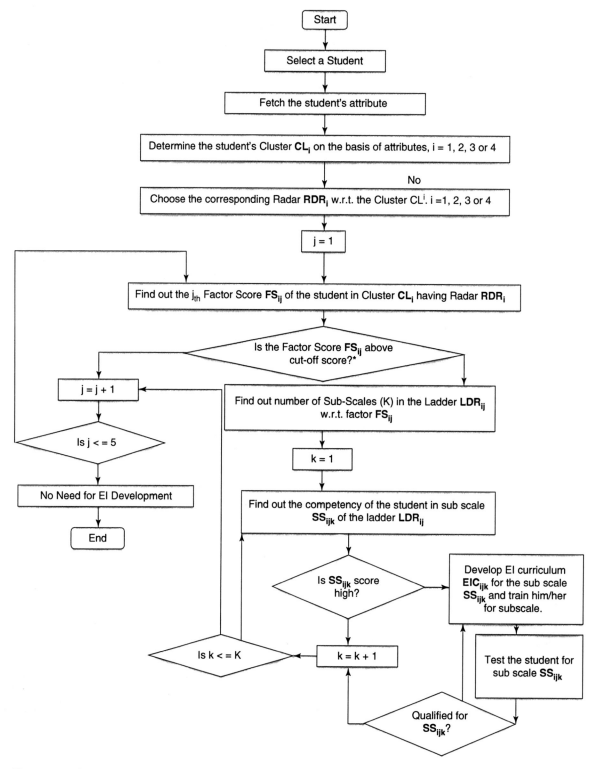

Figure 7.1   Computer-based Flow Diagram

Many researchers have viewed EI as critical to life success. Viewed from this perspective, we postulated that EI would be the compass by which the students may set their direction and the schools preparing them may adopt EI as its core curriculum to progress forward. EI will be the center of success of an individual. Hence, investment is necessary to teach students about the various factors of EI and the strategies for mastering them. Cluster analysis revealed that there are four clusters signifying the variances in family income, parental occupation, education, age, and gender. This analysis is a pointer to the educational policy makers to appropriately understand the imperatives of each cluster and innovate school and college curricula accordingly. The formation of clusters is the most focal points for description and study of factors that drive EI of students that represent diversity and plurality.

EI radar and EI ladder were formulated to address the above-mentioned issues to some extent. Cluster analysis is the means to one of these tools of discovery (EI radar). It may reveal associations and structure in data that, though not previously evident, nevertheless are sensible and useful once found. The results of cluster analysis may contribute to the definition of a formal classification scheme, such as indicating rules for assigning new cases to classes for identification and diagnostic purposes. Thus, we could summarize that cluster analysis is an exploratory data analysis tool that aims at sorting different objects into groups in a way that the degree of association between two objects is maximal if they belong to the same group and minimal otherwise.

Clustering techniques have been applied to a wide variety of research problems. In general, whenever one needs to classify a "mountain" of information into manageable meaningful piles, cluster analysis is of great utility. In sections below, cluster analysis revealed four clusters for school students (aged 9–14 years) and professional students (aged 21–27 years). The formulation of the EI radar, ladder, and curriculum could be specified in Fig 7.1.

7.2 DATABASE DEVELOPMENT

A database is a collection of interrelated data items that can be processed by one or more application systems. A database system (Hansen and Hansen, 2006) is comprised of a database, general-purpose software called the database management system (DBMS). DBMS manipulates the database and appropriate hardware. A DBMS is usually purchased from a software vendor and is the means by which an application program or an end user views and manipulates data in the database. A properly designed database system integrates data common to several functional units of an organization and facilitates the manipulation of data. In addition to simplifying the insertion, deletion, and updating of records, database systems facilitate identifying and quantifying derived relationship between data items, compiling statistical summary information, and drawing inferences about business trends. So, a database system transforms raw data into information. Database systems eliminate problems with data redundancy and data control by supporting an integrated centralized data structure. For easy retrieval of data of an individual student, database development was done using Visual basic*. Microsoft access was used at the front end to construct form 1 and form 2. Form 1 presented the data for professional students and form 2 presented data for school students. The EQ and factor scores along with the socio-economic background are obtained. The curriculum to be followed for a particular student is also featured in the program. Fig 7.2 shows the flow of data in this research.

A pictorial representation is done in Fig 7.2.

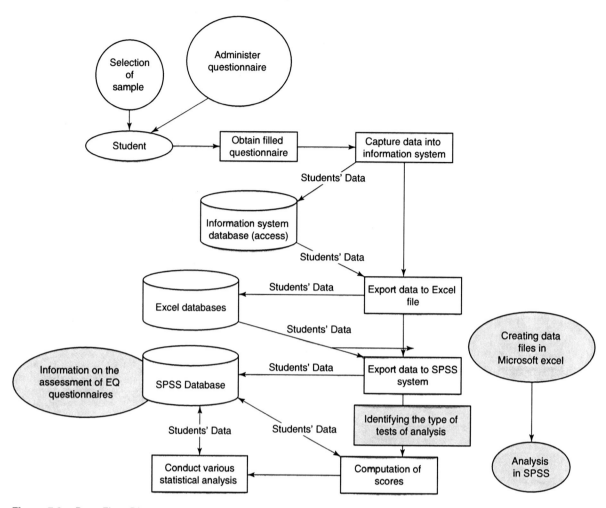

Figure 7.2   Data Flow Diagram

7.3 SAMPLE OF STUDENTS OF AGE GROUP 9–14 YEARS

Schools were based on Maharashtra State Board of Secondary and Higher Secondary Examination pattern (Secondary School Certificate Examination [SSC]) and Indian central board schools (Indian School Certificate Examination [ICSE] and Central Board of Secondary Education [CBSE]). In Mumbai, different school types like missionary, municipal, private trusts, and government-aided, exclusively boys, girls convent were considered. Schools having Muslim trusts and Jewish trusts were also included. Similarly, there were three tribal and three residential school students too in our sample. Data of students in schools of some rural areas and some cities of Maharashtra like Pune, Nasik, and Nagpur were also considered.

To summarize, schools of different ethnic groups are considered. Our various classifications included urban-rural students, residential-nonresidential students, tribal-nontribal students, government-private schools, and schools adhering to central-state board pattern as shown in Table 7.1. These students represent diverse socio-economic background characterized by upbringing of students in a rural/urban area, along with differing levels of parental literacy, parental occupation, and family income.

Table 7.1 Criteria for Classification of Students (9–14 years)

Criterion	Type of School Students
Examination pattern	SSC (state board)-ICSE and CBSE (central board)
Location	Urban-Rural
Ethnicity	Tribal-Nontribal
Boarding	Residential-Nonresidential
Management of schools	Government aided-Privately managed trusts

Table 7.2 Criteria for Classification Based on Parental Characteristics

Criterion	Parent	Level	Category
Literacy	Father	1	Up to 10th grade
		2	Graduate
		3	Postgraduates/professional education
	Mother	1	Up to 10th grade
		2	Graduate
		3	Postgraduates/professional education
Occupation	Father	0	Father has expired
		1	Father in janitorial jobs
		2	Father in service
		3	Father manages business
		4	Father is a professional
	Mother	0	Mother has expired
		1	Mother is housewife
		2	Mother in service
		3	Mother manages business
		4	Mother is a professional
Family income	–	1	Up to ₹ 100,000 (low income group)
		2	₹ 100,000 and 500,000 (medium income group)
		3	Above ₹ 500,000 (high income group)

These three parameters are also considered for classification of student type. Based on the data collected, parental categorizations are shown in Table 7.2. Literacy and occupation of each parent were considered. Based on the economic data for taxable incomes, categorization of household income was done. As discussed earlier, purposive quota sampling technique was used for this study and the questionnaires have been administered among 5,732 students.

About 268 students did not complete the main battery of tests. Hence the sample size was reduced to 5,464 (61.035% of respondents were male and 38.965% female) in the age group of 9–14 years representing 28 schools. Participants were asked if they would volunteer to study "emotional intelligence."

The stability and equivalence aspect of reliability was maintained in the procedure for data collection by personally administering the questionnaires. Workshops and personal interviews too were conducted personally, ensuring the authenticity of data collection. Also, age groups of 8 years were not considered as their comprehensibility of the questionnaire was doubtful. Similarly, age groups of 15–18 years too were not considered as

Table 7.3   Ratio Analysis for 9–14 Years

Age	Total	Ratios
9 years	120	2.19%
10 years	469	8.58%
11 years	948	17.34%
12 years	1015	18.57%
13 years	1254	22.95%
14 years	1658	30.34%

they were likely to be studying in class 10th to 12th, which are academically crucial years of their life. Similarly, age groups 21–27 years would have engineering, management and information technology students.

The results of the ratio analysis reveal that the quotas selected for this study are uniform. There is an increase observed in the number of 14-year-old students as they are able to comprehend and understand the questionnaires better than 9-year-olds. Hence, there was found to be uniform increase in the number of students as presented in Table 7.3.

Table 7.4 depicts the categorywise classification statistics for students (9–14 years) (n = 5,464) based on their gender, occupation of father and mother, and literacy levels of father and mother.

7.4 SAMPLE OF STUDENTS OF THE AGE GROUP 21–27 YEARS

The sample size comprised a total number of 761 students from 7 different types of professional colleges. Nine students did not complete the main battery of measures could not be considered. Hence, the main sample size reduced to 752 students—all of them belonging to age groups 21–27 years. About 434 (57.712%) of respondents were male and 318 (42.288%) female.

Data of students in the age group of 21–27 years was collected from management institutes, engineering colleges, and colleges providing Master's in Computer Application degrees. Two institutes provided residential courses and three institutes provided autonomous education. Table 7.5 depicts the criterion for classification for students (21–27 years) based on the courses offered by institutes, boarding type of students, and differentiation of college students.

These students represent diverse socio-economic background characterized by upbringing of students with differing levels of parental literacy, parental occupation, and family income. The criterion for classification based on parental characteristics as shown in Table 7.2 above is also considered for this sample of students (aged 21–27 years).

Table 7.6 depicts the categorywise classification statistics for students (21–27 years) (n = 752) based on their gender, occupation of father and mother, and literacy levels of father and mother. Lastly, the count of students based on family income is also considered. Ratio analysis revealed that of 623 MBA students, 53.4% were males. Of the 83 MCA students, 68.67% were males and of the 26 engineering students, 92.3% were males. When open workshops were conducted, MBA students were more interested than MCA and engineering students.

7.5 COLLECTION OF DATA

A covering letter was drafted to the head of the institution—college and school, which included general information about the research work and instrument, purpose of the study, confidentiality of the responses, and request for returning the filled questionnaire. A workshop for students along with personal interviews for teachers and the principal were two additional activities that were conducted.

Table 7.4 Classified Students' Data (9–14 years) of 5,464 Samples

Criteria	Total	Urban Students	Rural Students	Nonresidential Students	Residential Students	Tribal Students	Nontribal Students	Government Schools	Private Schools
Male	3,335	3,035	300	3,031	304	313	3,022	1,757	1,578
Female	2,129	2,018	111	2,101	28	211	1,918	950	1,179
Father's occupation									
0	20	18	2	17	3	1	19	8	12
1	1,138	752	386	744	394	447	691	701	437
2	1,661	1,141	520	1,535	126	44	1,617	548	1,113
3	2,019	1,735	284	1,761	258	13	2,006	450	1,569
4	626	425	201	587	39	3	623	76	550
Mother's occupation									
0	9	6	3	9	0	1	8	2	7
1	4,555	3,446	1,109	3,904	651	502	4,053	1,640	2,915
2	591	366	225	487	104	4	587	132	459
3	196	167	29	160	36	1	195	8	188
4	113	86	27	84	29	0	113	1	112
Father's literacy level									
1	1,403	992	411	1,000	403	448	955	799	604
2	3,011	2,416	595	2,824	187	58	2,953	833	2,178
3	1,050	663	387	820	230	2	1,048	151	899
Mother's literacy level									
1	2,852	2,179	673	2,365	487	483	2,369	1,229	1,623
2	2,116	1,595	521	1,853	263	25	2,091	546	1,570
3	496	297	199	426	70	0	496	8	488
Family income									
Up to 1,00,000	–	2,261	961	2,950	272	4,041	1,068	289	1,782
1,00,000–5,00,000	–	1,998	725	2,068	655	34	1,821	511	1,351
Above 5,00,000	–	1,455	1,353	2,411	397	0	2,615	983	559

Table 7.5 Criterion for Classification for Students (21–27 years)

Criterion	Type
Degree/Diploma offered by institutes	University approved courses-AICTE approved autonomous diploma
Boarding	Residential-Nonresidential
Program	Management-Engineering-Computer application

- **Workshop for students**

  A workshop is an educational seminar or series of meetings emphasizing interaction and exchange of information among a usually small number of participants (*The American Heritage Dictionary*). Agreement of the principal led the researcher to conduct the test in his or her premises. A workshop was conducted for students to explain the contents of the questionnaire. The listening skills of the individuals were observed.

- **Personal interviews**

  Personal interview method requires a person known as the interviewer asking questions generally in a face-to-face contact to the other person or persons (Kothari, 1999). This sort of interview may be in the form of direct personal investigation or it may be an indirect oral investigation. In the case of direct personal investigations, the interviewer has to collect the information personally from the sources concerned. He has to be on the spot and meet people from whom data has to be collected and is suitable for intensive investigations. Direct personal investigations were conducted with teachers and the principals regarding the attitude and behavior of their students of their respective classes. Specific comments made by the teacher were noted.

7.6 ANALYSIS OF DATA

- Computation of scores—Coding is done as SPSS* 11.5 for MS Windows* was utilized. Having a sample of tables redone checked the accuracy of the tabulation.
- Database development—For easy retrieval of data of an individual student, database development was done using Visual basic*. Microsoft access was used at the front end to construct form 1 and form 2. The curriculum to be followed for a particular student also featured in the program.
- Descriptive statistics—Descriptive statistics concern (Kothari, 1999) the development of certain indices from raw data. The statistical measures used in this research were measures of central tendency (mean) and measures of dispersion (standard deviation). Mean is the arithmetic average and is defined by Kothari (1999) as the value we get by dividing the total of values of various given items in a series by the total number of items. Standard deviation is defined (Kothari, 1999) as the square root of the average of squares of deviation.

  The standard deviation of sampling distribution of a statistic is known as its standard error. The objective of standard error is to provide information about the reliability and precision of a sample. If the standard error is small, there is greater uniformity in the sampling distribution and hence reliability is greater.

- Reliability assessment—Reliability (Anastasi and Urbina, 2005) refers to the consistency of scores obtained by the same person when he or she is reexamined with the test on different occasions or different set of equivalent items or under other variable examining conditions. A measuring instrument is reliable if it provides consistent results. If the instrument satisfies the quality of reliability, it leads to sound measurement of the research question.

Table 7.6 Classified Students' Data (21–27 years) of 752 Samples

Criteria	Total Number of Students	MBA Students	MCA Students	Engineering Students	Residential Students	Nonresidential Students	Mumbai University Affiliated Colleges	AICTE Approved Autonomous Institutions
Male	434	333	57	24	196	238	224	210
Female	318	290	26	2	69	249	208	110
Father's occupation								
0	7	5	2	0	1	6	4	3
1	132	101	29	2	18	114	54	78
2	146	95	42	9	18	128	82	44
3	397	293	94	10	116	281	209	188
4	69	44	20	5	20	49	34	35
Mother's occupation								
0	2	1	1	0	0	7	1	1
1	688	505	161	22	167	521	345	343
2	50	25	22	3	6	44	32	18
3	5	4	1	0	1	4	1	4
4	7	4	3	0	0	7	4	3
Father's literacy level								
1	225	188	35	2	85	140	76	149
2	457	308	127	22	70	387	269	188
3	70	43	25	2	19	51	38	32
Mother's literacy level								
1	431	347	66	18	126	305	182	249
2	309	185	116	8	47	262	194	115
3	12	7	5	0	1	11	7	5
Family income								
Up to 1,00,000	752	539	187	26	174	578	383	369
1,00,000–5,00,000	161	119	40	2	21	140	69	92
Above 5,00,000	254	194	57	3	54	200	129	125

- Discriminant analysis—Cooper and Schindler (2007) describe discriminant analysis as a method to classify objects into two or more groups. Discriminant analysis joins a nominally scaled criterion or dependent variable with one or more independent variables that are interval or ratio scaled. This analysis is appropriate when the researcher has a single dependent variable, which can be classified into groups on the basis of some attribute. The objective of this analysis is to predict an entity's possibility of belonging to a particular group based on several variables.
- Cluster analysis—Cluster analysis described by Cooper and Schindler (2007) is a set of techniques for grouping similar objects and people. It identifies homogenous subgroups or clusters. It starts with an undifferentiated group of people, events or objects and reorganizes them into homogenous subgroups. This analysis is a multivariate procedure that involves combining similar objects like similar scores of EI and the factors, parental background and economic background.
- Construction of EI radar—Based on scores of the factors of EI, EI radar is constructed to provide a direction to academicians and parents for the path they need to adopt for the development of EI in students.
- Development of EI competency ladder—Upon identification of the strengths and weaknesses of an individual, an EI competency ladder is created with stepwise introduction and mastery of a concept, which considered together, could lead to an individual with high EI.

Fig 7.3 presents a system flow diagram of the research design and development, which is the entire research in a nutshell. The explanation for each of the above steps is given above step by step. Selection and administration is the first step followed by data entry with compilation of raw and standard scores. Classification of their scores categorywise based on the school is followed by organization of their scores. Database development and organization is the next step. After testing the reliability of the questionnaire,

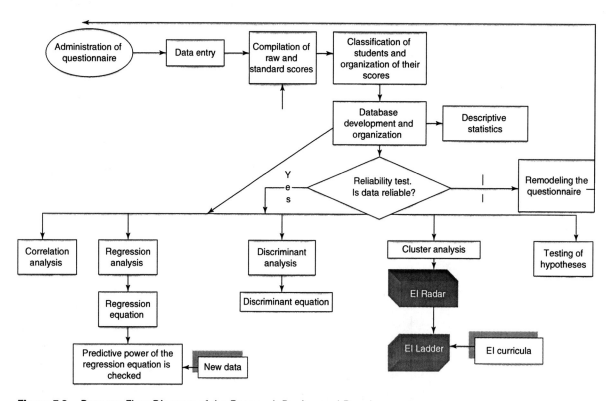

Figure 7.3   Process Flow Diagram of the Research Design and Development

different empirical analysis have been performed. If the reliability test would not have given higher values of Cronbach alpha the questionnaire would not be reliable and it would have led to the remodeling of the questionnaire and retesting. Correlation analysis leads to the identification of the significant factors that lead to the development of EI competency ladder. Regression and discriminant analysis led to the construction of regression and discriminant equations; the predictive power of the former is assessed upon collection of fresh samples. Clustering was done next with formation of four clusters, which lead to the formation of EI radar. EI radar and EI competency ladder led to the development of EI curriculum for specific categories of students.

The classifications of students were tested using analysis of variance technique. Database development is represented in the attached compact disc with categories, scores of EI, and curriculum codes assigned to specific students.

7.7 DESCRIPTIVE STATISTICS

7.7.1 Participants Group 1: 9–14 Years

In this step, scores were computed with the aid of SPSS* 11.5 for MS Windows. Table 7.7 describes the scores of the multiple factors along with EI. As per guidelines provided, the scores of EI (represented by total EQ) and its factors were computed. Students ranged from 9 to 14 years of age; the mean age was 12.34 years (SD = 1.55) for males and 12.57 years (SD = 1.63) for females.

Some features of the statistics similar to the results obtained in Parker et al. (2004a) are as follows:

a. The lowest score in case of EI is 65.
b. For intrapersonal EQ-i and adaptability EQ-i, 130 is the maximum score.
c. In case of general mood EQ-i, the maximum score is 122.
d. The maximum score of stress management EQ-i and interpersonal EQ-i is126 each.

7.7.2 Participants Group 2: 21–27 Years

Table 7.8 describes the scores of students for the multiple factors along with EI.

a. EI and its factors had 65 as lowest score.
b. In case of EI, intrapersonal EQ-i and adaptability EQ-i scores are 120, 165, and 111, respectively.
c. In case of general mood EQ-i, the maximum score is 75.
d. Stress management EQ-i and interpersonal EQ-i have maximum score of 81 and 123, respectively.

Table 7.7 Statistics for Students in the Age Group of 9–14 Years

	Minimum		Maximum		Mean		Std. Deviation		Std. Error	
	Male	Female	Male	Female	Male	Female	Male	Female	Male	Female
Age	9	9	14	14	12.41	12.55	1.55	1.63	0.20	0.30
EI	65	65	130	130	91.18	90.9	14.96	13.95	0.26	0.32
Intrapersonal EQ-i	65	65	130	130	97.85	96.32	14.42	14.02	0.24	0.30
Interpersonal EQ-i	65	65	125	125	90.06	90.88	16.94	17.98	0.29	0.36
Stress management EQ-i	65	65	126	126	88.31	87.55	13.47	12.54	0.22	0.28
Adaptability EQ-i	65	65	130	130	95.22	97.73	16.43	16.78	0.28	0.34
General mood EQ-i	65	65	122	122	87.92	88.54	15.09	15.87	0.26	0.31

Table 7.8 Statistics for Students in the Age Group of 21–27 Years

	Minimum		Maximum		Mean		Std. Deviation		Std. Error	
	Male	Female	Male	Female	Male	Female	Male	Female	Male	Female
Age	21	21	27	27	24.41	23.55	1.15	1.11	0.28	0.34
EI	76	79	130	130	94.18	96.9	14.68	13.51	0.26	0.31
Intrapersonal EQ-i	123	124	165	165	97.85	96.32	14.42	14.02	0.28	0.34
Interpersonal EQ-i	92	91	122	123	90.06	90.88	16.94	17.98	0.26	0.31
Stress management EQ-i	42	44	80	81	88.31	87.55	13.47	12.54	0.03	0.03
Adaptability EQ-i	65	65	111	111	95.22	97.73	16.43	16.78	0.26	0.32
General mood EQ-i	51	52	69	75	87.92	88.54	15.09	15.87	0.26	0.31

7.8 CLUSTER ANALYSIS

Cluster analysis is a multivariate procedure (Nargundkar, 2002) of grouping similar objects. Cluster analysis is an exploratory data analysis tool for solving classification problems. Its objective is to sort cases (people, things, and events) into groups, or clusters so that the degree of association is strong between members of the same cluster and weak between members of different clusters. Each cluster thus describes, in terms of the data collected, the class to which its members belong; and this description may be abstracted through use from the particular to the general class or type.

Cooper and Schindler (2007) have identified five basic steps:

a. Selection of sample to be clustered.
b. Definition of the variables on which to measure the objects.
c. Computation of the similarities through correlation.
d. Selection of mutually exclusive clusters.
e. Cluster comparison

7.8.1 Participants Group 1: 9–14 Years

Based on these steps, EQ-i and its factor scores of students in the age group of 9–14 years were classified as presented in Table 7.9.

The basic clustering methods (Nargundkar, 2002) used in computer packages are hierarchical clustering or linkage methods and Nonhierarchical clustering or nodal methods.

In this study, the second type including the K-means approach is considered where the number of clusters is specified in advance. The specified number of nodes and points closest to them are used to form initial clusters, and through an iterative rearrangement, the final K clusters are determined by SPSS* 11.5 for MS Windows*. K-means procedure generally gives more stable cluster, because it is an interactive procedure compared with the single-pass hierarchical methods.

Table 7.9 Categories of EQ-i and Its Factors

Student Scores	Total EQ-i	Intrapersonal EQ-i	Interpersonal EQ-i	Adaptability EQ-i	Stress Management EQ-i	General Mood EQ-i
65–89	Low	Low	Low	Low	Low	Low
90–110	High	High	High	High	High	High
Above 111	Very high	Very high	Very high	Very high	Very high	Very high

Table 7.10 depicts the number of cases in each cluster and signifies that each cluster is determined by significant number of cases.

Final cluster centers describe the mean value of each variable for each of the four clusters. The brief description of each of the four clusters as presented in Table 7.11 is given below:

Cluster 1

Students belonging to this cluster are males in the age group of 13–14 years. They have low EQ-i and low scores of intrapersonal EQ-i, interpersonal EQ-i, stress management EQ-i, adaptability EQ-i, and general mood EQ-i. They have high scores of RC. Unfortunately, their fathers have expired but mothers having undergone professional education results in family income below 100, 000 per annum.

Cluster 2

Students belonging to this cluster are males in the age group of 9–12 years. They have low EQ-i score and low scores of intrapersonal EQ-i, interpersonal EQ-i, stress management EQ-i, adaptability EQ-i, general mood EQ-i, and UC. They have high scores of RC. Their fathers manage a business and mothers are housewives. Both parents are graduates with total family income above 500,000 per annum.

Table 7.10   Number of Cases in Each Cluster

Cluster	1	1,127.000
	2	1,887.000
	3	979.000
	4	1,411.000
Valid		5,404.000
Missing		60.000

Table 7.11   Final Cluster Centers

	Cluster			
	1	**2**	**3**	**4**
Categories of total EQ-i	1	1	2	2
Age group	2	1	2	2
Category of intrapersonal EQ-i	1.64	1.64	2.27	2.12
Category of interpersonal EQ-i	1.26	1.31	2.12	2.10
Category of stress management EQ-i	1.35	1.34	1.70	1.65
Category of adaptability EQ-i	1.39	1.42	2.31	2.34
Category of general mood EQ-i	1.24	1.24	1.95	1.90
Category of UC	1.37	1.41	1.33	1.49
Category of RC	2.13	2.13	2.13	2.29
Father's occupation	0	3	2	3
Mother's occupation	4	1	1	3
Father's education	2	2	1	2
Mother's education	3	2	1	2
Income	1	3	1	3
Gender	1	1	2	1

Cluster 3

Students belonging to this cluster are adolescent females in the age group of 13–14 years. They have high EQ-i scores and high scores of intrapersonal EQ-i, interpersonal EQ-i, adaptability EQ-i, and RC. The scores of stress management EQ-i, general mood EQ-, and UC are low. Their fathers are in service and mothers are housewives. Both parents are educated till the 10th standard with their family income below 100, 000 per annum.

Cluster 4

Students belonging to this cluster are adolescent males in the age group of 13–14 years. They have high EQ-i scores and high scores of intrapersonal EQ-i, interpersonal EQ-i, adaptability EQ-i, and RC. The scores of stress management EQ-i, general mood EQ-i, and UC are low. Both parents are graduates and are occupied in managing business. Their total family income is above 500, 000 per annum.

7.8.2 Participants Group 2: 21–27 Years

In this study, there are four clusters of students according to the category of EQ-i scores and factors of EQ-i. The EQ-i scores for 21–27 years were classified as presented earlier in 7.7.2. Table 7.12 depicts the number of cases in each cluster and signifies that each cluster is determined by significant number of cases.

Final cluster centers describe the mean value of each variable for each of the four clusters. The brief description of each of the four clusters as depicted in Table 7.13 is given below:

Table 7.12   Number of Cases in Each Cluster

Cluster		
	1	227.000
	2	187.000
	3	196.000
	4	142.000
Valid		752.000
Missing		0.000

Table 7.13   Final Cluster Centers

	Cluster			
	1	2	3	4
Age	23	23	25	23
Gender	1	1	2	1
Category of intrapersonal EQ-i	2.20	2.12	1.64	1.64
Category of interpersonal EQ-i	2.45	2.01	1.31	1.26
Category of stress management EQ-i	2.70	2.25	1.34	1.35
Category of adaptability EQ-i	2.41	2.34	1.42	1.39
Category of general mood EQ-i	2.05	2.60	1.24	1.24
Category of total EQ-i	2	2	1	1
Father's occupation	3	2	1	3
Mother's occupation	1	1	2	1
Father's literacy level	2	2	2	2
Mother's literacy level	1	1	2	1
Income	2	2	2	3

Cluster 1

Students belonging to this cluster are 23-year males having high EQ-i score. They have high scores of intrapersonal EQ-i, interpersonal EQ-i, stress management EQ-i, adaptability EQ-i, and general mood EQ-i. Their fathers manage their own business and mothers are housewives. Fathers are graduates and mothers studied till the 10th standard with family income between 100,000 and 500,000 per annum.

Cluster 2

Students belonging to this cluster are 23-year-old males with high EQ-i score. They have high scores of intrapersonal EQ-i, interpersonal EQ-i, stress management EQ-i, adaptability EQ-i, and general mood EQ-i. Their fathers are in service with banks, in governmental organizations, or in private firms as officers, supervisor, and other clerical positions and mothers are housewives. Fathers are graduates and mothers studied till the 10th standard with family income between 100,000 and 500,000 per annum.

Cluster 3

Students belonging to this cluster are 25-year-old females with low EQ-i score. They have low scores of intrapersonal EQ-i, interpersonal EQ-i, stress management EQ-i, adaptability EQ-i, and general mood EQ-i. Their fathers are working for lowly jobs such as peons, sweepers, and watchman and mothers are housewives. Both parents are graduates with family income between 100,000 and 500,000 per annum.

Cluster 4

Students belonging to this cluster are 23-year-old males with low EQ-i score. They have low scores of intrapersonal EQ-i, interpersonal EQ-i, stress management EQ-i, adaptability EQ-i, and general mood EQ-i. Their fathers manage their own business and mothers are housewives. Fathers are graduates and mothers studied till the 10th standard with family income above 500,000 per annum.

7.9 FORMULATION OF EI RADAR

Radar is "radio, detection, and ranging" (Wikipedia, 2008). Radar is a system that uses electromagnetic waves to identify the range, altitude, direction, or speed of both moving and fixed objects such as aircraft, ships, motor vehicles, weather formations, and terrain. In simple terms, a radar system is used to detect the position and/or movement of objects. Much like a map, our radar—EI radar—displays the position of scores of EI and its factors for four clusters formed in cluster analysis. This tool presents and relates to all of the factors through which an individual can look for opportunities to increase EI. Based on the study conducted till date, we have developed and applied a new framework called the EI radar.

The following are the objectives of EI radar

  a. Understanding: Broaden and deepen the construct of EI.
  b. Managing: Identify dimensions, which contribute to managing EI.
  c. Improving: Identify best practices to improve EI related to culture and ethnicity of students.
  d. Institutionalizing: Develop framework for enhancing EI of students.

The usages of EI radars are explained in section 7.10.

7.9.1 Radar for School Students (9–14 years)

Based on the empirical analysis as discussed in section 6.6 of chapter 6, various factors affecting EI helped to identify and define the radar's five dimensions:

1. Intrapersonal EQ-i
2. Interpersonal EQ-i
3. Stress management EQ-i
4. Adaptability EQ-i
5. General mood EQ-i

We have identified four clusters and the cluster components are age, gender, father's occupation, mother's occupation, father's literacy, mother's literacy, and income. Similar to a map, the EI radar consists of five factors that serve as anchors to guide academicians to identify a methodology that would surely increase EI. EI radars are shown in Figs 7.4–7.7 for students (age group of 9–14 years).

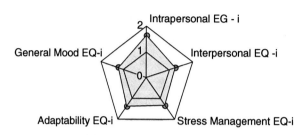

Figure 7.4   EI Radar for Students (9–14 years) in Cluster 1

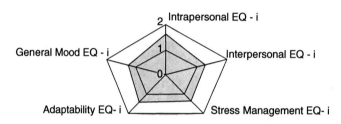

Figure 7.5   EI Radar for Students (9–14 years) in Cluster 2

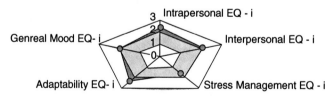

Figure 7.6   EI Radar for Students (9–14 years) in Cluster 3

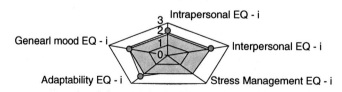

Figure 7.7   EI Radar for Students (9–14 years) in Cluster 4

Radars 1 and 2 have low scores of all the five factors: intrapersonal EQ-i, interpersonal EQ-i, adaptability EQ-i, stress management EQ-i, and general mood EQ-i resulting in subsequent display in radar 1 and radar 2. (Figs 7.4 and 7.5)

Clusters 3 and 4 have high scores of intrapersonal EQ-i, interpersonal EQ-i, adaptability EQ-i, and general mood EQ-i resulting in subsequent display in radar 3 and radar 4 (Figs 7.6 and Fig 7.7).

We are also investigating how academicians and EI practitioners can use the EI radar to construct a strategic approach to improve EI of students.

Specifically, the radar could help identify the strengths and weaknesses of each student as well as any promising capabilities, those overlooked by their parents and teachers.

7.9.2 Radar for Professional Students (21–27 years)

Various factors affecting EI helped to identify and define the radar's five dimensions:

a. Intrapersonal EQ-i
b. Interpersonal EQ-i
c. Stress management EQ-i

d. Adaptability EQ-i
e. General mood EQ-i

We have identified four clusters and the cluster components are age, gender, father's occupation, mother's occupation, father's literacy, mother's literacy, and income. Similar to a map, the EI radar consists of five factors that serve as anchors to guide academicians to identify a methodology that would surely increase EI. EI radars are shown in Figs 7.8–7.11 for students (age group of 21–27 years).

Radars 5 and 6 have high scores of all the five factors: intrapersonal EQ-i, interpersonal EQ-i, adaptability EQ-i, stress management EQ-i, and general mood EQ-i resulting in subsequent display in radar 5 and radar 6 (Figs 7.8 and 7.9).

Radars 5 and 6 have low scores of all the five factors: intrapersonal EQ-i, interpersonal EQ-i, adaptability EQ-i, stress management EQ-i, and general mood EQ-i resulting in subsequent display in radar 7 and radar 8. (Figs 7.10 and 7.11)

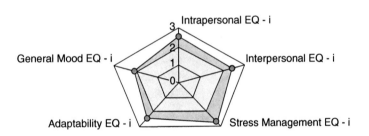

Figure 7.8   EI Radar for Students (21–27 years) in Cluster 1

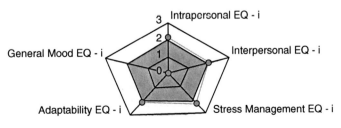

Figure 7.9   EI Radar for Students (21–27 years) in Cluster 2

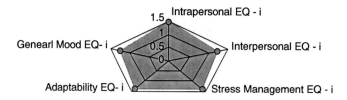

Figure 7.10 EI Radar for Students (21–27 years) in Cluster 3

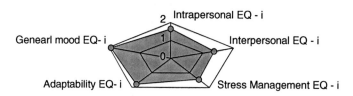

Figure 7.11 EI Radar for Students (21–27 years) in Cluster 4

7.10 USAGES OF EI RADAR

In this research, we are investigating how schools can use the EI radar to construct a strategic approach to competency and skills development. Specifically, the radar could help a school determine how its current scores of EI and the driving factors stack up. Using that information, the schools could then identify opportunities and prioritize on which dimensions to focus its efforts. Such analyses can reveal the strengths and weaknesses of each student as well as any promising opportunities, particularly those overlooked by the schools and parents as a whole. Traditionally, most schools do not engage in identifying the EI of students are the result of simple inertia or ignorance. But when a school identifies and pursues neglected EI dimensions, it can change the basis of human development, because each dimension requires a different set of capabilities that cannot be developed or acquired overnight. And developing along one dimension often influences choices with respect to other dimensions. Summarily, we can use the EI radar to visualize systematically, to brainstorm and explore the dimensions of EI, to diagnose and identify students with low scores, and to prescribe and suggest a curriculum for EI development. This radar may facilitate, develop, and navigate the position of each individual student to identify the strengths and weaknesses. This radar will promote a thorough understanding of EI. As discussed earlier, prior research has taken views on EI that tend to focus on what constitutes EI. We need to consider the how, who, and where of EI applications. This EI radar makes each factor of EI operational and is a pragmatic methodology for creating EI maps for each and every individual student. We have created a holistic conceptual framework through construction of radar to visualize, diagnose, and improve the EI of an individual student. Ultimately, the EI radar could guide the way academicians manage the increasingly complex student behavior and add value by building HC. In doing so, the framework of EI radar and EI ladder discussed in the subsequent section could become an important tool for students, EI trainers, and EI practitioners—anyone seeking development through EI.

7.11 EI COMPETENCY LADDER

Spencer and Spencer (1993) defined competency as an underlying characteristic of an individual that is causally related to criterion-referenced effective and/or superior performance in a job or situation. Underlying

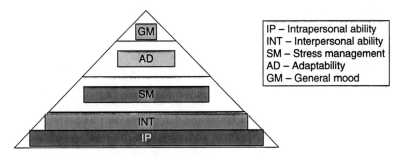

Figure 7.12   Importance of Factors of EI

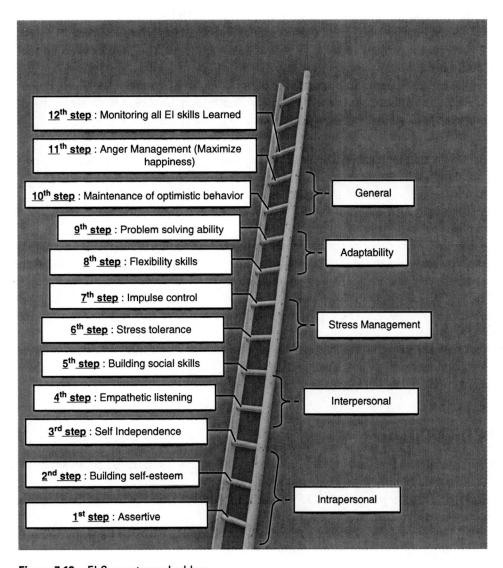

Figure 7.13   EI Competency Ladder

characteristic means the competency is a fairly deep and enduring part of a person's personality and can predict behavior in a wide variety of situations and job tasks. "Causally related" means that a competency causes or predicts behavior or performance. "Criterion referenced" means that the competency actually predicts who does something well or poorly as measured on a specific criterion or standard. Boyatzis (1982) defines a competency as an underlying characteristic of a person, which results in effective or superior performance. Competence is also defined as a set of behavior patterns that an incumbent needs to bring to a position in order to perform its tasks and functions in the delivery of desired results and outcomes (Bartram et al., 2002). A competency is a characteristic of an individual, which can be measured. It differentiates between superior and average or between effective and ineffective performances. To summarize, competencies are certain characteristics and abilities that enable an individual to perform appropriate actions. To increase the EI of students, a competency ladder is constructed based on the degree of association found between EI and its factors with correlation analysis. Goleman (1995) identified EI as a set of competencies by Goleman (1995). Similarly, our research has identified five competencies of EI: intrapersonal ability, interpersonal ability, stress management, adaptability, and general mood.

Fig 7.12 portrays the priority order of factors of EI for students. The priority is established based on correlation analysis.

Based on the earlier figure of importance of factors of EI, an EI competency ladder is constructed as presented in Fig 7.13 that discusses the steps of the ladder, which one needs to master one by one.

Each competency identified earlier is further characterized by specific skills.

- To master the competence of IP, one needs to master the art of assertive communication (step 1) and build high self-esteem (step 2).
- To master the competence of INT, one needs to master the self-independence (step 3) and empathetic listening (step 4). Building social skills and strengthening relationships (step 5) is also crucial if one needs to master the competence of INT.
- To master the competence of SM, which discusses methodology of tolerating and managing stress, we need to climb step 6 and step 7, which are stress tolerance and impulse control, respectively.
- To master the competence of AD, we need to climb step 8 (flexibility skills) and step 9 (problem-solving ability).
- To master our last competence of GM, we need to maintain optimistic behavior (step 10) and manage anger (maximize happiness, step 11).
- The last step analyzes the level of incorporation of eleven steps in an individual and thus monitors the level attained with practical suggestions. The EI radar and the EI ladder in conjunction form different curricula, which are student specific.

7.12 EI CURRICULA

Based on the dimensions identified in the EI radar and competencies in the EI competency ladder, an EI curriculum is designed to raise the EI scores of students.

Methodology: These steps would be incorporated in students with the help of case studies, exercises, live demonstrations, and lectures.

Duration: The steps vary in duration as the omission of a particular step depends on the individual's EI score.

* *The following are the curriculum codes for students in the age group of 9–14 years:*

The database representation on the compact disc comprises the description of the student with curriculum code C 1–C 27. Table 7.14 represents the rationale for elimination of steps if the scores are high.

Table 7.14 Rationale of Assignment of Curriculum Codes for Students (9–14 years)

Curriculum Code	Intrapersonal Ability	Interpersonal Ability	Stress Management	Adaptability	General Mood
C 1	< 90	> 89	> 69	> 89	> 69
C 2	< 90	< 90	> 69	> 89	> 69
C 3	< 90	< 90	< 70	> 89	> 69
C 4	< 90	< 90	< 70	< 90	> 69
C 5	< 90	< 90	< 70	< 90	< 70
C 6	> 89	< 90	> 69	> 89	> 69
C 7	> 89	< 90	< 70	> 89	> 69
C 8	> 89	< 90	< 70	< 90	> 69
C 9	> 89	< 90	< 70	< 90	< 70
C 10	> 89	> 89	< 70	< 90	> 69
C 11	> 89	> 89	< 70	> 89	> 69
C 12	> 89	> 89	< 70	< 90	< 70
C 13	> 89	> 89	> 69	< 90	> 69
C 14	> 89	> 89	> 69	> 89	< 70
C 15	> 89	> 89	> 69	< 90	< 70
C 16	< 90	> 89	< 70	> 89	> 69
C 17	< 90	> 89	> 69	< 90	> 69
C 18	< 90	> 89	> 69	> 89	< 70
C19	> 89	< 90	> 69	< 90	> 69
C 20	> 89	< 90	> 69	< 90	< 70
C 21	> 89	> 89	> 69	> 89	> 69
C 22	< 90	< 90	> 69	< 90	> 69
C 23	< 90	> 89	< 70	< 90	< 70
C 24	< 90	> 89	< 70	< 90	< 70
C 25	> 89	< 90	> 69	< 90	> 69
C 26	< 90	< 90	> 69	< 90	< 70
C 27	< 90	< 90	< 70	< 90	> 69

. * *The following are the curriculum codes for students in the age group of 21–27 years:*
One follows and masters the step and then goes to the next step.

a. If intrapersonal ability scores are high, steps 1–3 could be omitted. Steps 4–12 are to be followed.
b. If interpersonal ability scores are high, steps 4 and 5 could be omitted. Steps 1 and 2 and then steps 6–12 are to be followed.
c. If stress management scores are high, steps 6 and 7 could be omitted. Steps 1–5 and then steps 8–12 are to be followed.

d. If adaptability scores are high, steps 8 and 9 could be omitted. Steps 1–7 and then steps 10–12 are to be followed.

e. If the scores for general mood are high, then step 10 could be omitted. Steps 1–9 and then steps 11 and 12 are to be followed.

Table 7.15 represents the rationale for elimination of a step if the scores are high for students in the age group of 21–27 years.

One follows and masters the step and then goes to the next step.

a. If intrapersonal ability scores are high, steps 1 and 2 could be omitted. Steps 3–12 are to be followed.

b. If interpersonal ability scores are high, steps 3–5 could be omitted. Steps 1 and 2 and then steps 6–12 are to be followed.

c. If stress management scores are high, steps 6 and 7 could be omitted. Steps 1–5 and then steps 8–12 are to be followed.

d. If adaptability scores are high, steps 8 and 9 could be omitted. Steps 1–7 and then steps 10–12 are to be followed.

e. If the scores for general mood are high, then step 10 could be omitted. Steps 1–9 and then steps 11 and 12 are to be followed.

EI understands cognitively why they engage in effective and ineffective behaviors, and apply this wisdom in their daily lives and in the workplace.

The following are the five steps career counselors can use in helping their students gain personal, social, and career competence skills:

Table 7.15   Table Showing the Rationale of Assignment of Curriculum Codes for Students (21–27 years)

Curriculum Code	Intrapersonal Ability	Interpersonal Ability	Stress Management	Adaptability	General Mood
C 1	< 140	< 100	< 90	> 59	> 59
C 2	> 139	< 100	< 90	< 60	> 59
C 3	> 139	> 99	< 90	< 60	> 59
C 4	> 139	> 99	< 90	> 59	> 59
C 5	< 140	> 99	< 90	> 59	> 59
C 6	< 140	> 99	> 89	> 59	< 60
C 7	> 139	> 99	< 90	> 59	< 60
C 8	> 139	> 99	> 89	> 59	> 59
C 9	> 139	> 99	< 90	> 59	> 59
C 10	> 139	> 99	> 89	< 60	> 59
C 11	< 140	> 99	> 89	< 60	< 60
C 12	< 140	< 100	< 90	> 59	< 60
C 13	< 140	> 99	< 90	> 59	< 60
C 14	> 139	< 100	< 90	> 59	< 60

a. Understand the importance of EI skills. It is important to talk to the student about the importance of EI skills in attaining a job and succeeding in today's workplace. Students can benefit from seeing the EI framework and by identifying situations in which these EI skills might be helpful.
b. Identify deficits in EI skills. At this point, trying to assess the student's EI weaknesses is critical.
c. Assess the effect of EI skill deficits on career development. Once a skill deficit area is identified, a student usually needs assistance in exploring how lack of this skill is affecting his or her career development and how it could keep them from being successful in the workplace.
d. Usage of EI skills more effectively. In the career counseling process, students need help in learning to be more effective using the El skill. The role of the career counselor becomes one of a teacher and a model for the skill.
e. Practice of the EI skill. Social learning theorists (Vygotsky, 1978) believe that the best learning takes place not in isolation but in various social settings. On school and college campuses, there are immense opportunities to practice EI skills. Participation in hobbies, in leisure activities, in clubs, and in organizations can provide excellent opportunities for students to practice EI skills. In addition, interactions with others on campus or in residence halls can be opportunities to practice interpersonal skills.

To conclude, the overall physical health of such students would most likely be superior to students low in EI. If academia were indeed to incorporate an explicit focus on emotional intelligence, through what avenues could such a focus be implemented? One avenue is to require one or more classes on emotional intelligence, most likely as a lower division requirement, just as some universities require courses on critical thinking. Another avenue is to encourage the inclusion of a focus on emotional intelligence into existing courses where such a focus might be directly relevant (e.g., teaching conflict management skills in a psychology or sociology class).

In summary, the inclusion of a focus on emotional intelligence as part of the standard curriculum could lead to a variety of positive personal, social, and societal outcomes. Increasing emotional intelligence not only facilitates the learning process and improves career choice and likelihood of success, but also enhances the probability of better personal and social adaptation in general.

The educational experience would tend to be more balanced or holistic, as it would focus on educating the whole person. There could also be beneficial effects on the university milieu, improving the environment in which the educational experience occurs.

Emerging interdisciplinary research and studies from education, business, psychology, and behavioral medicine are showing clear and significant contributions of EI to human performance, personal health, and resilience.

Emotional knowledge, skills, and intelligence hold a major key to improving education and helping students, teachers, faculty, and student development professional attain higher degrees of achievement, career success, leadership, and personal well-being.

7.13 CONCLUDING REMARKS

EI radars are constructed based on cluster analysis of students. Based on significant factors of EI, sets of competencies are identified that increases EI scores. These competencies are presented as EI competency ladder.

The steps of the EI competency ladder will be useful to coach and counsel the students at a very young age to upgrade to higher level of EI. Accordingly, educational policy framework can be formulated for students to make them successful in life. Thus, the study contributes toward the HCD. These findings could be instrumental in designing interventions for those students who need to either reduce socially inappropriate emotion or induce socially appropriate emotions in themselves for social success. Further research, building from this model, must investigate the aspect of validating the scoring range of the instrument (very high, high, and low) in defining one's level of emotion management ability. A training manual should be developed using emotion management techniques and strategies, as an intervention or as social curriculum training.

References

Anastasi, A., and Urbina, S. (2005), Psychological testing, 7th edition, New Delhi: Pearson's Education, 84–154.

Bartram, D., Robertson, I. T., and Callinan, M. (2002), "Introduction: A framework for examining organizational effectiveness". In I. T. Robertson, M. Callinan and D. Bartram (Eds.), *Organisational effectiveness: The role of Psychology*, Chichestor, United Kingdom: Wiley, 1–12.

Boyatzis, R., (1982), The competent manager: A model for effective performance, New York: John Wiley and Sons.

Cooper, D., and Schindler, (2007), Business research methods, New Delhi: Tata Mcgraw hill, 138–170.

Goleman, D. (1995), Emotional intelligence, New York: Bantam Books.

Hansen, G. W., and Hansen, J. V. (2006), Data base management and design, New Delhi: Prentice hall of India Private limited, 3–99.

Kothari, C. R. (1999), Research methodology: methods and techniques, New Delhi: Vishwa Prakashan, 21–151.

Nargundkar, R. (2002). Marketing research: Text and cases, New Delhi: Tata Mcgraw-Hill.

Parker, J. D. A., Creque, R. E. Sr., Barnhart, D. L., Harris, J. I., Majeski, S. A., Wood, L. M., Bond, B. J., and Hogan, M. J. (2004a), "Academic achievement in high school: Does emotional intelligence matter?", *Personality and Individual Differences*, 37, 1321–1330.

Spencer, L., and Spencer, S. (1993), Competence at work: Models for superior performance, New York: John Wiley and Sons, 9–15.

Vygolsky, L. S. (1978), Mind in society, Cambridge, MA: Harvard University Press.

Wikipedia, the free encyclopedia downloaded on the 17th August 2008. http://www.thefreedictionary.com/workshop.

PART B

Methods to Manage the Steps of the EI Competency Ladder

This section discusses the methods to manage and regulate the steps of the EI competency ladder.

CHAPTER 8

Assertive Communication, Self-Esteem, Self-Independence, and Self-Regulation

8.1 INTRODUCTION

Assertive communication is a form of behavior and means of expression characterized by a confident declaration or affirmation of a statement without the need of proof (Holland and Ward, 1980). This affirm's the person's rights or point of view without either aggressively threatening the rights of another without assuming a position of dominance. It also does not submissively permit another to ignore or deny one's rights or point of views (Back and Back, 1986).

Assertive communication consists of sharing needs and wants honestly in a safe manner. This resumes respect for the boundaries of oneself and others. These boundaries include the physical self, possessions, and relationships. It also presumes an interest in the fulfillment of needs and wants through expression, coordination, and cooperation. Assertive communication of personal opinions, needs, and boundaries has been conceptualized as the behavioral middle ground. It lies between ineffective passive and aggressive responses of communication. Such assertive communication emphasizes expressing feelings forthrightly. The method or way of communicating is such that it will not spiral into aggression.

There could be instances wherein others' actions could threaten one's boundaries. Assertive communication would assist in preventing escalation of the situation. In contrast, aggressive communication judges, threatens, lies, breaks confidences, stonewalls, and violates others' boundaries. At the opposite end of the dialectic is passive communication. Victims may passively permit others to violate their boundaries. At a later time, they may come back and attack with a sense of impunity or righteous indignation. In our case, Susan had a passive aggressive type of personality. She could work on being assertive.

Assertive communication attempts to transcend these extremes by appealing to the shared interest of all parties. It focuses on the issue, topic, or problem under consideration, not the person. Aggressive and passive communication, on the other hand, may at times mark an end to a social relationship and reduce self-respect. There are instances wherein individuals confuse assertive communication with being right. They focus on winning, instead of focusing on the result that they really want to achieve. As a result of this, individuals don't listen to what is being said. The result of this is that they do not understand what the other person is trying to communicate to them. This is precisely where the whole conversation starts to break down. At a deep level, this sets up divisions on an emotional and psychological level.

Individuals are grown with this thought process of having inherent rights to not share matter or information, which is important to us. This comes from beliefs about scarcity and lack. These beliefs about scarcity and lack set the scene for conflict. The need for assertiveness comes out of a belief that there is a conflict. Scarcity, lack, conflict, and the need for assertive communication are just the beliefs in our society. A belief in scarcity and lack lead to resentment and insecurity. Individuals don't feel good about themselves and they go into fight or flight responses. Both the fight and the flight responses are defensive. It's the wait-and-negotiate phase that can be leveraged with assertive communication.

Assertiveness is the ability to express our needs and rights, positive or negative feelings, without violating the rights and limits of others. Taking the case of Susan, however, before one can comfortably express needs, one must believe that there is a legitimate right to have those needs. One has the right:

- To decide how to lead her life. This includes pursuing goals and dreams and establishing priorities.
- To own values, beliefs, opinions, and emotions—and the right to respect self for them, no matter the opinion of others.
- To refrain from justifying or explaining actions or feelings to others.
- To tell others how one wishes to be treated.
- To express self and to say "No," "I don't know," and "I don't understand," or even "I don't care." One has the right to take the time needed to formulate ideas before expressing them.
- To ask for information or help—without having negative feelings about needs.
- To change her mind, to make mistakes, and to sometimes act illogically—with full understanding and acceptance of the consequences.
- To like self even though not perfect, and to sometimes do less than one is capable of doing.
- To have positive, satisfying relationships within which one feels comfortable and free to express self honestly—and the right to change or end relationships if they don't meet her needs.
- To change, enhance, or develop our life in any way we determine.

When one doesn't believe that one has these rights, one may react very passively to circumstances and events in life as is Susan. When one allows the needs, opinions, and judgments of others to become more important than one's own, then one is likely to feel hurt, anxious, and even angry. This kind of passive or nonassertive behavior is often indirect, emotionally dishonest, and self-denying.

Many individuals feel that attending to their legitimate needs and asserting their rights translate to being selfish. Selfishness means being concerned about only your rights, with little or no regard for others. Implicitness in one's rights is the fact that one is concerned about the legitimate rights of others as well. That does not count for selfishness. Susan could look at her rights, needs, and wants.

8.2 SPECIFIC TECHNIQUES FOR IMPROVING ASSERTIVENESS

Given below are certain techniques for improving assertiveness for Susan.

a. Be as specific and clear as possible about what she wants, thinks, and feels. The following statements project this preciseness:
" I want to..."
" I don't want you to..."
" Would you...?"
" I liked it when you did that."
" I have a different opinion, I think that..."
"I have mixed reactions. I agree with these aspects for these reasons, however I am disturbed about these aspects for these reasons."
It can be helpful to explain exactly what one means and exactly what one doesn't mean, such as "I don't want to break up over this, however I'd like to talk it through and see if we can prevent it from happening again."

b. Be direct and deliver message to the person for whom it is intended.
If Solomon wants to tell Susan something, tell her directly. Telling everyone except Susan is a faulty methodology followed by Solomon. One cannot and should not tell a group of which Susan happens to be a member.

    c. "Own" our message. Acknowledge that our message comes from our frame of reference, our conception of good vs. bad or right vs. wrong, and our perceptions.

      One can acknowledge ownership with personalized "I" statements such as "I don't agree with you" as compared to "You're wrong" or "I'd like you to buy the groceries" as compared to "You really should buy the groceries, you know." Suggesting that someone is wrong or bad and should change for his or her own benefit when, in fact, it would foster resentment and resistance rather than understanding and cooperation.

To summarize, when individuals are expected to be open, attentive, and responsive to customers or colleagues, the disciplines of improvisation, presented effectively, are invaluable performance enablers. The essential benefits of practicing improvisation are that individuals develop transferable skills that enable them to:

- Work collaboratively with colleagues, family members, and customers.
- Trust and harness their creativity to solve problems and innovate.

8.3 HOW TO IMPROVE ASSERTIVENESS EVEN IF ONE IS SHY

One of the worst things about being shy is the feeling that results from not standing up for self when one knows that rights have been abused or violated. That's not to mention all of the lost opportunities that your shyness has prevented you from experiencing. What if there was a way to eliminate this shyness and the resultant bad feelings associated with not being assertive and standing up for your rights? There are various strategies to change our approach, outlook, and strategies to eliminate the shyness and improve your assertiveness. Individuals' lack of assertiveness is primarily the result of the three barriers they place between them and their assertiveness. These barriers are as follows:

    a. Negative self-concept
    b. Poor communication skills
    c. Lack of skill in handling conflict situations

Negative self-concept is the product of what others have told us about ourselves. It also includes our own observations of our actions and the resultant consequences of these actions. It takes many years to internalize and "believe" the judgments of others. Too often, individuals accept these judgments as "who one is" whether they are factual or not. How to change our self-concept or self-image in order to reduce our shyness and improve our assertiveness? There are two exercises that one can perform to change his or her self-image.

    1. One can reduce the number of times one said bad things to self about any weakness or fault one thinks that one may have.
    2. One can increase the number of times one says good things to self about any positive qualities possessed.

This simple exercise can dramatically improve your self-image. This is the first step to overcome our shyness and improve our assertiveness.

Poor communication skills are the next primary obstacle for those seeking to improve their assertiveness. The reason this is such a primary obstacle, especially for someone who is shy, is because of the verbal dialogue between persons. This being the case, the shy person can get seriously derailed from making his or her point effectively. Conversation can be objectionable and interruptible, not exactly the perfect "communication playground" for the shy person looking to be more assertive. However, there are exercises one can perform to increase the effectiveness of his or her communication skills. One particular exercise is scriptwriting. In this exercise, one develops different conversational scenarios and in essence practice various responses to each scenario created. It is imperative that one performs this exercise with one's viewpoint as well as that of the other party. This will help in improving one's communication skills because it allows one to develop the ability to see the viewpoint of the other individual.

The final major obstacle to improving assertiveness is a lack of skill in handling conflict situations. In certain stressful situations, some individuals literally cannot control themselves or their emotions. They just lose it. There are ways to reduce this negative occurrence over time. The most effective way is called desensitizing. This is a systematic approach that is similar to behavior therapy. In this approach, imagine a stressful event in one's life. One would then make a hierarchy of scenes of this event, from least intimidating to most intimidating. In one's mind, one would progress through each scene, giving sufficient time to adjust, cope, and relax in between scenes all the while building up to the crescendo of the final, most stressful, and unnerving scene. When practiced with scenarios from our life, this exercise can produce monumental gains in handling conflict situations and thus improving our assertiveness.

8.4 CONCLUDING REMARKS FOR ASSERTIVE COMMUNICATION

Assertiveness is an approach to communication that honors our choices as well as those of the person communicating with. It's not about being aggressive and steamrollering our colleague into submission in fact, it's about seeking and exchanging opinions, developing a full understanding of the issues, and negotiating a win-win situation, one that everyone can benefit from. As individuals practice assertive communication, they can almost see that little spark of self-respect glimmer, flicker, take hold, and burst into flame. Individuals can sense it when they respect themself, and they will treat others with respect; which is the ultimate goal of assertive communication.

In a business sense, improvisation of work helps individuals explore riskier and potentially more powerful ways to communicate. It builds trust around instinct, as often our first response is right. It helps individuals respond spontaneously in the moment and adapt to change. It opens them up to different options about how things are essential to communicate and convey ideas in a brief but confident manner so that our views are clearly expressed. It will help those who do not have the ability to honestly express their opinions, feelings, attitudes, and rights, without undue anxiety, in a way that doesn't infringe on the rights of others.

8.5 SELF-ESTEEM

Branden (1969) briefly defined self-esteem as the experience of being competent to cope with the basic challenges of life and being worthy of happiness. This two-factor approach, as some have also called it, provides a balanced definition that seems to be capable of dealing with limits of defining self-esteem primarily in terms of competence or worth alone. According to Branden, self-esteem is defined as a basic human need making an essential contribution to the life process and is indispensable to normal and healthy self-development with a value for survival. Self-esteem is an automatic and inevitable consequence of the sum of individuals' choices in using their consciousness (Branden, 1995).

Self-esteem is related to our self-worth and our value (Baumeister et al., 2003). Building esteem is a first step toward our happiness and a better life. Self-esteem increases confidence. If one has confidence, he or she will respect self. If one respects self, he or she can respect others, improve relationships, achievements, and happiness.

Low self-esteem causes depression, unhappiness, insecurity, and poor confidence. Other's desires may take preference over ours. Inner criticism, that nagging voice of disapproval inside, causes one to stumble at every challenge, and challenges seem impossible (Trzesniewski et al 2013). Self-esteem isn't bragging about how great one is. It's more like quietly knowing that one is worth a lot. Most individuals feel bad about themselves from time to time. Feelings of low self-esteem may be triggered by being treated poorly by someone else recently or in the past, or by a person's own judgments. This is normal. However, low self-esteem is a constant companion for too many individuals, especially those who experience depression, anxiety, phobias, psychosis, delusional thinking, or who have an illness or a disability. Low self-esteem keeps one from enjoying life, doing the things one wants to do, and working toward personal goals. One has a right to feel good about self. However, it can be very difficult to feel good about self when one is under the stress of having symptoms that are hard to manage, when one is dealing with a disability, or when one is having a difficult time. At these times, it is easy to be drawn into a downward spiral of lower self-esteem.

They will diminish as one feels better and better about self. To help relieve these feelings, let friends know what one is going through. Have a good cry at times. Do things to relax, such as meditating or taking a nice warm bath. The way we view and feel about ourselves has a profound effect on how we live our lives. These opinions are shaped by experiences in the family, at school, from friendships, and in wider society. Self-esteem involves our ability to think, to deal with life, and to be happy. From infancy we look for encouragement and approval. Yet our culture does not readily give this. Parents can be tough taskmasters in seeking the best for their children. Young individuals have a tendency to be intolerant of difference and often mock their peers who are clever or hard working. The educational system with its emphasis on league tables implicitly demands more and more and leaves less scope for valuing improvement. Personal acknowledgement of ability and pride in oneself can be regarded as being arrogant, boastful, or conceited. Rejection or loss at any age is likely to undermine self-esteem. Events like parents separating, being ostracized by friends or picked on by peers, dealing with an unsuccessful application, having an accident, a burglary, or coping with a death are likely to provoke feelings of loss and threat. For some, this is temporary, while for others the effects are long-lasting. Conversely, success is a great ego booster, and academic achievement can be an obvious signal of success. However, the wealth of talent and competitive environment can easily lead to self-doubt and insecurity. There is a lot of pressure on students to do well for the sake of family, college, and the university. Other individuals overestimate our ability and this burden of expectation can lead to a sense of failure and impossibility. However, what we feel about ourselves is not based solely on what we do. It usually involves our relationships with others and whether we feel worthwhile as individuals. We have a basic human need to be wanted, noticed, and included. We want to contribute, to be of value, and make a difference—in other words to matter.

Our self-esteem will continually fluctuate and is affected by events and encounters with other individuals. We are also constantly judging and evaluating ourselves, often in comparison with others. Observing ourselves in relation to other individuals can be a helpful source of learning and feedback (Turner et al, 1994). Yet all too often comparison slips into competition and others become a yardstick by which we evaluate ourselves as good or bad, competent or inadequate. The reality is we are all different. Each of us has strengths and limitations that we need to learn about and learn to live with. There are aspects of our behavior and appearance we may seek to change or develop, but a sense of self is also based on self-awareness and self-acceptance (Trzesniewski et al, 2003).

Self-esteem is an automatic and inevitable consequence of the sum of individuals' choices in using their own consciousness. Something experienced as a part of, or background to, all of the individual's thoughts, feelings, and actions (Turner and Onorato, 1999).

8.6 HOW TO IMPROVE OUR SELF-ESTEEM

Ways to increase self-esteem at work, enjoy presentations, and improve relationships are given below:

1. Face fears—They are not as bad as one thinks they are. Facing our fears increases our confidence.
2. Forget failures—Learn from them. Avoid making the same mistakes again but don't limit our self. Try again as an individual is turned more wise and stronger.

3. Know what one wants and asks for it. One deserves dreams to come true.
4. Reward self on the success of a particular task or event—no one else will.
5. Talk—We often make assumptions about a situation or person, which are not true. This can be solved in two ways:
   a. Get help from teachers, professors, and other helpers
      Go to professors, advisors, or tutors to ask for help in classes if this is a problem. If one lacks self-confidence in certain areas, take classes or try out new activities to increase one's sense of competence (e.g., take a math class, join a dance club, or take swimming lessons)
   b. Talk to a therapist or counselor

Sometimes low self-esteem can feel so painful or difficult to overcome that the professional help of a therapist or counselor is needed.

Talking to a counselor is a good way to learn more about one's self-esteem issues and begin to improve our self-esteem.

Change is not easy. It means stepping into the unknown and taking a risk. Inevitably this means that some initiatives will work well while others don't work out as one hoped. One can help self by being realistic in one's choices and seeing each success as a step in the right direction. Remember that small changes add up. Call on other individuals to help by being encouraging, taking an interest, giving feedback, and making suggestions (Trzesniewski et al, 2003). The following are some important suggestions for increasing self-esteem:

1. Do things for pleasure, for fun—Think about ways one enjoys. Put effort into making life pleasurable and satisfying. Arrange to be in situations that are playful and make one laugh. Learn something new.
2. Look after self physically—Eating regularly, thinking about the sort of food one eats, and making sure one tries to get the amount of sleep one needs. Exercise and toning muscles can give confidence and help to feel good about our body. Pay attention to how one stands and walks. Think tall.
3. Use rewards, but avoid punishments—Reward self in other ways. Listen to how one treats self—the internal conversation. Low self-esteem makes it difficult to identify strong points but it does not mean one does not have them—only that they are unfamiliar to one.
4. Avoid as much as possible situations and individuals that leave one feeling bad about self and spend more time concentrating on experiences that are likely to be successful and rewarding.
5. Take responsibility—It is not good to wait for others or circumstances to leave us feeling better about ourselves. So, accept responsibility for our own actions; as we cannot make other individuals change, we need to make the changes ourselves.
6. Make anxiety our ally—Write down our worries for 30 days. Nagging concerns that loom so large in our imagination lose their power on paper. Amazingly, after writing those down, the anxieties begin to fade.
7. Recognize that mistakes are opportunities—Keep the setback in perspective. Most mistakes are not personal tragedies; rather they are problems one now has the opportunity to solve. Success is often a string of failed attempts to get it right.
8. Compete to improve our self not to beat someone else.
9. Be ambitious—When setting goals, remember that one is distinct from what one has and what one seems to be. If one let others define who one is, one may not find happiness. Pursue our own dreams—not our parent's or our best friend's.
10. Be brave and take risks—Do not be afraid of mistakes. Risk-taking builds confidence. When considering any risk, define a clear goal. Review the positive, practical, and potential losses. Determine whether the risk is one of trust, identity, or something larger. When one focuses on

risks that have a larger purpose, one can't go wrong. Even if the risk doesn't turn out as one hoped it would, one will gain from it. Act. Take a risk. Be confident—one has earned it.

11. Think and speak positively—If one hears a compliment or positive statements about someone, one knows to pass that compliment on to that person. An Arabian proverb puts it neatly: Blessed is he who speaks a kindness; thrice blessed he who repeats it.

12. Learn something new—Create a new hobby. Increase our vocabulary one word a week. Take on a new physical challenge or activity.

13. Spend time investing in your personal growth—This enables joy to flourish amid the fears and difficulties of life. Read self-help books and act on the knowledge.

14. Decisions—The next time one ponders on a decision, think of everything that could go right.

15. Smile and be courteous—Use the words please and thank you consistently.

16. Keep good company—Positive feeds positive and negative breeds negative. If one chooses to be around positive individuals, we in turn will become more positive.

17. Reward yourself—Give self and others positive rewards for being and doing well.

18. Don't accept messages that damage our own self-esteem—It is much easier to improve or change one's behavior when one believes that one is lovable and capable.

19. Be aware of the different messages—One should hear and remember to turn up the volume on the messages that contribute to our positive self-esteem and to turn down the volume on any message that encourages to think negatively about our worth or ability.

20. A small success can bring big feeling of competence—Small steps lead to more steps. Pat our self on the back every time one makes a small success. Every step counts. Take one step at a time in a positive direction; this is the practice of self-esteem.

8.7 CONCLUDING REMARKS FOR SELF-ESTEEM

Self-esteem is not only important for individuals in their life but also it is important in the organizations as well. It reflects a person's overall self-appraisal of his or her own worth. Self-esteem encompasses both beliefs and emotions. Self-esteem, however, is something more fundamental than the normal ups and downs associated with situational changes. For individuals with good basic self-esteem, normal ups and downs may lead to temporary fluctuations in how they feel about themselves, but only limited extent. In contrast, for individuals with poor basic self-esteem, these ups and downs may make all the difference in the world.

It is needed to pass the judgments in the life; none is more important than the judgment we pass on ourselves. It impacts every moment and every aspect of our existence. Our self-evaluation is the basic context in which we act and react. During the study from various references, we learnt that there are six pillars on which health self-esteem depends: living consciously, self-acceptance, self-responsibility, self-assertiveness, living purposefully, and personal integrity. Also, research has proven that low self-esteem can have devastating consequence and can create anxiety, stress, loneliness, and increased likelihood for depression. It can cause problems with friendship and relationships (Turner and Onorato, 1999). Also, it can seriously impair academic and job performance.

To summarize, there are suggestions of some tools for Susan to develop self-esteem, figure out what the problem is, accept responsibility, recognize that mistakes are opportunities, and make list of the stuff one is good at (Trzesniewski et al 2013).

8.8 INTRODUCTION: SELF-INDEPENDENCE

Self-independence (SI) could be defined as the ability to work on our own and achieve the desired result. One must not rely on anyone, and one must face the outside world. Being self-independent teaches one a lot of things. It teaches us not to rely on anyone but to go on without any fear. We must be self-independent. Even students must not rely on their parents or teachers for school studies. They must be independent in whatever they wish to do. SI is self-reliance that is achieved when one frees self from social and psychological barriers. From a political point of view, SI can be achieved when a country is independent of the help aids in various forms, from other nations. In psychological terms, it is about having control over one's self.

8.8.1 Drawbacks of not Being Self-independent

Taking others' advice is sometimes beneficial; however, one must not totally rely on them and do what they say because they may be saying the wrong thing. One must think wisely and then decide because only thinking will bring us to some conclusion and this is then what will make us different and independent. Being self-independent teaches one to be patient and teaches not to fear. Those who fear reach nowhere. One must plunge ourselves into the air and try to reach our goal or aim in life independently as every cloud has a silver lining. When things get down, one should not put him- or herself down, but instead should work harder as the world out there is not any easy game! One must be independent in everything that is done, whether it is his or her favorite hobby or passion. If one goes as others say, he or she will never learn to be independent and will always be stationed behind those who are. It helps us to believe in ourselves and leaves a mark on others and gives them some inspiration.

8.9 INTRODUCTION: SELF-REGULATION

Self-regulation is a dynamic reciprocal interaction between person, environment, and behavior. Self-regulation often improves competition by creating or disseminating truthful information, valued by consumers. It can provide a dangerous opportunity for rivals, often out of public sight, to damage rivals that they fear they cannot defeat in the marketplace. Self-regulation implies to the concepts of goal setting, self-monitoring, activation and use of goals, discrepancy detection and implementation, self-evaluation, self-efficacy, and metaskills. A clear focus on the goal is done by right treatment and adaptation for a specific behavior. In other words, too much deviation from the original path may lead to never finding the same path again. Thus, clear and defined goal setting is essential in the initial approach to self-regulation. Once goal setting has been developed, the ability to self-monitor becomes essential because attention to internal and external cues, through greater self-awareness, leads to faster and more appropriate control of intervention strategies.

Activation of goal-directed behaviors guides individual responses to task performance. After self-monitoring over a given period, internal and external cues initiate a modulation of thought, affect, or behavior under goal-setting directives. These responses are presumably stored in long-term working memory that can constantly scan psycho-physiological content during activity and alert the individual. An important feature in self-regulation is detecting discrepancies between ideal behavior and current behavior according to goal-setting objectives. It appears to be affected by motivation and knowledge of results when comparing ideal and current behavior. Self-evaluating detected discrepancies along a spectrum of favorable to unfavorable behavior, and then self-cons equation by reinforcing or reducing behavior through positive or negative self-communication, influences the self-regulatory strategies. Metaskills or metacognition are those skills required in the self-regulatory process that govern the holistic coordination of self-regulation. Memory retrieval and correct temporal activation, forethought, self-reflectiveness, the capacity to learn vicariously, use of imagery and language, and emotional and intellectual intelligence are needed in a coordinated approach for volitional freedom to exercise self-influence in self-regulation.

Healthy self-regulation is related to the capacity to tolerate the sensations of distress that accompany unmet needs. Self-regulation also applies to the emotional development of a being; it also helps as an anticipatory commitment in the business conduct and helps in the economic development. The essence of self-regulation rejuvenates need to make good public relationship and consumer-friendly environment that is from single codes to group initiatives, from single issues to a broad array, from autonomous to embedded within government and international organization policy. The trend of self-regulation is much bigger than most individuals realize and is becoming more institutionalized and global. Self-regulation renders social responsibility and codes for the correct conduct as a means to reduce costs, increase profits, build reputation trust, and reduce risk. This is an ongoing conversation individuals have with themselves, which frees them from being prisoners of their feelings. Individuals with a high degree of self-regulation are more capable of facing the ambiguities of an advancing industry than those whose degree of self-regulation is low. Furthermore, individuals with a high level of self-regulation can help to enhance the integrity of an organization by not making bad decisions through impulse behavior. Self-regulation will help individuals stay in control of their feelings and make thoughtful decisions. Emotional intelligence is based on the idea that one must first become aware of his or her emotions before being able to alter one's behavior for better results. Studies show that managers who maintain a high level of self-regulation possess more aspects of emotional quotient (EQ) and are therefore rated as more effective by both superiors and subordinates. Self-regulation is not getting carried away with emotions, but rather objectively managing them in order to take control of the subsequent actions resulting from these emotions. By acknowledging our emotions, we can manage them; deal with them, and then move on. This is very difficult for some individuals to do. It is much easier at times to just ignore, deny or rationalize our emotions. It is crucial, however, for us to develop an understanding of what we are feeling in order to use our emotions intelligently.

8.10 DEFINITIONS OF SELF-REGULATION

Self-regulation is the ability to control potentially disruptive emotions and impulses (Zimmerman, 2000). These potentially disruptive emotions can result in a viewpoint that the manager is not yet ready to be a leader in an organization. Leaders exhibiting characteristics consistent with self-regulation or self-control are considered by peers to be trustworthy, conscientious, and able to adjust to changing situations. Self-regulation is also characterized by a readiness to seize opportunity and a drive for excellence. Self-regulation refers to individuals monitoring, controlling, and directing aspects of their learning for themselves. The skills of planning, monitoring, evaluating, and reinforcing are involved in self-regulation.

Goleman defined self-regulation as the ability to control or redirect disruptive impulses and moods and the propensity to suspend judgment and to think before acting. Hallmarks include trustworthiness and integrity; comfort with ambiguity; and openness to change. Through self-regulation (or consciously choosing emotional responses to individuals and events), individuals are able to foster an environment of trust and fairness where efficiency and productivity can flourish. Time is not wasted on negative emotions that can cripple organizational efforts. This attribute flows from self-awareness, but runs in a different direction. Individuals with this trait are able to control their impulses or even channel them for good purposes. Self-regulation includes the following:

1. Self-control—Managing disruptive impulses.
2. Trustworthiness—Maintaining standards of honesty and integrity.
3. Conscientiousness—Taking responsibility for our performance.
4. Adaptability—Flexibility in handling changes.
5. Innovation—Being open to new ideas.

8.11 STRATEGIES FOR SELF-REGULATION

First of all, individuals who are in control of their feelings and impulses are able to create an environment of trust and fairness. In such an environment, politics and infighting are sharply reduced and productivity is high. Talented individuals flock to the organization and are not tempted to leave. Self-regulation has a trickledown effect. No one wants to be known as a "hothead" when the boss is known for "calm approach."

Fewer bad moods at the top mean fewer throughout the organization. Second, self-regulation is important for competitive reasons. Everyone knows that business today is prevalent with ambiguity and change. Companies merge and break apart regularly. Technology transforms work at a dizzying pace. Individuals who have mastered their emotions are able to roll with the changes. When a new program is announced, they do not get panic, instead, they are able to suspend judgment, seek out information, and listen to executives explain the new program.

The signs of emotional self-regulation are not hard to miss (Bembenutty, 2009): a propensity for reflection and thoughtfulness; comfort with ambiguity and change; and integrity, an ability to say no to impulsive urges. Like self-awareness, self-regulation often does not get its due. Individuals who can master their emotions are sometimes seen as cold fish; their considered responses are taken as a lack of passion. Individuals with fiery temperaments are frequently thought of as "classic" leaders. Their outbursts are considered hallmark of charisma and power. But when such individuals make it to the top, their impulsiveness often works against them. According to Goleman, extreme displays of negative emotion have never emerged as a driver of good leadership.

Individuals with high skill levels of self-regulation demonstrate the following qualities:

1. They foster a climate of trust and fairness
2. They draw talented individuals to themselves
3. They focus on issues, not on politics and turf battles
4. They are role models for professional demeanor and behavior
5. They adapt quickly and frequently initiate changes
6. They resist temptation to violate their ethics
7. They build relationships that endure

The managers have to learn the following emotional competencies that have been identified after a detailed research. These competencies are as follows:

Tackling emotional upsets: This means tackling frustrations, conflicts, inferiority complexes, etc. It also means avoiding emotional exhaustion such as stress, burnout, and negativity of emotions. Individuals in conflict are generally locked into a self, perpetuating emotional spiral in which the genesis of the conflict is usually not clear. Finding ways to deal with anger, fear, anxiety and sadness are essential signs of emotional competency. For example, learning how to manage when upset is one such asset. Being able to channel emotions to a positive end is another key skill to raise your EQ. Under some conditions, inferiority complex arising from issues such as knowledge, education, physical characteristics, religion, region, caste, sex, and creed are not uncommon. Inferiority complex is also reflected in the low self-esteem, negative feelings, and low opinion about oneself. Research shows that a high level of emotional intelligence helps to overcome inferiority complex.

High self-esteem: Many managers often give themselves a negative feedback (Aron and McLaughlin-Volpe, 2001). On the other hand, there are those who believe that optimism can be a useful asset. Research done in organizations has indicated that leaders should learn to be optimistic to boost their self-esteem. High self-esteem gives a manager realistic confidence to perceive challenges as learning opportunities. As a result, one constantly grows and improves. High self-esteem is the greatest gift a manager can give to himself. Unfortunately, most of us suffer from a wounded self-esteem that often leads to a psychological invalidation of the self.

Susan should learn to acquire high self-esteem, which is reflected in the feelings of confidence and competence.

Tactful response to emotional stimuli: This means being creative and practical toward emotional prompts elicited from the inner self and the immediate environment. An emotionally intelligent manager will try to manipulate the ongoing environment to his or her advantage by reacting appropriately.

Handling egoism: Egoism is based on the view that the fundamental motive behind all emotional conduct is self-interest. A self-centered manager talks incessantly of himself and his doings and is interested in only his own concerns. Tackling ego problems without hurting one's self-esteem is the key to success. An "I am never wrong" attitude may be harmful in many situations. One should not be an egoist. It is the root cause of problems in interpersonal relations. Taking the initiative to resume dialogue and breaking the ice in situations where both parties have stuck to their original stand and have refused to budge is a sign of emotional competency.

8.12 CONCLUDING REMARKS FOR SELF-REGULATION

SI is achievable when we push self beyond our ordinary threshold. In extreme situations, we would have probably noticed that virtually anything can't intervene in our way and our body can reveal almost superhuman capacities. Our mind is capable of supporting itself as well. So, in order to drive away the negative impacts from our lives, we must be self-independent.

Individuals with a high degree of self-regulation are more capable of facing the ambiguities of an advancing industry than those whose degree of self-regulation is low. Furthermore, individuals with a high level of self-regulation can help to enhance the integrity of an organization by not making bad decisions through impulse behavior. Self-regulation will help individuals stay in control of their feelings and make thoughtful decisions.

Self-regulation is the ability to control one's emotions (Zimmerman {2002, 2008}). This is important because it helps one to create an environment of trust and fairness. The lead by example rule applies nicely in this situation. More importantly, this serves as a role model for everyone. The second aspect of self-regulation is that it assists in competitive situations. Individuals who have a strong control over their emotions will be able to handle new situations comfortably. Rather than getting panicked or worried, they will seek out the information they need and figure out how to work through the situation. The final aspect of self-regulation is integrity. Individuals with self-regulation are more apt to avoid tempting situations that might present themselves. Those with lower impulse control might just say "yes" and both the individual and the company will suffer. The basis of both SI and self-regulation is self-monitoring. There are several issues that appear to have no consensus in the literature concerning self-monitoring. These issues are as follows:

1. Defining self-monitoring—High and low self-monitors are categorized on different bases (Alberti and Emmons, 1974). For example, high self-monitors possess more public awareness than low self-monitors; however, low self-monitors possess more private awareness than high self-monitors. If the definition of self-monitoring is the ability to observe oneself, that is one's psycho-physiological processes, then high self-monitors are actually low self-monitors and low self-monitors are high self-monitors. This is because high self-monitors concern themselves with more external than internal events, and low self-monitors with internal rather than external events. Therefore, future research should explore the various facets of psycho-physiological events from a phenomenological perspective.
2. Method of self-monitoring—The methods of current research in self-monitoring display many different approaches. The validity and reliability of self-reports, inventories, and a questionnaire is debatable because of inherent and constructed biases of culture, meaning, and subjectivity. Videotape and task performance feedback were also offered as a correlate with self-monitoring/self-regulating ability. During all these data-gathering methods, no distinctions were made between

real-time and reflective self-monitoring that may be important for successful implementation of a self-regulation program (Bembenutty, 2011).

References

Alberti, R., and Emmons, M. (1974), Your perfect right, San Luis Obispo, CA: Impact.

Aron, A., and McLaughlin-Volpe, T. (2001), "Including others in the self: Extensions to own and partner's group memberships", In C. Sedikides and M. B. Brewer (Eds.), Individual self, relational self, collective self, Philadelphia, PA: Psychology Press, 89–108.

Back, R., and Back, K. (1986), Assertiveness at work – A practical guide to handling awkward situations, London: McGraw Hill.

Baumeister, R. F., Campbell, J. D., Krueger, J. I., and Vohs, K. D. (2003), "Does high self-esteem cause better performance, interpersonal success, happiness, or healthier lifestyles?, Psychological Science in the Public Interest, 4, 1–44.

Bembenutty, H. (2009), "Self-regulation of homework completion", Psychology Journal, 6, 138–153.

Bembenutty, H. (2011), "The last word: An interview with Harris Cooper—Research, policies, tips, and current perspectives on homework", Journal of Advanced Academics, 22, 342–351.

Branden, N., (1969), "The psychology of self-esteem", New York: Bantam.

Branden, N. (1995), The six pillars of self-esteem, New York: Bantam, 27.

Holland, S., and Ward, C. (1980), "Assertiveness: A practical approach", Bicester: Winslow Press.

Trzesniewski, K., Donnellan, B., and Robins, R. W. (2013), "Development of self-esteem", In V. Zeigler-Hill (Ed.), Self-esteem, New York, NY: Psychology Press, 60 –79.

Trzesniewski, K. H., Donnellan, M. B., and Robins, R. W. (2003), "Stability of self-esteem across the life span", Journal of Personality and Social Psychology, 84, 205–220.

Turner, J. C., Oakes, P. J., Haslam, S. A., and McGarty, C. (1994), "Self and collective: Cognition and social context", Personality and Social Psychology Bulletin, 20, 454–463.

Turner, J. C., and Onorato, R. S. (1999), "Social identity, personality, and the self-concept: A self-categorization perspective", In T. Tyler, R. M. Kramer, and O. P. John (Eds.), The psychology of the social self, London: Erlbaum, 11–46.

Zimmerman, B. J. (2000), "Attaining self-regulation: A social cognitive perspective", In M. Boekaerts, P. R. Pintrich, and M. Zeidner (Eds.), Handbook of self-regulation, San Diego, CA: Academic Press, 13–39.

Zimmerman, B. J. (2002), "Achieving self-regulation: The trial and triumph of adolescence", In F. Pajares and T. Urdan (Eds.), Academic motivation of adolescents, Vol. 2, Greenwich, CT: Information Age, 1–27.

Zimmerman, B. J. (2008), "Investigating self-regulation and motivation: Historical background, methodological developments, and future prospects", American Education Research Journal, 45, 166–183.

CHAPTER 9

Empathetic Listening, Building Social Skills, Stress Tolerance, and Self-awareness

9.1 WHAT IS EMPATHETIC LISTENING?

Empathy is generally defined as the extent to which one has the ability to understand and accept another's feelings and emotions. Some view empathy simply as one's ability to put him- or herself in another's shoes and view the issue from another's perspective. However, some researchers suggest that perspective-taking is a cognitive process that precedes empathy, which is an affective or emotion-based response to perspective-taking.

From a moral development perspective, individuals are thought to progress from an egocentric form of morality toward a level of moral development where one examines issues from a variety of perspectives. Although technical skills are considered less important as a person rises within an organizational hierarchy, the ability to empathize is thought to be a more important determinant of success. Empathy is considered to be a quintessential managerial competence because it is a fundamental individual skill.

Empathy is thought to have both a genetic and an experiential foundation. However, Goleman (1995) stresses that as a capability, empathy can be enhanced through desire and training. Research indicates that self-awareness is positively related to empathy, suggesting that empathy may be a function of the degree to which a person can read and manage his own emotions. Training that focuses on empathy building has been suggested as a means of fostering this social skill.

A person who is skillful at empathizing makes others feel respected and worthy of attention. The development of this skill requires effective communication. Thus, training managers in communication techniques such as active listening may contribute to building empathic competence. Research examining empathy has largely been embedded within efforts to gain a greater understanding of emotional intelligence. Studies indicate that empathy is positively related to intrinsic motivation and effective problem-solving, supporting the view that empathy is an important aspect of effective leadership. The need for empathy is increasingly important in the workplace as the use of teams and self-directed work groups, where social competencies are a critical factor in success, are on the rise. Globalization, and the difficulties associated with intercultural relationships, also makes empathy an increasingly critical managerial competence.

Empathy is particularly important today as a component today as component of leadership for at least three reasons: the increasing use of teams; the rapid place of globalization; and the growing need to retain talent. From a traditional business perspective, empathy may seem inappropriate. However, empathy is a critical skill, helping individuals address today's challenges. Empathy is a core skill required as individuals work in teams by sensing and understanding the views of everyone, experience globalization through cross-cultural sensitivity, and retain talent with coaching and mentoring.

9.2 MORE DATA ON EMPATHY

Empathy is a person's ability to feel how others feel about a certain situation. Many individuals are blessed with the gift of empathy and are called empathic. Almost every one of us has empathy to some degree; however, learning to listen to that and learning about it are the challenges that many face. This is why they come to psychic readers with that ability. Many individuals with a keen sense of empathy have problems in crowds because of their ability to feel what everyone is thinking and feeling about. It can be very overwhelming to be empathic and many have to learn to turn this off while in situations like that.

According to Bar-on (2004), Empathy is one's ability to recognize and understand the emotion of another. As the states of mind, beliefs, and desires of others are intertwined with their emotions, one with empathy for another may often be able to more effectively divine another's modes of thought and mood. Empathy is often characterized as the ability to "put oneself into another's shoes," or experiencing the outlook or emotions of another being within oneself, a sort of emotional resonance. While the ability to imagine oneself as another person is a sophisticated imaginative process that only fully develops with time, as later on in life, or with considerable training, or investigation, or imagination, the roots of such ability are probably innate to the empathizer's life, training, or investigation.

Human capacity to recognize the emotions of another is related to one's imitative capacities and seems to be grounded in one's innate capacity to associate the bodily movements and facial expressions one sees in another with the proprioceptive feelings of one's corresponding movements or expressions. Humans also seem to make the same immediate connection between the tone of voice and body language of another and one's inner feeling. Hence, by looking at the facial expressions or bodily movements of another, or by hearing another's tone of voice, one may be able to get an immediate sense of how another seems to feel on the inside. One experiences this as anything in a range from understanding to directly experiencing or to feeling another's emotion—for example, sadness or anger, rather than just noting the behavioral symptoms of another's emotion. However, clinicians must take care not to overinvest their own emotions at the risk of draining away their own resourcefulness; thus, awareness of one's own limitations is prudent in a clinical situation, as in care giving.

More fully developed empathy requires more than simply recognizing another's emotional state. Since emotions are typically directed toward objects or states of affairs, either real or imaginary, the empathizer first requires some idea of what that object might be. Next, the empathizer must determine how the emotional feeling will significantly affect the way in which he perceives the other person. The empathizer needs to determine the aspects of the person upon which to focus. Hence, he must not only recognize the person toward which the other is directed, but also then recognize the bodily feeling and add these components together. Next, the empathizer needs to find the way into the loop where perception of the other person generates feeling. That feeling affects the perception of the other person. This process occurs before taking in account the character of the other person as well as his or her wider nonpsychological context such as being short or being a lawyer.

9.3 HOW TO BECOME EMPATHETIC?

Meditation is a great way to work on empathy. As one meditates about a certain person, one begins to pick up empathy for a certain person and messages. Many disregard this as imagination when it usually isn't. It is all about what they are feeling. To work on our ability to be empathic and have empathy for individuals, we must meditate quite often approximately once per day and use the technique of focusing on one certain person. To some this comes easy, and to others it is much more difficult. At any rate, empathy is something that should be worked on by all individuals to create a more caring and loving world.

"Idealists" are individuals who use empathy to engender trust and build bonds, catalysts that are able to create positive communities for the greater good. But even if empathy does not come naturally to some of us, it's firmly believed that we can develop this capacity.

Here are a few practical tips one might like to consider:

1. Listen—Truly listen to individuals. Listen with ears, eyes, and heart. Pay attention to others' body language, to their tone of voice, to the hidden emotions behind what they are saying, and to contextual aspects.
2. Don't interrupt individuals. Don't dismiss their concerns off hand. Don't rush to give advice. Don't change the subject. Allow individuals their moment.
3. Increase the ability to understand others' nonverbal communication, because often individuals don't communicate openly what they think or feel.
4. Use individual's names. Remember the names of individual's spouse and children so that they could be referred by name.
5. Be fully present when one is with individuals. Don't check emails, look at the watch or take phone calls when a direct report drops into our office to talk. Put self in their shoes. How would we feel if our boss did that to us?
6. Smile at individuals.
7. Encourage individuals, particularly the quiet ones, when they speak up in meetings. A simple thing like an attentive nod can boost individual's morale.
8. When one gives praise, spend a little effort to make our genuine words memorable for the constituents.
9. For example say things like: "You are an asset to this team because. . . ."; "This was pure genius"; or "I would have missed this if you hadn't picked it up."
10. Show individuals that they are cared by taking a personal interest in them. Show genuine curiosity about their lives. Ask them questions about their hobbies, their challenges, their families, and their aspirations.
11. Spend time with the individuals who work for us. Get out from behind our desk and walk around and meet them in their turf. Talk to them. Sit down for a moment so that both at the same level while talking.
12. Have the finger on the pulse of our department or organization. Learn to read the mood of a group.
13. Be sensitive to diversity. Make an effort to understand constituents of different cultures.

9.4 CONCLUDING REMARKS FOR EMPATHY

Empathy is the ability to be aware of and appreciate others' feelings—an ability to show caring. It has both positive and negative faces:

Positive: Helps with anticipating and understanding the perspectives of customers, team members, and key stakeholders.

Negative: Can run rough shod over others. Poor empathy often feeds off of poor self-awareness.

Empathy is a very important parameter for growth of any organization. Empathy is a valued relationship currency. It allows us to create bonds of trust; it gives us insights into what others may be feeling or thinking; it helps us understand how or why others are reacting to situations; and it sharpens our individual acumen and informs our decisions. It's very important in decision-making, to handle stress situation, and to handle relations among individuals.

9.5 A SOCIAL FRAMEWORK

A network is generally defined as a specific type of relation linking a defined set of persons, objects or events. Social skills or social relationships (SR) are an integral part of higher mammalian societies and can be used to explain why societies as entities function the way they do. From a social network analysis point of view, a society can be expressed as patterns of relationships between interacting units (Petit et al., 1994). Social networks were considered in multiagent systems, and concepts such as reputation and trust were explored. Social networks connect individuals with all different types of interests, and one area that is expanding in the use of these networks is the corporate environment (Dodge et al., 1986). Businesses are beginning to use social networks as a means to connecting employees together and helping employees to build profiles so that they can be searchable and be connected with other business professionals. These networks act as a customer relationship management tool for companies selling products and services. Companies can also use social networking in the form of banner and text advertisements. Because businesses are expanding globally, social networks make them easier to keep in touch with the other contacts around the world. Negotiation, cooperation, mutual respect, and trust are the strongest links. The implementation of these skills will improve existing relationships and help build new relationships that are lasting and fulfilling. Those who feel they have inputs in the direction of an organization will feel better about their relationships with other members of the organization when their input is solicited and valued.

High scorers (Harrist et al., 1991) will believe that SR are very important and will therefore spend time and energy on establishing and developing relationships with others. They are usually skilled communicators and can motivate and lead others effectively. They generally enjoy social occasions, working together in groups and teams and are effective and skilled communicators. Low scorers find that they work better on their own rather than with others whether in couples or in teams. Often, they can be less interested in communicating and prefer to keep themselves and their views to themselves. In social settings, they are not too loud or pushy and may prefer to stay in the background and are less likely to speak in public (Mize and Pettit, 1997).

The important thing is that emotionally intelligent individuals know themselves and know which aspects of them to use and show others at appropriate times. Just to emphasize, these aspects can be developed if you feel comfortable with this and feel it is necessary. What ties information architecture, knowledge management, and social networks more closely together is the reciprocal relationship between individuals and content. Success of an organization largely depends on what other individuals know and who the other individuals know. This demands good search, navigation, and content management systems, which can only be achieved if strong relationships exist in the organization. Successful business concerns appealed to communities of interest and claimed to establish meaningful connections across distances and differences. They built firm relationships taking into consideration that a community has both emotional and behavioral manifestations when a person feels a sense of belonging, which causes them to volunteer their time and resources to help follow community members.

SR have four central elements (Harrist et al., 1994):

1. Membership—A feeling of belonging or sharing present or potential relatedness. Associations provide a space for individuals to connect around shared identity and relatedness.
2. Influence—A sense that one matters and that what one does make a difference. Association enacts this as voice in the form of lobbying, advertising, and advocacy.
3. Integration and fulfillment of needs—Confidence that membership in the group will fulfill needs and expectations. Associations accomplish this by providing members with venues for learning, advocacy, and interpersonal exchange.
4. Shared emotional connection—Trust on the part of members that they have shared and will share history of experiences. Sentiments of members manifest itself in the form of voluntarism, engagement, and increased willingness to commit and contribute to resources and group. This includes the measure of the level of confidence that individuals have in staff and leaders, the

extent to which they experience organization as responsive, and the degree to which they feel valued by others, which can in turn effectively predict critical outcomes such as the intent to renew, to attend meetings, and to volunteer.

9.6 TRAITS THAT HELP BUILD SOCIAL SKILLS

The following are the traits that help build social skills:

a. A tolerance for unreliable behavior
   In most groups of friends, there's the person (Mize and Pettit, 1994) who's consistently fifteen minutes late. A little less common, but still not unheard of, is the unreliable friend who makes plans and never follows through on them, or who doesn't show up when they say they will. Another type is the slightly eccentric guy who marches to the beat of his own drum and who does things like going to another bar without telling to anyone.
   All these things are annoying but one has to not let them get to oneself too much (Pettit et al, 1991). Most of this stuff just comes up from time to time. It's much easier to get over it quickly and get on with our plans. Of course, there is a point where lateness or unreliability go too far and one needs to put one's foot down, and maybe even hang out with the person less; but if one does this for every little instance of unreliability, one is going to run out of friends.

b. A tolerance for unpredictability or the ability to go with the flow
   Plans can change; new ideas come up, and things not under our control happen. Sometimes, the opinion of the group outvotes our personal preferences. One can't let these things get to us. Never resent our mates over it. Just loosen up and go with it. One never knows the new plans may take one somewhere much more fun than the original ones (Pettit et al, 1997).

c. The ability to amuse self when one has to
   One can't count on other individuals to entertain at all times (Putallaz, 1987). One has got to cultivate the ability to find one's own fun and the skills to make it happen. If our friends all decide they want to play pool for the next two hours, and pool bores you to tears, then it's good to have a backup plan. One could chat up random individuals. That takes a certain amount of spine, and a gift for the gab, but with practice one can get better at it. Or if one finds our friends always want to play pool, one could give it a chance and play with them. Being able to meet some interesting new friends and get in their good books quickly is also a good skill to know.

d. A tolerance for other individual's stupidity instances of being drunk, reckless, and messy
   Sometimes other individuals act stupid and annoying. They get drunk and become loud, retarded liabilities. They do reckless idiotic things on a whim because they amuse them somehow. They're too messy when they come over to your apartment. It's just one of those things that happens from time to time. Be laid back about it.

e. A thick enough skin to not take joking too seriously
   Individuals are going to joke around at our expense—poking fun, busting balls, taking the piss, and winding one up. Even when they seem quite serious, they're often just kidding around with one. One can't be too touchy or defensive about these things. If someone makes a joke with friendly intentions and one turns around and bites their head off, or sulk about it, they're not going to see one in the best light. The best response is to make a funny comeback or just laugh it off. Sometimes their cutting remarks have a valid point. It keeps one honest, and so just smile and shake your head.

f. Not being too stingy with money

Lots of the things individuals want to do cost money to one degree (Parke and Bhavnagri, 1989) or another. If our love of saving money keeps one from taking part in these things, then one is holding self-back. Individuals are going to want to eat out, they're going to want to go to a club with a slightly high cover and that charges too much for drinks, they're going to want to get another round, and they're going to want to see movies in the pricier theater. Don't worry too much and just go along. When one is a little generous with money, things have a habit of evening out.

g. One can throw self into what everyone else is doing and not get stuck in our head

Everyone would be talking, partying, or having fun, and one could be lost in one's own thoughts, cut off from everyone else. The solution was simple. It was to consciously force oneself to stay in the moment and tune into what the others were doing. One could focus on the conversation and keep wondering thoughts in check. Another thing that helps is being able to hold our own in whatever the group is doing. If they all want to dance, then it's good if one can dance too. If they're all joking around about a certain show, then it helps if one is up to date on the show (Robinson, 1982).

h. One is not too self-focused

A couple of times individuals have been caught off guard. They were picking up on the fact that one is such an introverted, solitary person. One has to do little things to show that he or she is thinking about other individuals.

i. One can contribute to individual's conversations

Individuals also commented that one is quiet. It's honestly not that insulting a thing to say, but it makes one feel defensive. It's amazing how quickly individuals notice someone who's keeping silent and not contributing to the discussion. One may think that someone is sitting back and observing, occasionally chipping in with a poignant comment. But no, they think one is quiet. One thing that helps with this is just pulling out of our own mind and paying attention to what individuals are saying. Another is to realize that one has to say something every now and then. If one doesn't then one gets that quiet label (Dunn et al, 1987). A lot of the time several things to say will be running through our head, but we "veto" them for various reasons. Just say these things. Don't worry about whether they're stupid or boring. Saying anything to socialize with someone else is better than saying nothing and not socializing.

Usually individuals get quiet (Pettit and Mize, 1993) when they're first around a new group of individuals who all know each other. In this situation, it can feel okay to sit back and watch, but it's really the time to jump in and become a member of that group, at least for that day. One needs to say a few things so that one can work our way into the conversation and become an active member of it. The onus is on us to participate. The group has enough to talk about among themselves that they probably won't go too much out of their way to include one who is an outsider.

Having a varied amount of general knowledge and life experience to draw on helps a lot here. Whatever the group is talking about, one will be more likely have something to contribute about the topic. Individuals also get quiet when they perceive that they don't "belong" to the group, or like they don't have much common ground with the group they're with. A lot of this is in the head. It can also become a self-fulfilling prophecy when one thinks that one has nothing in common with them so one keeps quiet and act sullen. One could make a poor impression and they then subtly reject the person.

j. A willingness to give new individuals a chance

Being down on new individuals is another case where self-fulfilling prophecies can arise. For one, if one never gives someone a chance, one can never confirm or deny that our first impression of them is correct. Also, if one has a bad attitude toward someone, then it can lead to unfriendly behavior to them (Quick et al, 1997). They'll sense our unfriendliness and be unfriendly back.

k. A willingness to give certain activities a chance
A lot of shyer individuals have a negative attitude about many of the activities more "mainstream" individuals enjoy.
One thing we don't quite "get" is the idea of just socializing for the sake of socializing. It's just fun. Spending three hours sitting around and having a hilarious conversation with three of our friends is just inherently good. Then there are all those "mindless fun" activities such as drinking, dancing, gossiping, and talking about "shallow" things. First, what's wrong with having mindless fun? Isn't playing video games or watching anime just as much "mindless fun" as partying? If something "shallow" is enjoyable to discuss, then why not talk about it? Just because someone talks about shallow things doesn't mean they're shallow. But in small doses is it really the end of the world? Does it automatically mean one can't have a good time if there's some shallowness in the air? Do individuals always have to talk about deep philosophical issues or devote all their time to important problems?
A lot of the so-called mindless activities are actually pretty enjoyable if one gives them a chance. No one can like everything of course, but it never hurts to broaden our horizons and the same goes for the stuff one likes and other individuals don't seem to understand.

l. One must have the rest of one's life in order as much as possible
The theme running through all these things was to lighten up about individuals and their behaviors. Sometimes because one is too negative, but other times because one is naive about what was normal behavior from individuals. Focus a lot less on that stuff, and more on all the good things that are happening around us.

9.7 MISTAKES LONELY INDIVIDUALS OFTEN MAKE

These are some mistakes some individuals make (Black and Logan, 1995):

a. They hide from the world because they are embarrassed about being lonely and having no life. No one who doesn't live with can tell (or really cares) whether one has a lot of friends or not.

b. They become experts at distracting themselves from their loneliness.
It's relatively easy to throw our spare hours away in front of the television or personal computers. Obviously this doesn't fix the problem.

c. They expect other individuals to do all the work of inviting them out. Sometimes we will meet someone we get along with and they'll make all the effort of getting our contact information and inviting us out with them, but often this doesn't happen. Individuals are usually pretty busy and already have social lives of their own. They're often on a kind of auto-pilot where they won't think of one as a potential buddy unless we get them thinking that way. If we want to get a circle of friends together, assume we have to do all the work.

d. They think they have to be super cool to have friends. Pretty much anyone can have friends if they want to. An annoying person who makes an effort to be social and makes plans with individuals will often have friends.

e. They actually aren't that much interested in hanging around individuals. Individuals who become lonely tend to be more shy, anxious, and introverted in the first place and don't have as much of a built-in need to be social. They're also more likely to have been ostracized in one form or another when they were growing up leaving them a bit bitter and weary toward other individuals.

f. They may feel the painful effects of loneliness and isolation and want to escape them, but at the same time they're not 100% keen on being around other individuals. This causes them to make initial steps toward getting a social life, and then not following through on them.

g. They have a negative attitude toward individuals. Studies have shown that lonely individuals tend to be more negative toward other individuals. This could be a cause or effect of being lonely, or both. In practice this manifests in a picky, superior, or snobby attitude. It may be an overcompensation for insecurity, anxiety, or low self-esteem. It may also have routes in somewhat justified feelings of being different, left-out, and alienated.

9.8   HOW TO GET A SOCIAL LIFE?

Most of the individuals make friends easily and keep them for years. If you are one of those shy, loner types, then certain tips would definitely help you.

a. Take the attitude that you have just moved into a new town and need to make a new circle of friends from scratch.
b. Get an outside life of your own.
c. Even if you don't talk with everyone, just being with them would boost confidence and have the advantage of meeting new individuals.
d. Understand that a man's friendship is different from that of a woman's.
e. You should meet new individuals and if you are too shy to meet them, then you can meet your current contacts.
f. Potential friends may or may not last for long in one's life. You must understand and see the bigger picture and not get demotivated by not being able to stay in touch with them.
g. Our initial goal is to just set our social life brooding. You may not stay with them for long but at least going out with them instead of sitting at home outweighs this.
h. You should never turn down an invitation. You never know what fun it is to go out unless and until you do not go out. You should not rationalize but take a chance anyways.
i. Maintain friendships. Once you become friends with someone, you must maintain friendships by way of emails, Yahoo messengers, Facebook, SMS (messaging on a mobile phone), Twitter, WhatsApp, Instagram, and phone. You should also try and hang out with them on a regular basis.
j. Don't be needy and pester the friend too much to stay in touch with you or to meet all your social and entertainment needs. You should keep in touch with all new friends and acquaintances because building up social life does take time.

9.9   CONCLUDING REMARKS FOR BUILDING SOCIAL SKILLS

Deterioration of interpersonal relationships can devastate a business. Both the direct and opportunity costs in such cases can be monumental. If the members spend just one hour per day bickering, avoiding each other, or talking to others about family problems, the cost of lost productivity is measurable based on a person's salary. Perhaps even more costly can be the opportunities that will be missed because of the conflicts. Whatever impacts the employees and their relationships is likely to reverberate through the business and vice versa (Putallaz and Gottman, 1983).

There are skills which can be taught to make working together and living together more rewarding and enjoyable. Bond between members (MacDonald, 1987) is the currency of any voluntary association. Quite consistently, business concerns receiving favorable scores on member satisfaction, commitment of resources, and voluntarism are those where the bonds between members are sufficiently strong to motivate members to make contact with each other outside formal association meetings and sponsored events (Putallaz and Heflin, 1986). Cooperative relationships are formed with the aim to achieve some common objectives, by means of the combination or the use of the resources and/or capabilities of each of the members, existing therefore, a mutual interdependence paving way to an organization's success.

9.10 THREE MAJOR APPROACHES TO STRESS MANAGEMENT

Refers to various efforts used to control and reduce the tension that occurs in these situations. Stress management involves making emotional and physical changes. The degree of stress and the desire to make the changes will determine the level of change that will take place. Identifying unrelieved stress and being aware of its effect on our lives is not sufficient for reducing its harmful effects. Just as there are many sources of stress, there are many possibilities for its management. However, all require work toward change: changing the source of stress and/or changing the reaction to it. The aim of stress management is to help balance the various aspects of life, work, leisure, and their relationships, and to balance the physical, intellectual, and emotional aspects of life. Individuals who effectively manage stress consider life a challenge rather than a series of irritations, and they feel they have control over their lives, even in the face of setbacks (Davis et al, 1995).

A. Action oriented: In this approach, we seek to confront the problem causing the stress, changing the environment or the situation—best where one has some control. To be able to take an action-oriented approach, we must have some power in the situation. If we do, then action-oriented approaches are some of the most satisfying and rewarding ways of managing stress. These are techniques that we can use to manage and overcome stressful situations, changing them to our advantage.

B. Emotion oriented: In this approach, we do not have the power to change the situation, but we can manage stress by changing our interpretation of the situation and the way we feel about it. Emotion-oriented approaches are subtle but effective. If one does not have the power to change a situation, then one may be able to reduce stress by changing the way one looks at it, using an emotion-oriented approach. Emotion-oriented approaches are often less attractive than action-oriented approaches in which the stresses can recur time and again; however, they are useful and effective in their place.

C. Acceptance oriented: Where something has happened over which we have no power and no emotional control, and where our focus is on surviving the stress—when there's no valid alternative. Sometimes, we have so little power in a situation that all we can do to survive it. This is the case, for example, when loved ones die. In these situations, often the first stage of coping with the stress is to accept one's lack of power.

These different orientations to stress management address our definition of stress in different ways: the action-oriented approach helps us to manage the demands upon us and increase the resources we can mobilize; the emotion-oriented approach helps us to adjust our perceptions of the situation; and the acceptance-oriented approach helps us survive the situations that we genuinely cannot change.

9.11 METHODS OF STRESS MANAGEMENT

A. Awareness of our stressors and our emotional and physical reactions.
   Notice distress. Don't ignore it. Don't gloss over problems.
B. Recognize what one can change (Seward, 1999).
   Can one change your stressors by avoiding or eliminating them completely?
   Can one reduce their intensity (manage them over a period of time instead of on a daily or weekly basis)?
   Can one shorten your exposure to stress (take a break, leave the physical premises)?

Can one devote the time and energy necessary to making a change (goal setting, time management techniques, and delayed gratification strategies may be helpful here)?

C. Reduce the intensity of emotional reactions to stress.

The stress reaction is triggered by our perception of danger, physical danger and/or emotional danger.

Work at adopting more moderate views; try to see the stress as something one can cope with rather than something that overpowers one.

Try to temper excess emotions. Put the situation in perspective. Do not labor on the negative aspects and the "what if's."

D. Learn to moderate physical reactions to stress.

Slow, deep breathing will bring heart rate and respiration back to normal.

Relaxation techniques can reduce muscle tension. Electronic biofeedback can help gain voluntary control over muscle tension, heart rate, and blood pressure.

Medications, when prescribed by a physician, can help in the short term in moderating physical reactions. However, they alone are not the answer. Learning to moderate these reactions voluntarily is a preferable long-term solution.

E. Building our physical reserves (Snyder and Pulvers, 2001).

Exercise for cardiovascular fitness regularly (moderate, prolonged rhythmic exercise is best, such as walking, swimming, cycling, or jogging). Eat well-balanced, nutritious meals.

Maintain ideal weight.

Avoid nicotine, excessive caffeine, and other stimulants.

Mix leisure with work. Take breaks and get away.

Get enough sleep. Be as consistent with sleep schedule as possible.

F. Maintain emotional reserves.

Develop some mutually supportive friendships/relationships.

Pursue realistic goals that are meaningful, rather than goals others have that one doesn't share.

Expect some frustrations, failures, and sorrows. Always be kind and gentle with one—be a friend to oneself.

9.12 REDUCING STRESS

If one feels that one is suffering from stress, try to identify the aspects of one's life that are causing it. Sometimes one may not be able to change or avoid them, but at other times simple lifestyle adjustments can make all the difference. Many stresses can be changed, eliminated, or minimized (Williamson and Dooley, 2001). Awareness about our own reactions to stress is the first step. Then reinforce positive self-statements. Focus on our good qualities and accomplishments. Avoid unnecessary competition. Recognize and accept our limits. Remember that everyone is unique and different. Plan ahead and avoid procrastination. Make a weekly schedule and try to follow it. Set realistic goals. When studying for an exam, study in short blocks and gradually lengthen the study time. Take frequent short breaks. Some more suggestions to reduce stress are given below:

a. *Support systems:* We need someone in our life to whom we can rely on when we are having a hard time. Minimal or absent support systems make stressful situations more difficult to deal with. One of the most effective things we can do when we are stressed is to talk from our heart to a friendly listener who remains calm and listens in a way that makes us feel understood. Studies show that individuals who are active socially are most capable of dealing with stressful situations and major illnesses. To help reduce stress, develop a network of friends and family members to turn to when stress threatens to overwhelm you. If one is a naturally private or independent person, it might seem challenging to build a support system. In order to cultivate a circle of friends, we need to take the first step. Our efforts to create a strong social network will serve well when we are confronted with serious stress. Think of individuals who care and with whom one can share most personal thoughts. Reach out to those individual. Call them; be open and available to them. Be sure to include some individuals at least a generation younger so that one won't outlive one's buddies and be left alone. Build relationships based on emotional honesty. Members of inner circle should know how to listen without judging, giving advice, or comparing experiences to theirs.

b. Relaxation: Individuals with no outside interests, hobbies, or means of relaxation may be unable to handle stressful situations because they have no outlet for stress.

c. Journalizing: It has many benefits that include improvement in cognitive functioning, health benefits, and the gift of introspection. The act of writing about feelings of stress, as well as exploring potential solutions to these problems, can soothe and help process difficult feelings and also take proactive steps against future stress. Writing things down has a marvelous way of putting things in perspective. Putting worries into words may help see that one doesn't really have that much to worry about, or it may help get organized and manage stress, rather than letting it manage one. Regardless, keeping a journal should help identify concerns and establish a plan for moving forward. List the situations that produce stress in life (e.g., moving to a new location, work or school demands, balancing priorities, or job promotion).

d. Meditation: There are many ways to meditate; the practice of meditation can greatly reduce stressful feelings that one is experiencing and counteract some of the negative effects of stress. Meditation can also be a tool for introspection; one can meditate on the cause of stress that one is experiencing, and as one relaxes, answers may come with ease and clarity.

e. Self-hypnosis: Self-hypnosis is much like meditation, in that it involves unconscious mind and carries many of the same benefits. However, one can also use self-hypnosis to address the root cause of stress that one experienced by working on changing habits that may be causing stress, such as negative thought patterns or disorganization, while relieving current stress.

f. Affirmations: Negative self-talk can cause more stress than most individuals are aware of. It's the little voice in our head that evaluates things positively or negatively, and tells about things one is experiencing and about oneself. One great way to change negative self-talk is to practice positive affirmations. It may take a little self-exploration to decide which affirmations to choose, but the results can be stress relief and growth.

g. Assertiveness: If we're feeling overscheduled and overstressed, it's definitely time to learn how to say no to individual's demands on our time. One would feel powerful as one does so, and one can prevent the overly busy lifestyle that keeps the cycle of stress going. One can look within to see why one may say "yes" too often, and take steps to feel better right away.

h. Reassess areas of self-destruction: How often does one get so stressed that one lashes out at individuals without meaning to? If it's a regular event, one may be suffering from self-destructive thought patterns that cause additional mental and emotional stress. One can look within and change these patterns, reducing future stress in oneself—and those around him or her.

i. Time management: It may also be necessary to reorganize schedules in order to maintain a more balanced life. Some strategies for time management include:
   a. Make a "to-do" list.
   b. Check items off as one completes them.
   c. Prioritize tasks and then work on the most important ones.
   d. Be assertive.

    e. Delegate less important tasks.

    f. Schedule extra time for tasks, in case of interruptions.

    g. Take frequent breaks and schedule time for relaxation.

  j. Developing coping skills for stress relief: Our attitude has a lot to do with whether events and occurrences produce a feeling of stress. Once we admit that we are not able to control everything, we will be better equipped to handle unexpected situations. Stress management comes down to finding ways to change our thinking and manage our expectations. Other important ways to adjust our attitude include the following: Be realistic. Shed the Superman/Superwoman image. Don't expect too much of ourselves or others. Nobody's perfect! Try to be assertive rather than passive or aggressive. Be flexible. Give in sometimes. Rehearse/prepare for presentations and interviews. Think positively. Look at each stressful situation as an opportunity to improve our life. Don't take work problems home or home problems to work. Rely on humor to relieve tension. Organize and simplify our life. If one of our main sources of stress is the sheer number of things that need to be done, getting organized should help feel more at peace. A good sense of organization will also make one more efficient. Simplifying life also should help one feel less overwhelmed. Plan the day. Learn to prioritize. Do what is most important first and realize that some things can wait until later. Cut out some activities and delegate tasks. Break large demands into small, manageable parts. Work through tasks one by one. Organize one's home and workspace so that you know where things are. Keep one's personal belongings in working order to prevent untimely, stressful repairs.

  k. Nurturing oneself: Taking care of our body, mind, and spirit can help reduce feelings of anxiety and frustration that often accompany stress. One might be surprised by how much stress relief a long bubble bath or a quick catnap will provide. Practice relaxation techniques such as controlling breathing, clearing our mind, and relaxing our muscles. Get enough sleep. Have a balanced diet and exercise. It relieves tension and provides a timeout from stressful situations. Reduce or eliminate caffeine (coffee, black and green tea, cola drinks, and chocolate). Because caffeine is a stimulant, it can make you feel more anxious. Avoid or reduce intake of alcohol, tobacco, and recreational drugs. Get a massage to relieve tension. Read a good book or see an upbeat movie. Consider getting a pet. A pet's love is unconditional.

  l. Taking a break: Try to take time every day to slow down and do something one enjoys for a few minutes. Reading a magazine, playing with dog, reading a book to our children, or any other activity that helps us forget the stresses of the day and helps us remember what is important. Stop for several minibreaks during the workday. Take thirty seconds to look out the window or stretch. Set aside some personal time, but limit time spent with negative individuals. Go for a walk. Listen to music. Socialize. Indulge in sports and recreation. Take some time off to rejuvenate—even if it's just one day midweek or a long weekend. If possible, go on vacation. Do volunteer work or start a hobby. Soak in a hot bath. Pray or meditate. Do Yoga or Tai Chi. As we have seen, positive stress adds anticipation and excitement to life, and we all thrive under a certain amount of stress. Deadlines, competitions, confrontations, and even our frustrations and sorrows add depth and enrichment to our lives. Our goal is not to eliminate stress but to learn how to manage it and how to use it to help us. Insufficient stress acts as a depressant and may leave us feeling bored or dejected; on the other hand, excessive stress may leave us feeling "tied up in knots." What we need to do is find the optimal level of stress which will individually motivate but not overwhelm. There is no single level of stress that is optimal for all individuals. We are all individual creatures with unique requirements. As such, what is distressing to one may be a joy to another. And even when we agree that a particular event is distressing, we are likely to differ in our physiological and psychological responses to it. The person who loves to arbitrate disputes and moves from one job site to other job site would be stressed in a job, which was stable and routine, whereas the person who thrives under stable conditions would very likely be stressed on a job where duties were highly varied. Also, our personal stress requirements and the amount which we can tolerate before we become distressed changes with our ages. It has been found that most illness is related to unrelieved stress. If one is experiencing stress symptoms, one has gone beyond optimal stress level; one needs to reduce the stress in life and/or improve the ability to manage it.

9.13 CONCLUDING REMARKS FOR STRESS MANAGEMENT

When one is in the midst of a stressful situation, it's hard to determine whether one is simply feeling stress or something more serious. Stress doesn't just go away. Instead, it goes to work inside the body. The longer it's there, the more likely it is to produce physical and psychological illness. The latest research shows that stress can cause damage to the brain, heart, joints, digestive system, and immune system. If one thinks that one would benefit from help, either in identifying the things that are causing stress, or in learning techniques to help relax, there are many individuals who can give professional assistance in these areas.

It's time to seek professional help if one feels that stress is affecting one's health; feels that it will never end; feels so desperate that one thinks about quitting the job, running away, taking a drug overdose, or injuring oneself; feels depressed, sad, tearful, or that life is not worth living, loses appetite and find it difficult to sleep; is overeating, drinking alcoholic beverages, smoking, or using recreational drugs in abnormally large amounts; has worries, feeling, and thoughts that are hard to talk about; hears voices telling what to do. Professional help is particularly important if one feels depressed or extremely anxious. These conditions can be triggered by stress and often are overlooked. Stress-induced conditions can be managed and treated, but one must be patient. Stress tolerance does not always come easy. It takes time and practice to reduce anxiety, depression, and stress.

9.14 IMPLICATIONS OF SELF-AWARENESS

Self-awareness is the first component of emotional intelligence, which makes sense when one considers that the Delphic oracle gave the advice to know self, several thousands of years ago. To understand the concept, self-awareness means having a deep understanding of one's emotions, strengths, weaknesses, needs, and drives. Individuals with strong self-awareness are neither overly critical nor unrealistically hopeful. Rather, they are honest with themselves and with others. Individuals who have a high degree of self-awareness recognize how their feelings affect them, other individuals, and their job performance. Thus, a self-aware person who knows that tight deadlines bring out the worst in him plans his time carefully and gets his work done well in advance. Another person with high self-awareness will be able to work with a demanding client. She will understand the client's impact on her moods and the deeper reasons for her frustration. She would probably try to go one step further and convert her anger into something constructive. Self-awareness extends to a person's understanding of his or her values and goals. Someone who is highly self-aware knows where he is headed and why; so, for example, he will be able to be firm in turning down a job offer that is tempting financially but does not fit with his principles or long-term goals. A person who lacks self-awareness is apt to make decisions that bring on inner turmoil by treading on buried values. The decisions of self-aware individuals mesh with their values; consequently, they often find work to be energizing. How can one recognize self-awareness?

1. First and foremost, it shows itself as candor and an ability to assess oneself realistically. Individuals with high self-awareness are able to speak accurately and openly—although not necessarily effusively or confessional—about their emotions and the impact they have on their work. For

instance, one manager was skeptical about a new personal-shopper service that her company, a major department-store chain, was about to introduce. Without prompting from her team or her boss, she offered them an explanation: "It's hard for me to get behind the rollout of this service," she admitted, "because I really wanted to run the project, but I wasn't selected. Bear with me while I deal with that." The manager did indeed examine her feelings; a week later, she was supporting the project fully.

Such self-knowledge often shows itself in the hiring process. Ask a candidate to describe a time he got carried away by his feelings and did something he later regretted. Self-aware candidates will be frank in admitting to failure—and will often tell their tales with a smile.

2. One of the hallmarks of self-awareness is a self-deprecating sense of humor.

3. Self-awareness can also be identified during performance reviews. Self-aware individuals know—and are comfortable talking about—their limitations and strengths, and they often demonstrate a thirst for constructive criticism. By contrast, individuals with low self-awareness interpret the message that they need to improve as a threat or a sign of failure.

4. Self-aware individuals can also be recognized by their self-confidence. They have a firm grasp of their capabilities and are less likely to set themselves up to fail by, for example, overstretching on assignments. They know, too, when to ask for help. And the risks they take on the job are calculated. They won't ask for a challenge that they know they can't handle alone. They'll play to their strengths.

Consider the actions of a midlevel employee—Susan who was invited to sit in on a strategy meeting with her company's top executives. Although she was the most junior person in the room, she did not sit there quietly, listening in awestruck or fearful silence. She knew she had a head for clear logic and the skill to present ideas persuasively, and she offered cogent suggestions about the company's strategy. At the same time, her self-awareness stopped her from wandering into territory where she knew she was weak. Despite the value of having self-aware individuals in the workplace, research indicates that senior executives don't often give self-awareness the credit it deserves when they look for potential leaders. Many executives mistake candor about feelings for "wimpiness" and fail to give due respect to employees who openly acknowledge their shortcomings. Such individuals are too readily dismissed as "not tough enough" to lead others. In fact, the opposite is true. In the first place, individuals generally admire and respect candor. Further, leaders are constantly required to make judgment calls that require a candid assessment of capabilities—their own and those of others. Do we have the management expertise to acquire a competitor? Can we launch a new product within 6 months? Individuals who assess themselves honestly—that is, self-aware individuals—are well suited to do the same for the organizations they run.

9.15 METHOD TO DEVELOP SELF-AWARENESS

Surely, twenty-first-century leadership calls for a new type of leader who understands him/herself well and can call others into a higher state of being, rather than the old-style leader who simply knows how to manage finance, sales, and marketing processes. It calls for leaders who can engage the hearts and minds of all members within the organization, facilitating the psychological contract, so important for winning the market wars. But how can this journey be started? And what tools are available to assist? The Enneagram gives chance to invoke our true reservoir of talents and skills, instead of operating out of habit from comforting convictions (Daniels, 2000). A centuries old eastern wisdom, the Enneagram has the power to help make this journey. A tool that not only helps uncover the real "you," but then calls out on to a higher plain, from where one becomes more real, more content, and often, more effective in whatever one does.

For Connelly and Diaz, the Enneagram has been both a powerful personal transformational tool and one which they have used to support many individuals become more effective at work and at home. The Enneagram describes nine basic worldviews and nine ways of doing business. Each of the nine personality types is something of a pathway through life, with likely obstacles and pitfalls along the way. Each style has its own natural gifts, limitations, blind spots and its own distinctive ways of thinking, acting, and being.

The Enneagram builds upon the law of attention, which states that: energy follows attention to move attention and energy requires self-observation. Self-observation never becomes habitual. So, in order to transform what one does, one must first become aware of where we place our inner attentions—what are feelings and thinking—often paraconsciously. The more one does this, the more natural and habitual it will become and the more one would give self the chance to truly change his or her behavior. The Enneagram is both a very simplistic tool, describing nine world views, and a very complex tool, allowing for the fact that no two individuals are exactly the same. And here in lies one of its main differentiators from many of the other more common personality profiling tools (Wiltse and Palmer, 2011). Not only can one fall generally within a particular personality profile, but the system accepts that one will have shades of at least four other types within one's make-up, plus one of three subtypes. To summarize, two individuals of the same basic type can act quite differently at times. The self-awareness program developed at executive awareness is designed to lead one out of these shackles, by way of simple self-awareness exercises, which one can use at any time of the day. One wants to always remain in control. Soon one will be able to stop self-doing what comes automatically and change one's behavior to one which may be more appropriate to the person or situation. The Enneagram obviously lends itself, therefore, to helping leaders become more effective and can also be used most effectively within team development: executive/management teams, project teams, client teams, and process teams.

References

Bar-On, R. (2004), "The Bar-On Emotional Quotient Inventory (EQ-i): Rationale, description and summary of psychometric properties", In G. Geher (Ed.), *Measuring Emotional Intelligence: Common Ground and Controversy*, New York: Nova Science Publishers, Inc, 115–145.

Black, B., and Logan, A. (1995), "Links between communication patterns in mother-child, father-child, and child-peer interactions and children's social status", *Child Development*, 66(1), 255–271.

Daniels, D. (2000), The essential enneagram, California: HarperOne.

Davis, M., Eshelman, E. R., and McKay, M. (1995), The relaxation and stress reduction workbook, Oakland, CA: New Harbinger Publications, Inc.

Dodge, K. A., Pettit, G. S., McClaskey, C. L., and Brown, M. M. (1986), "Social competence in children", *Monographs of the Society for Research in Child Development*, 51, 1–85.

Dunn, S. E., Putallaz, M, Sheppard, B. H., and Lindstrom, R. (1987), "Social support and adjustment in gifted adolescents", *Journal of Educational Psychology*, 79, 467–473.

Goleman, D. (1995), Emotional intelligence, New York: Bantam Books.

Harrist, A. W., Pettit, G. S., Dodge, K. A., and Bates, J. E. (1994). Dyadic synchrony in motherchild interaction: Relations with children's subsequent kindergarten adjustment, *Family Relations*, 43, 417–424.

MacDonald, E. B. (1987), "Parent-child physical play with rejected, neglected, and popular boys", *Developmental Psychology*, 23, 705–711.

Mize, J., and Pettit, G. S. (1997), Mothers' social coaching, mother-child relationship style, and children's peer competence: Is the medium the message? *Child Development*, 68, 312–332.

Parke, R.D. and Bhavnagri, N. (1989). "Parents as Managers of Children's Peer Relationships", in D. Belle (Ed.) *Children's Social Networks and Social Supports*. New York: John Wiley

Pettit, G. S., Harrist, A. W., Bates, J. E., and Dodge, K. A. (1991), "Family interaction, social cognition, and children's subsequent relations", *Journal of Social and Personal Relationships*, 8, 383–402.

Pettit, G. S., & Harrist, A. W. (1993). Children's possessive and socially unsaved playground behavior with peers: Origins in early family relations. In C. H. Hart (Ed.), Children on playgrounds: Research perspectives and applications, Albany: State University of New York Press, 240–270.

Pettit, G.S. & Mize, J. (1993). Substance and style: Understanding the ways in which parents teach children about social relationships. In S. Duck (Ed.), *Understanding relationship processes. Vol 2: Leaming about relationships*, Newbury Park, CA: Sage, 118–151.

Pettit, G. S., Laird, R. D., Bates, J. E., and Dodge, K. A. (1997), "Patterns of after-school care in middle childhood: Risk factors and developmental outcomes", *Merrill-Palmer Quarterly*, 43, 515–538.

Putallaz, M., and Gottman, J. M. (1983), "Social relationship problems in children: An approach to intervention", In B. B. Lahey and A. E. Kazdin (Eds.), *Advances in clinical child psychology*, Vol. 6, New York: Plenum Publishing Corporation.

Putallaz, M., and Heflin, A. H. (1986), "Toward the development of a model of peer acceptance", In J. M. Gottman and J. G. Parker (Eds.), *Conversation of friends: Speculations on affective development*, New York: Cambridge University Press.

Putallaz, M. (1987), "Maternal behavior and children's sociometric status", *Child Development*, 58, 324–340.

Quick, J. C., Quick, J. D., Nelson, D. L., and Hurrell, J. J. (1997), Preventive stress management in organizations, Washington, DC: American Psychological Association.

Robinson, J. W. (1982), Stress and how to live with it, Edited by Cheryl Tevis, Lowa: Meredith Corp.

Seward, B. L. (1999), Managing stress: Principles and strategies for health and well-being, 2nd edition, Sudbury, MA: Jones and Bartlett.

Snyder, C. R., and Pulvers, K. M. (2001), "Dr. Seuss, the coping machine, and 'Oh the Places You'll Go,'" In C. R. Snyder (Ed.), Coping with stress: Effective people and processes, Oxford: Oxford University Press, 3–29.

Williamson, G. M., and Dooley, K. (2001), "Aging and coping: The activity solution." In C. R. Snyder (Ed.), *Coping with stress: Effective people and processes*, Oxford: Oxford University Press, 240–258.

Wiltse, V., and Palmer, H. (2011), "Hidden in plain sight: Observations on the origin of the Enneagram", *The Enneagram Journal*, 4(1), 4–37.

CHAPTER 10

Impulse Control, Flexibility Skills, Maintenance of Optimistic Behavior, and Anger Management

10.1 INDIVIDUAL IMPULSE CONTROL

In this dimension of controlling the impulse, this chapter will discuss how an individual behaves in best possible manner to control his or her impulses (Denson et al 2011, Black, 2001).

a. Time factor: When one has to control the impulses it cannot be controlled by underestimating the time. Change is part and parcel of the time, it will not wait. One has to take control of one's impulses.
b. Priority factor: When one has to accomplish certain critical amount of task and then at that time, if he or she loses the control over impulses that will result in unwanted situations and therefore when one does try to impulse control, one has to take into account the actual prioritization of tasks.
c. Interest factor: Unless and until one has interest in doing it, else will lose all the threads of controlling impulses.

10.2 SOME POINTS TO CONTROL THE IMPULSE DISORDER

1. Awareness of the problem, and when and under what circumstances the behavior occurs, is the first step to control it.
2. Regular exercise may help to control impulse disorder.
3. Being a social person and talking with friends or consultation with family member will help to reduce the impulse disorder.
4. Going for a walk away from the home will help to reduce the impulse disorder.
5. Take up enjoyable hobbies and interests to provide distraction and enhance self-esteem "positive self-talk."
6. Celebrate successes and acknowledge the hard work one has put into resisting the urges.

10.3 SUGGESTIONS FOR INCREASING CONTROL OF IMPULSES

The possible measures of impulse control management are given below:

a. Journal: Keep a journal to keep track of the impulses so that one can monitor changes and see any improvements, for instance, less frequent behaviors. Mark achievements in this diary and see what one can learn from them. An achievement might consist of resisting the urge to carry out the problem behavior for a whole day, week, or month. Awareness of the problem and when and under what circumstances the behavior occurs is the first step to controlling it. Celebrate successes and acknowledge the hard work one puts into resisting the urges.

    b. Distraction: This is possible with the following steps:

      1. Regular exercise may help because it releases natural endorphins ("feel-good" chemicals) into the body.

      2. When urges are great, do something else. Call a supportive friend or family member or a telephone counseling service, such as lifeline, and talk until urge passes; go for a walk away from temptation; or do something else that requires your concentration such as playing a musical instrument or reading a good book. One might find it helpful to make up a list of distractions that you can refer to quickly when one needs to.

      3. Take up enjoyable hobbies and interests to provide distraction and enhance self-esteem positive self-talk.

      4. Try to catch self when one thinks or says negative things about self and replace them with more positive and realistic things.

      5. Avoid punishing self when one has engaged in the impulsive behavior; research has shown that punishment is not an effective tool for changing human behavior. It is better to reward self at times when one has managed to resist the impulses.

      6. It is often too overwhelming to try to simply stop the behavior and can be more effective to do this gradually. Try to resist engaging in the problem behavior for a shorter time period and remember that by resisting one is gradually gaining control; in time these periods can get longer.

      7. If one slips and engages in the problem behavior, it does not mean it is hopeless or one has failed. Try to put it behind, forgive self, and wipe the slate clean.

      8. Accept that one has an impulse control disorder and "externalize" it.

      9. Enlist support from family members and friends by explaining the disorder to them and what one is doing to try to overcome it. They may need education about the disorder, and so try showing them this fact sheet.

    c. Families and friends

      10. Impulse control disorders may be frustrating and difficult to understand, particularly when one sees the negative effects of the behavior on his or her relative. It can be hard to understand why they can't just stop.

      11. Read up on the disorder to enable one to understand it.

      12. Encourage the person in any efforts he or she makes to resist the impulses and support any treatment he or she is receiving.

      13. Avoid enabling the person to continue with his or her impulsive behaviors. This doesn't mean that one can stop or control the person but one can control how one responds to it. For example, do not lend or give the person money to gamble with or agree to make excuses for that person.

      14. Celebrate small successes with the person. A day without engaging in the problem behaviors may not seem a long time, but could be a significant achievement for the person.

10.4 CONCLUDING REMARKS FOR IMPULSE CONTROL

This section helps us to know and to understand impulse control disorders from their very base. It tells us that impulse control disorders are basically psychological disorders and what exactly the causes and symptoms may be for these impulse control disorders. Basically with causes, symptoms, and types, one can get a good knowledge of how exactly such disorders may exist. The report also includes a brief overview of the various treatments that prove to be useful for controlling these types of disorders (Duckworth and Seligman 2005).

    It also gives an idea about how these disorders can create trouble for individuals at individual, organizational, and societal levels and also how one can control them at such levels.

10.5 FLEXIBILITY SKILLS: THE ELEMENTS OF SUCCESS

The research suggests that three critical elements contribute to the successful integration of flexibility initiatives in the workplace (Masley, Roetzheim and Gualtieri, 2009). These elements include the following:

1. A workplace culture that supports flexibility and provides clear guidelines for its practice;
2. Sufficient support and training for managers; and
3. An appropriate balance between the life patterns of the employee and the dynamic needs of the organization.

10.5.1 The Role of Workplace Culture

Studies have found that formal flexibility policies alone do not suffice as an indicator of flexibility. A more precise measure is the extent to which employees feel free to utilize such policies, whether formal or informal. The research literature concurs that an organization's informal culture is more important than formal policies in shaping employees' behavior.

In some cases, employees find that formal flexibility policies are discouraged in practice and may even have negative career effects. At the other end of the flexibility continuum, some supervisors permit more flexibility than is formally allowed and encourage employees to take time off unofficially, thus making flex invisible to higher level managers. Even informal policies may not be enough to create "felt" flex. On a day-to-day basis, managers often express ambivalence about whether to promote flex policies.

This demonstrates that while formal flexibility policies are important, so is the perceived ability to use such policies and the importance of developing clear guidelines and parameters.

10.5.2 Managerial Support and Guidance

Approach to the structure of work, which is defining work by hours spent in the workplace, rewards for long hours, the lack of formal guidelines to demonstrate leadership commitment, and organizational myths about the availability, acceptability, and career implications of alternative schedules (Kriete and Noelle, 2005). These barriers exist in varying degrees throughout large organizations, leading to inconsistency across departments, divisions, and teams.

In a Catalyst survey (1997), managers expressed interest in learning the flex negotiation and approval process, coordinating alternative arrangements for work groups and teams, and redesigning work responsibilities. The degree of support, guidance, and appropriate tools has been correlated to managers' effectiveness in implementing alternative work arrangements.

10.5.3 Balancing Employee Needs and Organizational Needs

An analysis of studies in the field showed that flexible work schedules had positive effects on employee productivity, job satisfaction, satisfaction with work schedule, and employee absenteeism. Both flextime and compressed workweek schedules showed primarily positive and no negative effects on work-related criteria. These positive benefits are consistent with historical trends in favor of more alternative work schedules.

Researchers caution that, in reviewing flexibility proposals, human resource practitioners must analyze the work that needs to be done and the degree of interdependence between jobs. Jobs with high levels of autonomy and routine might be more conducive to such arrangements than jobs with high interdependencies and nonroutine demands. Flexible arrangements for employees with highly interdependent jobs may require more managerial support (Masley, Roetzheim and Gualtieri, 2009).

Well-implemented flexibility initiatives offer enormous potential for improved staff retention, enhanced productivity, and increased job satisfaction. In terms of management and organizational development, the main benefit of flexibility is a fundamental shift from counting resources to measuring results. As one manager noted, in a recent Catalyst study (1997), "The truth is, the part-time arrangements forced us to be a little more deliberate about how we ordered priorities and what we did. It has forced us to stop managing by spasm."

10.6 CONCLUDING REMARKS FOR FLEXIBILITY

Above section shows flexibility is essential at the individual level and the organizational level. Being flexible means drifting a little bit from set boundaries, which will make our work easier and faster. This concept of being flexible is adopted by not only individuals but also organizations.

10.7 OVERVIEW OF THE PROBLEM-SOLVING STAGES

To be a successful problem-solver, one must go through these stages:

- Recognizing and defining the problem
- Finding possible alternative solutions
- Choosing the best solution
- Implementing the solution

10.7.1 Recognizing and Defining the Problem

Obviously, before any action can be taken to solve a problem, one need to recognize that a problem exists. A surprising number of problems go unnoticed or are only recognized when the situation becomes serious. Opportunities are also missed. There are specific techniques one can use to help recognize problems and opportunities. Once one has recognized a problem, we need to give it a label—a tentative definition. This serves to focus our search for relevant information, from which one can write an accurate description or definition of the problem. The process of definition differs for closed and open-ended problems. With closed problems, one needs to define all the circumstances surrounding the deviation from the norm. Sometimes, this will provide strong clues as to the cause of the problem. Defining open-ended problems involves identifying and defining our objectives and any obstacles that could prevent reaching them. The problem definition provides the basis for finding solutions.

10.7.2 Finding Possible Solutions

Closed problems generally have one or a limited number of possible solutions, whereas open-ended problems usually can be solved in a large number of ways. The most effective solution to an open-ended problem is found by selecting the best from a wide range of possibilities. Finding solutions involves analyzing the problem to ensure that one fully understands it and then constructing courses of action, which will achieve our objective.

Analyzing the problem involves identifying and collecting the relevant information representing it in a meaningful way. Analyzing closed problems helps to identify all the possible causes and confirm the real cause, or obstacle, before looking for a solution. With open-ended problems, one is looking for information that will help to suggest a range of possible ways to solve the problem. Analysis also helps to decide what the ideal solution would be, which helps to guide our search for solutions. Constructing courses of action to solve the problem involves discovering what actions will deal with any obstacles and achieve our objective. Workable solutions are developed by combining and modifying ideas and a range of creative techniques are available to help in this process. The more ideas one has to work with, the better the chances of finding an effective solution.

10.7.3 Choosing the Best Solution

This is a stage at which evaluates the possible solutions and select that which will be most effective in solving the problem. It's a process of decision-making based on a comparison of the potential outcome of alternative solutions. This involves the following:

- Identifying all the features of an ideal solution, including the constraints it has to meet.
- Eliminating solutions which do not meet the constraints.
- Evaluating the remaining solutions against the outcome required.
- Assessing the risks associated with the best solution.
- Making the decision to implement this solution.

A problem is only solved when a solution has been implemented. In some situations, before this can take place, one should gain acceptance of the solution by other individuals, or get their authority to implement it. This may involve various strategies or persuasion.

10.7.4 Implementing the Solution

This involves three separate stages:

- Planning and preparing to implement the solution.
- Taking the appropriate action and monitoring its effects.
- Reviewing the ultimate success of the action.

Implementing our solution is the culmination of all our efforts and requires very careful planning. The plan describes the sequence of actions required to achieve the objective, the timescale and the resources required at each stage. Ways of minimizing the risks involved and preventing mistakes have to be devised and built into the plan. Details of an alternative action pathway called as contingency plan, in case things do not proceed as envisaged, are also included.

Once the plan has been put into effect, the situation has to be monitored to ensure that things are running smoothly. Any problems or potential problems have to be dealt with quickly. When the action is completed, it's necessary to measure its success, both to estimate its usefulness for solving future problems of this type and to ensure that the problem has been solved. If not, further action may be required.

These stages provide a very flexible framework that can be adapted to suit all problems. With closed problems, for example, where there is likely to be only one or a few solutions, the emphasis is on defining and analyzing the problem to indicate possible causes. Open-ended problems, on the other hand, require more work to develop a large range of possible solutions. At any stage in solving the problem, it may be necessary to go back and adapt work done at an earlier stage. A variety of techniques and strategies are available to help one at each stage.

10.8 PROBLEM-SOLVING SKILLS

The nature of human problem-solving methods has been studied by psychologists over the past hundred years. There are several methods of studying problem-solving: introspection, behaviorism, simulation and computer modeling, and experiment.

Problem-solving requires two distinct types of mental skill: analytical and creative. Analytical or logical thinking includes skills such as ordering, comparing, evaluating, contrasting, and selecting. It provides a logical framework for problem-solving and helps to select the best alternative from those available by narrowing down the range of possibilities. Analytical thinking often predominates in solving closed problems, where the possible causes have to be identified and analyzed to find the real cause. Creative thinking is a divergent process, using the imagination to create a large range of ideas for solutions. It requires us to look beyond the obvious, creating ideas that may, at first, seem unrealistic or have no logical connection with the problem. There is a large element of creative thinking in solving open problems. The creative thinking skills can be divided into several key elements:

- Fluency—producing many ideas
- Flexibility—producing a broad range of ideas
- Originality—producing uncommon ideas
- Elaboration—developing ideas

10.9 DEVELOPING PROBLEM-SOLVING ABILITY

Learning to become a good problem-solver is a means to developing critical and logical thinking and discovering new mathematical ideas.

The goal is for all individuals to become increasingly able and willing to engage with and solve problems. Critical thinking is the intellectually disciplined process of actively and skillfully conceptualizing, applying, analyzing, synthesizing, and/or evaluating information gathered from, or generated by, observation, experience, reflection, reasoning, or communication, as a guide to belief and action. In its exemplary form, it is based on universal intellectual values that transcend subject matter divisions: clarity, accuracy, precision, consistency, relevance, sound evidence, good reasons, depth, breadth, and fairness.

10.9.1 A Brief Conceptualization of Critical Thinking

Critical thinking is self-guided, self-disciplined thinking that attempts to reason at the highest level of quality in a fair-minded way. Individuals, who think critically, consistently attempt to live rationally, reasonably, and empathically (Baumeister and Vohs, 2007). They are keenly aware of the inherently flawed nature of human thinking when left unchecked. They strive to diminish the power of their egocentric and sociocentric tendencies. They use the intellectual tools that critical thinking offers—concepts and principles that enable them to analyze, assess, and improve thinking. They work diligently to develop the intellectual virtues of intellectual integrity, intellectual humility, intellectual civility, intellectual empathy, intellectual sense of justice, and confidence in reason. They realize that no matter how skilled they are as thinkers, they can always improve their reasoning abilities and they will at times fall prey to mistakes in reasoning, human irrationality, prejudices, biases, distortions, uncritically accepted social rules and taboos, self-interest, and vested interest. They strive to improve the world in whatever ways they can and contribute to a more rational, civilized society. At the same time, they recognize the complexities often inherent in doing so. They strive never to think simplistically about complicated issues and always consider the rights and needs of relevant others. They recognize the complexities in developing as thinkers, and commit themselves to lifelong practice toward self-improvement. They embody the Socratic principle:

10.10 DISCUSSION OF THE PROBLEM-SOLVING GUIDELINES

10.10.1 Problem Exploration

The problem is investigated, broken into subproblems, and the terms are defined. A determination is made about the nature of the problem that could be sociological, personal, technological, and historical. Some research is made into whether or not it has been met in the past, and if so, how.

10.10.2 State the Problem

State what the problem is. Questions could be answered—Does it have multiple aspects? If so, what are they? This should include a written description of the problem in the clearest way it can be put. The statement might begin with the problem as given; put in quotation marks to remind one that that's the way it was received. But the problem should always be stated in our own words too. Make the problem our own, and do not let it become attached to the verbal clothing in which it was originally delivered to one.

A useful aspect of any definition or problem statement is to state what the thing is not. By clearly identifying what is not the problem, one will clarify what it is. Restate the problem in entirely different words, or in a completely different way. Do this several different times, generally three to eight is recommended. Again, the purpose of this process is to break the problem away from confusing or restricting verbal maps of it so that the problem in itself can be isolated.

State the problem more generally or more broadly. Put it abstractly or even philosophically. The idea here is to find out whether the given wording of the problem is really only a specific statement of a more general problem. Often, general statements allow the problem to be seen in entirely different terms and therefore suggest solutions that otherwise wouldn't be thought of.

10.10.3 Clarify the Problem

Define the key terms of the problem. Use synonyms; move from genus to species or species to genus. Continue to define in more and more general or specific ways. This kind of definition allows the breaking of the problem into attributes, components, and general features. The result is to shake loose some possible solutions.

Clarify anything about the problem that is ambiguous or uncertain. Often, problems as given are unclear in their original form. Articulate the assumptions being made about the problem and describe the way a solution would have to work. Assumptions can be tricky because they tend to be automatic and submerged—not consciously made. This articulation step in the problem-solving procedure involves the conscious listing of all assumptions that can be identified. The listing is without prejudice or judgment or hostility. A suggestion is to list as many as can be thought of.

It is especially important when listing assumptions to list the extremely obvious ones, because often it is those that later turn out to be alterable. Examine these assumptions to discover if they are necessary, not necessary, or uncertain as to their necessity. Many assumptions are quite necessary, of course. In the problem, develop a better way to destroy kidney stones, one obvious and necessary assumption is that the patient should be alive after the procedure. But often assumptions turn out to be made for no good reason—that is they are not necessary assumptions. These can be challenged and new routes to success can then be discovered. Obtain needed information. Research into past approaches to the problem or to similar problems will help get new ideas as well as gain understanding of the nature and environment of the problem itself.

10.10.4 Explain the Problem

Discuss the problem with someone else. Explain it carefully. Listen to our own explanation. Discussion has two important features. First, there is the possibility that one will find a solution in the head of another person. Discussion enables one to get information, suggestions, and ideas. Important: even if the ideas have nothing to do with the problem, or if they are in themselves unworkable, they can still be valuable stimuli because they will show a new approach to the problem or they will suggest something practical to you. So, even though our friend can never understand our problem technically, emotionally, intellectually, artistically, or whatever, one can still gain valuable insight by discussing it and by hearing a response.

Secondly, discussing our problem with someone allows seeing what one really thinks. Philosophers and writing theorists have long noted that individuals think and work out ideas as they talk. Francis Bacon noted that one value of friendship was to have someone to talk to so that one can see how our ideas look when they are turned into words. Some individuals have reported remarkable insights just by talking to their pets, where no intellectual feedback from the "listener" was possible. So, when one discusses problems or idea, listen to self as well as to the other person.

Explain why the problem is a problem. What are its negative or undesirable features? One, by explaining why the problem is problematic, one discovers more about its nature and whether it really is a problem. Research claims that there have been a lot of solutions to problems that didn't exist. So, this explanation phase allows one to discover just whether a problem is real.

Next, by explaining in detail the negatives of the problem, a set of more specific targets can be identified, thus better lending themselves to being solved. Look at the problem from different viewpoints. Remember that our view of reality, as an intelligent, concerned, conscientious, middle class person, is only one view. By imaginatively taking on the viewpoints of various other individuals affected by a particular problem, one can sometimes discover solutions that one would never think of.

The importance of being able to see different sides or angles has been reinforced in folk wisdom worldwide. Ask a series of clarifying whys. By asking "why" of every statement of the problem, possible solution, or identified goal, clearer definitions are made. Asking why can serve a purpose similar to that of broadening the definition of the problem, and can lead to new ways of looking at the problem and at possible solutions.

10.10.5 Put the Problem in Context

The first question is what is the history of the problem? Knowing where it came from can help focus our efforts toward a solution to try or away from a solution not to try. If a particular solution has been tried already and met with a sensational disaster, one might not want to try it again.

Some more questions to be answered are what is the problem environment? What are the surrounding contexts? Are there associative factors that helped cause or perpetuate the problem? Have there been similar problems and solutions that may be useful in solving this one? An understanding of contributing or perpetuating factors will help one to take steps to prevent a problem from coming right back once solved it. Similarly, studying how similar or analogous problems have been solved may lead to a shortcut solution to this one. List the constraints of the problem. What limitations are imposed, what is required, what must be observed in solving the problem? This is pretty straightforward. Constraints are givens that must be followed—a budget one cannot exceed legal or contractual requirements that must be met and so on.

For example, if the problem in the case is to find an apartment on lease by Susan and Solomon in a short time span. Constraints are simply requirements to keep in mind, part of the problem's basic dimensions. Of course, writing them down helps to keep them in the foreground as one works toward solutions. Occasionally, the identified constraints turn out, upon listing and examination, not to be necessary after all. They can be eliminated or worked around.

10.10.6 Goal Establishment

- Consider Ideal Goals—We too often set our goals as the solving of the immediate problem or the minimum solution rather than considering how we would like reality to be ideally.
- Establish Practical Goals—What are the goals to be achieved that would make this problem be declared solved? The listing of definite and precise goals is useful in problem-solving because the attempts at solution can then be measured against the goals to see how much progress is being made.

Setting up goals helps to clarify the direction to take in solving the problem and gives you something definite to aim at. What will the solution be like? That is, what will occur as a result of the solution? Describe the world as it will be after the solution is implemented (Baumeister and Vohs, 2007).

In our unemployment example above, we could say the solution will involve setting up a permanent job-finding service that will continue to operate after the goal is met, to insure that unemployment (the problem) doesn't return later on. The solution might also include educational services to train workers or to train individuals in job-finding strategies. Note that the description of the solution here can be pretty vague and dreamy if necessary, because sometimes you will have only an uncertain notion of what that solution will ultimately be. But try to be as specific as possible.

Idea Generation

- Generate Ideas for Possible Solutions. Read, research, think, ask questions, and discuss. Look for ideas and solutions. Begin with a period of information gathering and mental stimulation. Knowledge is power. Get facts. Learn as much as one can about the problem.
- Use idea generation techniques such as brainstorming, forced relationships, and random stimulation. Generate a large number of ideas of all kinds so that one will have a good selection to choose from, adapt, or stimulate other ideas. Don't worry about whether the ideas are practical or wild at this point.
- Allow time to incubate during various phases of idea generation. The major cycle of creativity that has long been identified is preparation—initial thought, research, study, work, and incubation—time to let the unconscious work, insight, implementation, and evaluation.

Small problems will require only a short period of incubation. Difficult problems will require longer periods. Some individuals require longer periods than other individuals. The main thing is to remember the cycle of work and incubate. Susan could allow time for incubation, though. When she has worked a long time and is up against a wall, she could leave the problem and go out and do something relaxing. Then return to the problem. The idea of sleeping on a problem is excellent.

Idea Selection

Evaluate the Possibilities: Evaluate the collection of ideas and possible solutions and approaches. What possible solutions, either individually or in conjunction with each other, will solve this problem? An important thing to remember here is not to get fixated on the single solution idea. One may want to adopt two or three separate solution paths at the same time—kind of like the triple antibiotic ointment approach. Susan might also want to set up a plan B, a possible solution approach that can be implemented if our main plan does not work. So in our evaluation, don't focus on choosing just one solution and tossing the others away.

When one evaluates, find the solution that will be the most effective, works best, efficient costing the least, in terms of money, time, or emotions, and have the fewest drawbacks or side effects.

10.10.7 Choose the Solutions

Select one or more solutions to try. In the above evaluation, Susan should establish some rank ordering. Choose from among those near the top of the list. Something to be noted is that the very top ranked solution is not always the one to get chosen for implementation. Subjective, emotional factors, sudden changes, peculiar circumstances, the desire for beneficial side effects not directly related to the solution, and intuitive feeling often shift the choice to something ranked below number one or two.

- Allow others to see and criticize our selected solution and to make suggestions for improvements or even alternatives. The best way to turn our idea light bulb into a chandelier or floodlight is to let other individuals comment on it. This takes a certain amount of ego strength, since only intermediate friends will say how good the idea is. Strangers and close friends will quickly point out absurdities and weaknesses. But that's good, because one will have a chance to improve our solution idea before attempting to implement it.

One has to walk a narrow path here. Don't be swayed too easily by criticism to change an idea that one is confident is really good. After all, the typical person is not a creative visionary and will be controlled by the prejudices of ordinariness. One can expect resistance to good new ideas. On the other hand, don't be so in love with our idea that one cannot see the legitimacy of criticisms that point our genuine weaknesses. It is suggested to be willing to incorporate new ideas and improvements from fresh minds looking at the problem and solution from a different perspective.

Implementation

a. Try out the solution. Experiment it—Do it, fix it, and try it.
   The real test of an idea is to try it out. The key concept here is action. Get going and begin the solution. Once one chooses a solution path, get to work on it. Don't worry if objections or problems remain. Start working. Susan noted that if all possible objections to a proposal must first be overcome, nothing would ever be attempted. And remember to give our solution sufficient time to work. Too hasty an abandonment of a solution or solution path is as common a problem as too obsessive a commitment to a particular solution path. A solution may take weeks or months (or years) to work, and so use judgment in determining how long to wait before abandoning the choice.
b. Make adjustments or changes as needed during implementation.
   Remain flexible in this application phase. Practically, every solution needs some modification in the process of being put into effect. Blueprints are changed, scripts are rewritten, and our parenting methodology is adjusted. Don't expect that our solution will be exactly as one originally proposed. Remember that the goal is to solve the problem, not mindlessly to implement the solution exactly as proposed.
c. Evaluation—Investigate to determine whether the solution worked.
   Investigate to determine whether the solution worked, to what extent. Do modifications need to be made? Do other solutions need to be selected and tried? Is a different approach needed? One of the most frequent failures of problem-solving is the lack of evaluation of the implemented solution. Too often in the past, once a solution has been chosen and implemented, individuals have wandered off, assuming that the problem was solved and everything was fine. But the solution may not have worked or not worked completely, or it may have caused other problems in the process. Staying around long enough to evaluate the solution's effectiveness, then, is an important part of problem-solving.
d. Remembering that many solutions are better described as partially successful or partially unsuccessful, either in success or failure division.
   If one proposes a solution that reduces drug addiction by even 10%, your solution is a good one, even though it didn't work for other 90% of cases. In many cases, an incomplete remedy is better than none at all.

10.11 TECHNIQUES FOR GROUP PROBLEM-SOLVING

The two major group techniques designed specifically for problem-solving are brainstorming and Synectics. Quality circles are primarily concerned with problem-solving but serve additional.

Brainstorming and Synectics use a common method for giving direction to the problem-solving activity. First, the problem is defined in terms of "How to . . .?" This wording has the advantage that it doesn't have to be realistic statement of what the group wants to achieve; so, it doesn't need to be justi-fied and impractical ideas are not discouraged. Then, solutions to this problem definition are sought in response to the question "In how many ways can we . . .?" This takes the group from formulating goals to suggesting ways to achieve them. Both group techniques help to stimulate the imagination of participant by displaying permanently all the ideas as there produced.

10.11.1 Brainstorming

The technique of brainstorming, which was devised in the advertising agency, is designed to generate a large number and range of ideas in a short time. This is achieved by concentrating solely on idea generation and creating a light-hearted, free-willing atmosphere. The number of individuals in a brainstorming session varies between five and twenty, with an optimum of about twelve. Everyone present in the session contributes ideas, including a leader, because nonparticipating observes can have an inhibiting effect. Sessions are held in a room away from destructions, with chairs arranged in U shape and a flip chart with something like newsprint, which can be used to record ideas and then torn of, is pinned to the walls. Session can last anything up to two hours; although the longer they are, no difficult it is to sustain the flow of ideas. The finishing time should be left open so that it does not curtail a fruitful session.

The leader's role begins with preparation for the session, gaining a full understanding of the problem, and selecting and inviting participants who are given a brief description of the problem. During the session, the leader contributes, stimulates, and record ideas; constant structure stimulation is needed to keep the ideas flowing and everyone participating.

There are four basic rules to be followed in a brainstorming session and it is a leader's job to enforce them:

- **Suspend judgment**
  No evolution is allowed during the session and the leader must be able to enforce this rule even with very high ranking individuals.
- **Free-wheel**
  This is the lowering of barriers in inhibitions about what is practical and what is impractical so that the mind can wander freely. It is encouraged by the suspense judgment rule and by humor and laughter in response to silly ideas.
- **Cross-fertilize**
  Participants are encouraged to modify and develop other individual ideas and to express any further ideas.
- **Quantity**
  Participants are encouraged to produce a large number of ideas irrespective of whether they are practical or impractical. A good session can produce hundreds of ideas.

    All energy in a brainstorming session is directed toward producing ideas for solving the problem, which involve the following status:
  - Defining and discussing the problem
  - Restating the problem
  - Warming up
  - Brainstorming
  1. Defining and discussing the problem—The problem is described briefly by someone with knowledge of the situation, giving enough information for the order to understand it but not enough to inhibit his or her ideas for a solution. This stage usually takes around five minutes.

2. Restating the problem—Group members restate the problem, looking at it from different angles and phrasing it in terms of "how to . . .?" The leader writes these down on newsprint. Throughout the session, all ideas are numbered serially to make them easier to identify later. Restatement continues until all ideas are exhausted. This should result in at least twenty-five restatements often many more.

3. Warming up—At this stage, it is useful to use one of the fluency exercises, such as "other user for . . . and the consequence of bizarre situation." This helps to get the group members in free-wheeling frame of mind; none of these ideas are recorded.

4. Brainstorming—One of the restatements is selected either by wrong or by voting or by the leader, who then writes it down on a new sheet of paper beginning with the words "In how many ways can we . . .?" The leader reads the restatement and asks for ideas, writing them down as they are called out. When a sheet is full displayed prominently on the wall to act as a stimulus to further ideas have been exhausted another restatement is selected, as remote as possible from the first one, and the process is repeated; three or four restatements are treated in this way.

There are various things the leader can do to stimulate the group: repeating ideas as they are written down, asking for variation on an earlier idea, and calling for another warming-up exercise. The leader can also suggest the ideas, which lead the group into new areas. When ideas dry up, the leader asks the group to select the wildest idea from the lists and to select useful variation. A couple of the wildest ideas are treated in this way before the leader ends the session with a description of the evaluation process.

Evaluation starts a few days after the brainstorming session, once a list of all the ideas produced has been typed. There are two methods of evaluation: by a small team of individuals selected from the original session, including the leader and committed to solving the problem, and by all the participants individually. Using both methods helps to prevent potentially useful ideas being discarded.

The list of the ideas produced is sent to individual participants who are asked to select a small proportion of the ideas they feel could be useful in solving the problem. They send the numbers of these ideas to the leader, who collates them and discards ideas that received few votes for this purpose.

Under some circumstances, brainstorming sessions can be conducted successfully in a less structured way. One particular application is the creation of brand names—starting with a product description under the creation of brand names. Group members explore all the associations that a product might inspire in the mind of the consumer. Visual image of various lifestyles associated with the product can be used to help stimulate ideas for names.

A two-hour session, with several products under consideration, may generate around 2,000 names. Already in use and checking by linguists to ensure that translations into different languages would not create a disastrous associated with the product.

10.12 CONCLUDING REMARKS FOR PROBLEM-SOLVING ABILITY

Problem-solving forms part of thinking. Apart from being considered as the most complex of all intellectual functions, problem-solving has been defined as higher order cognitive process that requires the modulation and control of more routine or fundamental skills. It occurs if an organism or an artificial intelligence system does not know how to proceed from a given state to a desired goal state. It is a part of the larger problem process that includes problem-finding and problem-shaping. It helps in finding best solution for problem.

Problem-solving involves realization of goals that cannot immediately be attained. Gestalt approach emphasized need to restructure problems to gain insight into solution. Problem-solving is inhibited by functional fixedness. Information processing emphasized exploration of problem space using heuristics. Problem-solving ability is crucial in every aspects of life from individual to group to organization.

Individuals have some problem-solving skill and it is a very individualized process. Problem-solving is something that occurs regularly every day, yet little emphasis has traditionally been given to its improvement. Recent studies and theories have provided new insight into how individuals solve problems. From this has come a clearer understanding of the problem-solving process, an understanding that problem-solving is based upon skills and that new skills can be learned to increase problem-solving effectiveness. The key points to be learned are as follows:

   a. Understanding the problem-solving process, from problem awareness through evaluation.
   b. Learning the structures and skills that facilitate the use of the problem-solving process.
   c. Practicing flexibility in utilizing both the structure and the process to become a better problem-solver.

10.13 ANGER MANAGEMENT

Anger is a strong feeling of displeasure caused by disappointment. It has many adverse effects and results in destructive activities. The process in which there is combination of methods and procedures for controlling anger in known as anger management. Anger management is the compilation of stress reduction techniques for channeling one's angry feelings into socially acceptable directions. It is the ability to cope and deal with stress (Wright, Day and Howells 2009). There are certain techniques and methodologies to train our brain to stay calm. It helps in executing anger management. Anger management is required anywhere and everywhere, round the clock to gain professional, social, and personal achievements.

In many arguments, a person brings up old issues from previous disputes. That expands the argument and creates too many issues to resolve at one time. If the other person tries to bring up other issues, use the broken record technique, repeatedly politely insisting that one would stick to the first issue and will deal with the others only after the main issue has been resolved. Likewise, if the other person attacks one personally, one must resist the temptation to stop and defend self until the main point has been worked out. Once drawn into an enlarged discussion or put on the defensive, one has lost the ability to manage and resolve the argument. Making eye contact and saying, "I understand what you're saying," or "I understand that you feel such-and-such," helps calm the other person down and helps clarify misunderstanding, often laying the groundwork for him to listen to us after he has calmed down. Silly humor can help defuse rage in a number of ways. For one thing, it can help one get a more balanced perspective. When one gets angry and calls someone a name or refers to that person in some imaginative phrase, stop and picture what that word would literally look like. If we are at work and think of a coworker as a dirt bag or a single-celled life form, for example, picture a large bag full of dirt or an amoeba sitting at our colleague's desk, talking on the phone, and going to meetings. Do this whenever a name comes into our head about another person. If we can, draw a picture of what the actual thing might look like. This will take a lot of the edge off our fury; and humor can always be relied on to help unknot a tense situation. The underlying message of highly angry individuals is "things ought to go their way." Angry individuals tend to feel that they are morally right, that any blocking or changing of their plans is an unbearable indignity, and that they should not have to suffer this way.

When one feels that urge to be angry, picture self as a god or goddess or a supreme ruler, who owns the streets and stores and office space, striding alone and having our way in all situations while others defer to us (Wright, Day and Howells 2009). The more detail one can get into our imaginary scenes, the more chances one has to realize that maybe one is being unreasonable; one will also realize how unimportant the things one is angry about really are. There are two cautions in using humor. First, don't try to just laugh off problems. Use humor to help self-face them more constructively. Second, don't give in to harsh, sarcastic humor because that is just another form of unhealthy expression of anger. These techniques have in common is a refusal to take one too seriously. Anger is a serious emotion, but it's often accompanied by ideas that, if examined, can make one laugh.

10.14 ANGER-MANAGEMENT TRAINING

The effectiveness of anger-management training depends on a number of factors. They are as follows:

a. Length of treatment: The effectiveness of anger-management training depends on how many sessions are provided. By holding booster sessions 1 year after the initial intervention, improves the long-term outcomes. Thus, this suggests that greater number of sessions along with booster sessions after 1 year will contribute to the effectiveness of intervention.

b. Framing the training: To enhance the effectiveness of anger management, the training must be relevant to the students being trained. For example, aggressive students tend to have a strong need for retaliation. They often consider having the last word or striking the last blow to be a win. Trainers can work with students to help them understand that, if they respond when provoked, they have been manipulated by other into losing control of themselves. In order to win, they must learn to walk away. Hence, framing the training in terms of youth's understanding seems to increase the effectiveness of intervention.

c. Supplemental interventions: According to this, the benefits of anger management grow manifold when supplemented with other interventions. For example, students who were asked to set weekly goals along with anger management training showed greater decreases in their disruptive behavior. Anger replacement training is a more comprehensive approach that incorporates moral education and structured training with anger management. Students who received anger replacement training showed increases in moral reasoning, engaged in more productive interactions with others, and improved their ability to solve social problems.

Most anger management programs use techniques borrowed from cognitive-behavioral therapy to help individuals deal with anger. Some strategies to keep Susan's negative emotions in check are given below:

a. She could reframe the situation. Instead of seeing every inconvenience or frustration as a personal affront, she should imagine a benign explanation.

b. She could find a constructive solution to issue at hand. By finding a reason to be normal in odd situation, she will be able to shift focus from ways to punish the members of her family by finding ways to behave in a healthy way.

c. By keeping an anger log to monitor what makes one angry, she would be able to identify and avoid the triggers.

d. She should be aware that anger tends to rise in increments. By evaluating her anger on a scale of 1 (frustration) to 10 (rage), and if one can catch oneself at 3 or 4, it means that the person can think more rationally about the situation.

e. If she feels that a blow up is about to come on, then giving a time-out before acting on it will prove to be useful. Hence, waiting fifteen minutes before she says something, or an hour before one sends an email. This helps in keeping options open.

f. It is important to get a health checkup done as medical problems, such as diabetes or chronic pain, can make individuals very irritable. Anger, either repressed or unleashed, can cause medical problems too. About 30,000 heart attacks each year are triggered by momentary anger.

g. She should be aware of how to talk to self. Feeling victimized tends to make one get all the angrier.

h. She should not ruminate on past affronts or injustices.

i. She could recognize patterns. One should not rely or recall on past incidents, which make him or her angry. It is essential to move on and think about the present to act rationally.

j. She must calculate what anger is costing her. Many individuals with anger problems think anger gives them an edge, and establishes superiority. Instead, it makes them look like a fool.

k. She cannot get physical, without fists. When our primitive brain senses a threat, it sets off the "fight or flight" cascade of hormones. Opt for flight instead of fight and burn off the extra adrenaline and cortisol with exercise. Even a brisk walk will help calm one down.

l. The ultimate lesson for Susan is to pay more attention to the important things in life and recognize that most frustrations, inconveniences, and indignities are trivial and temporary.

m. She could make use of six seconds technique—Count 1–10 and the time taken is six seconds to cool down anger.

10.15 EARLY IDENTIFICATION AND INTERVENTION

School violence is a result of anger and sudden rage. Students who do not know how to manage their anger are at risk of displaying aggression and even violent explosive behavior at home as well as in school. Anger management teaches such students with high levels of aggression how to control their emotions and understand and manage their feelings in order to avoid escalating negative feelings, which may result in serious confrontations with peers, teachers, etc.

In anger management, students are taught strategies like problem-solving skills that enable them to control their anger in case of conflicts (Redford 2001).

It helps students alter their perceptions toward individuals, things, and situations. First, they develop an ability to understand the perspective of others by putting themselves in other's shoes. Second, students learn to be cognizant of their emotional and physical states when they are angry. Also, relaxation techniques are adopted to teach students the art of self-control. Students are trained in problem-solving skills:

1. Identifying the problem
2. Generating alternative solutions
3. Considering the consequences of each solution
4. Selecting an effective response
5. Evaluating outcomes of that response

Anger management programs generally include activities like group discussion, role-plays, modeling of appropriate behavior, simulation games, and examples on videotape. Usually, such sessions are conducted in a small group of six to eight individuals in order to provide individual attention to all. Sessions generally have one leader or two, including a psychologist, counselor, or a mental health professional.

Anger management training is aimed at curbing the aggression of individuals in the short term. It is especially effective in case of youths as they are able to improve themselves faster at a tender age. Students trained in anger management have been found to decrease their disruptive and aggressive behaviors both at home and at school and tend to display greater self-control.

Researchers have found that the short-term benefits of anger management are apparent; however, long-term results have been found to be inconsistent, for example, a three-year follow-up study of aggressive elementary school boys showed decreased drug and alcohol involvement and improved self-esteem, but no change in delinquent behavior.

Anger management is beneficial for many individuals who get themselves into difficulties with their anger. Just as some individuals make their lives difficult through the way they manage their money, some of us mismanage our anger and create all kinds of problems. One might get angry too often or not often enough; one might become threatening to others or terrify self; one might always show one's anger at the wrong time or never to the right person. This is the story of managing anger differently for each individual. In the same way that money management is not about stopping individuals making and spending money, anger management does not stop one feeling and expressing anger. Along with fear, joy, and sadness, anger is one of the four most basic human emotions and is usually a natural and healthy process. To "manage" being angry well is to "spend" anger wisely.

Process is a key word in anger management. The emotion of anger is a motion—an action, not a thing. It is an important communication about how you are dealing with a situation. When someone is happy or angry or sad, he or she is giving vital information about the way he or she relates to other individuals. This information is both internal, which signals to us, and external, which messages to others. Learning about our anger process means exploring two crucial areas: our thinking style and our communication skills. Anger does not operate in isolation from other emotions. Deep sadness due to grief, perhaps, or severe disappointment is often associated with anger. Some individuals who have anger management sessions are surprised to find that when they recognize and accept other strong feelings that they usually suppress, this emotional integration helps them to control their anger more easily. Anger is controllable. With a little help, most of us can learn how to process our anger authentically and usefully, depending on our individual needs and desires. Anger management offers three main benefits:

1. Personal understanding of the meaning and purpose of our anger and other emotions.
2. Knowledge of what happens in our brain and body when one responds angrily to current situations or memories.
3. Increased self-responsibility for our angry feelings and more choices about how to use them positively in all areas of our life.

Empower self and educate self that this is a problem not to be ignored and there are so many ill consequences, psychologically, emotionally, and spiritually. We are upset about things that are completely unimportant and they are hurting us. Just remember that the fire that one burns in our heart for our enemy will often burn us first.

Know our anger-warning signs: edginess, headache, perspiration, teeth grinding, muscle tension, and lightheadedness can signal when one is close to the edge. Stop, breathe, and then leave. Stop from saying or doing anything one knows one will regret. Breathe deeply and slowly. Count to 10, recite a mantra, and say a favorite prayer to take our mind off the stress. Remove self from the source of the stress. Leave the room, take a walk, go somewhere, and cool down.

10.16 CONCLUDING REMARKS FOR ANGER MANAGEMENT

Anger is one letter shorter than danger, and to avoid this danger we should call up the Two Fs—Forget and Forgive. We should concentrate on anger management.

Through anger management and practicing "Cooling Off," one can attain the divine bliss of mind (Snyder, Kymissis and Kessler, 1999). It is good for the physical health as it cancels the probability of various anger-borne diseases. It increases your mental stamina and improves your personality. Most importantly, it enhances your social acceptance.

Through anger management, we can achieve soul-satisfaction and self-contentment. As per Addison, A contented mind is the greatest blessing a man can enjoy in this world.

Anger management empowers students to control their actions and reactions in case of a conflict or an altercation. Overall, anger management is a promising intervention that curbs disruptive and violent behavior in aggressive students.

Conventional anger management programs teach relaxation techniques and impulse control skills, but critics point out that these classes skim the surface of rage, mostly helping those individuals who are already determined to change. The root cause of anger is that it strikes too quickly for cognitive control and boiling over before the rational brain can stop it. Also because anger is often fueled by guilt and shame, making individuals feel bad about their behavior does not work either as it reinforces the angry person's sense of victimhood. Hence, to get to the root of anger, a step-by-step process called HEALS can be adopted (Redford 2001).

HEALS works on the philosophy—compassion can cure anger. The process goes in the following manner for Susan:

H: At the first sign of anger, Susan should call up the word in her mind. If she is angry at someone, then try to picture that person with the word on her face.

E: Explain to herself the core problem for the person to feel hurt, such as feeling unloved, disregarded, or neglected.

A: The third step is to access her core values, which makes her life worth living. This includes her good deeds, loving relationships, or values one likes to uphold, such as honesty and bravery.

L: This step tells to love self.

S: Solve the problem. Address the conflict that underlies her anger.

A repetition of the abovementioned process on a daily basis, she would train angry individuals to automatically draw on this process during moments of stress enabling individuals to identify personal hurts fueling their anger and to develop a quick and automatic response to defuse anger triggers.

10.17 CONCLUDING REMARKS FOR CASE STUDY ON SUSAN

The late Earl Nightingale states "We become what we think about." It is our thoughts that determine who we are. Susan can create tomorrow based on what we are thinking today. So, simply by changing her thoughts, Susan can change who she is and hence change every aspect of her life. For Susan, the most important point right now is a strong sense of human beings' desire to excel comes with ones' need to feel worthy, important, and respected by ourselves and others. Susan strives on for one success after another hoping that she will succeed one more time. In today's world, many individuals equate sense of self with their possessions and what they do for a living. Susan has to be aware that sooner or later, Murphy's Law will pay a visit: whatever can go wrong, eventually will go wrong. When she fails, she had negative thoughts and feelings. She begins to feel unworthy, undeserving, and unimportant. In contrast, if she has a strong sense of self, she would stop linking her success or failures to self-worth and self-esteem.

References

Baumeister, R. F., and Vohs, K. D. (2007), "Self-regulation, ego depletion, and motivation", *Social and Personality Psychology Compass*, 1, 115–128.

Black, D. W. (2001), "Compulsive buying disorder: definition, assessment, epidemiology and clinical management", *CNS Drugs*, 15(1), 17–27.

Denson, T. F., Capper, M. M., Oaten, M., Friese, M., and Schofield, T. P. (2011), "Self-control training decreases aggression in response to provocation in aggressive individuals", *Journal of Research in Personality*, 45, 252–256.

Duckworth, A. L., and Seligman, M. E. P. (2005), "Self-discipline outdoes IQ in predicting academic performance of adolescents", *Psychological Science*, 16, 939–944.

Kriete, T., and Noelle, D. C. (2005), "Impaired cognitive flexibility and intact cognitive control in autism: A computational cognitive neuroscience approach", In Proceedings of the 27th annual conference of the cognitive science society, 1190–1195.

Masley, S., Roetzheim R., Gualtieri, T. (2009), "Aerobic exercise enhances cognitive flexibility", *Journal of Clinical Psychology in Medical Settings*, 16, 186–193.

Plummer, D. M. (2008), Anger management games for children, London, GBR: Jessica Kingsley Publishers.

Redford, P. C. (2001), Anger: A cross-cultural investigation, *Unpublished doctoral dissertation*, University of Sussex, Brighton, United Kingdom.

Snyder, K., Kymissis, P., and Kessler, K. (1999), "Anger management for adolescents: Efficacy of brief group therapy", *Journal of the American Academy of Child and Adolescent Psychiatry*, 38(11), 1409–1416.

Wright, S., Day, A., and Howells, K. (2009), "Mindfulness and the treatment of anger problems", *Aggression and Violent Behavior*, 14(5), 396–401.

CHAPTER 11

Study of Selected Global Business Changers

11.1 INTRODUCTION

Emotionally intelligent leaders are business changers. They communicate effectively, are self-aware, are motivated to inspire others, have means of managing stress, form strong relationships, and create powerful coping strategies. Emotionally unintelligent people have a tough time—no matter how high their IQs (Bar-On, 2000; Bar-On, 2004).

The study involves the exploration of selected global business changers with reference to the EI competency ladder. Its purpose is to show that the way a leader conducts himself at work affects the organization directly. This section also includes the effects of their individual behaviors on their organization's overall success. The project highlights the perspectives of EI competency ladder on business challenges and the way leaders confront those challenges.

How were the people investigated qualitatively chosen for this chapter? The selections were made largely on the basis of their impact on positive social change. The use of their products and services was another factor considered. Other factors were considered as follows:

1. How influential had the person become in his lifetime?
2. Did the person or his or her organization transform lives of the general public in any significant way?
3. Did they alter our professional lives to facilitate more productivity, emotional enhancement, or innovation?

Admittedly, the answers to these questions are entirely subjective and needs further elaboration. So, too, are the choices of entrepreneurs listed in this chapter. All of them are global business changers whose products and services have found their way into our lives and enhanced them for the better. The goal was to bring entrepreneur's experience and wisdom for the benefit of others—to understand, to inspire, to motivate, to learn, and to achieve. Although much work has gone into the development and application of EI in people's lives, we took a different perspective for this paper. Our goal is to add to independent, systematic analysis of the claim that EI increases individual performance over and above the level expected from traditional notions of general intelligence.

Each of these world changers is influential in his or her ways and deemed to be emotionally intelligent. This research will discuss the attributes of EI based on situations and actions displayed by our world changers. Most importantly, we will discuss how these attributes helped to shape them, their careers, businesses, and ultimately shaped them to become the world changers that they are.

Adaptation of "Cognitive and Noncognitive Competencies of Selected World Business Changers," by Shamira Malekar and Tatiana Burks, which was published in The International Journal of Transformative Emotional Intelligence, May 11, 2016. Adapted and reprinted by permission.

This intellectually stimulating and thought-provoking research can assist in developing skillsets that are the epitome of success. This research emphasizes the EI attributes that have contributed to the success of these entrepreneurs and their businesses. Real-life examples and situations have been studied to understand the impact of their EI in business-related risk taking, decision-making, and critical thinking. To start with, two eminent global business changers, Ratan Tata of Tata Group and Michael Dell of Dell Inc., are discussed.

11.2 MICHAEL DELL AND RATAN TATA

Michael Dell and Ratan Tata are both well-known and respected business men. Michael Dell's idea of business was to sell computers directly to the customers; he bypassed the middleman and the markups. His idea was one of a kind for its time in the 1980s. Today, Dell Inc., is one of the best known companies; the way he thinks with EI is one of the root cause. Ratan Tata on the other hand started out working in an entry level position at a family run company. He worked his way up to take over after his uncle J.D.R Tata. In this case, there is research on these two men who are running their business by understanding their EI, stress tolerance levels, empathetic listening, and social skills.

While Michael Dell was in college, he found the niche that would eventually become his boom. The PC world was still young and Dell realized that no company had tried selling directly to customers. Bypassing the middleman and the markups, Dell tapped his savings account for $1,000 and started building and selling computers for people he knew at college. His emphasis, however, was not just on good machines, but on strong customer support and cheaper prices (Dell, 2004). Soon, he had accounts outside of school and it was not long before Dell dropped out and focused all his efforts on his business. He dropped out of school when he realized his business needed him more than he required a medical school education; this decision can be construed both as strategic and rational. No smart person who is in medical school would drop out on a whim, he obviously thought it out. After weighing all the different aspects, he came to a conclusion that dropping out of school and selling computers was the right decision. The proof, as they say, is in the pudding.

Ratan Tata was an opportunistic owing to the fact that perhaps the secret lies in his ability to think big and small. While he guides the Tata Group to pick up the luxurious Pierre Hotel in New York, he is also driving the launch of the budget Ginger hotels in India. He has the ability to envisage an automotive business that encompasses diverse businesses such as the iconic Jaguar and Land Rover Marques on one hand, the world's cheapest car the Nano on the other, and hardy, rough-road trucks sandwiched in between. It's no secret that the genesis of the Tata Group's blockbuster moves can be traced to him. Tata's first global venture—the February 2000 purchase of Tetley—had begun 5 years earlier when Tata made a $318 million bid for the tea company. In the end it costs much more; however, it is a wonderful expression of how Tata valued the opportunities available. Under his care, the Tata Company has grown tremendously and has become a global force.

Given below are similarities and instances based on the lives on Ratan Tata and Michael dell researched considering the steps of the ladder.

11.2.1 Step 1: Assertive Communication

Being assertive is a core communication skill. Assertive communication focuses on expressing effectively and standing up for our point of view. There involves a degree of respecting the rights and beliefs of others. Assertive communications can also help boost our self-esteem and earn others' respect.

Michael Dell	Ratan Tata
He is known to be outspoken. He presents facts and brings out the matter as is. He is a great motivator. He has earned the respect of all those he meets. He firmly believes that to be successful one doesn't have to be a genius, a visionary, or even a college graduate. All that is required is a framework and a dream. Michael Dell, the chief executive officer (CEO) of Dell Inc., displays his assertiveness by being conscious of costs the organization may incur. He avoids expenses that may hurt the company's financial position. In 2006, for instance, he sent out a memo to Dell employees informing that the organization will be reducing the bonus amounts given that year (Dell, 2008). He also announced reducing managerial level staff. This memo was the result of the previous year's disappointing earnings reports and eroding market shares. Although his decision may have been disappointing to his employees, Dell took his position as a leader of the organization to get it back to good standings despite its effect on others.	He is a very assertive and has a confident personality. He has respect for others and in return receives a lot of praise. He is known to speak as it is. He is an Indian businessman, philanthropist, investor, and Chairman of Tata Sons. He had a difficult time adjusting in 1991. Earlier he was introverted and not comfortable talking to people. So, he relied on support from other directors to get his innovative business ideas across. In other words, he was aware of a quality he lacks and turns to other resources to help shape his vision. It was in 1983, as a youngster in the company, he suggested that the group expands internationally. In 2000, they acquired a company and created Tata Tea of Tetley. In 2004, Tata ought South Korea's Daewoo Motors. In 2005, Tata Steel acquired the Singapore-based NatSteel. In 2005, Tata Chemicals secured Brunner Mond Group, UK. In 2007, the largest acquisition, Tata Steel took Corus, the Anglo-Dutch giant. It was a landmark deal. In 2008, Tata Motors added the Jaguar and Land Rover Brands to its stable. These are all examples of how Tata began with a vision and took action to bring his vision to life. He believed it was possible and made it happen.

11.2.2 Step 2: Self-Esteem

Self-esteem reflects a person's overall subjective emotional evaluation of one's own worth. It is a judgment of self as well. It is also our attitude toward self.

Michael Dell	Ratan Tata
He is known to have great self-confidence. His parents wanted him to pursue the medical profession and be a leading practitioner. However, his heart lay with the computer business. He was sure that he would be a great business owner that he dropped out of a premier university. Dell agreed to go back on the condition only if summer's sales proved disappointing. In the first month, Dell sold some $180,000 worth of PCs. This is a reflection of his psychology. He has discussions on the significance of having a belief system. Michael mentions that although he values customer feedback, he does not consider the things that would deter the direction in which he wants to take the organization. He works on improving product development and increasing revenue. There were times that other teams were working on innovative projects and those projects either failed or had to be scrapped. It takes a great leader to motivate the teams to work better on their next project, even though the last one may have failed. One important aspect of motivators, therefore, is their ability to create and nurture resiliency in individuals and teams.	He is viewed as the visionary. Though Ratan Tata was judged earlier to have risen because of his last name, the world saw through his excellent vision and leadership as the Empire reached the top in the Indian Economy. A true businessman with a clear strategy, vision, and commitment, Rata Tata stands as an example of true success achieved with what it takes. He has great self-esteem, as well as self-confidence. Before transitioning to what is now Tata Motors, Telco business in the flagship of Tata sons developed its first Indigenous car with a brand name, Indica. It was introduced in the small car market. The production of this car resulted in India losing credibility in the motor manufacturing market due to its low quality problems and returns being less than half of its expected share in the domestic market. This led to predictions that India would be unsuccessful in the motor industry. Despite its unpleasant reputation in the motor market, a sleek silver prototype of a sport utility and saloon crossover vehicle was one of the stars at a car show in Geneva. Its production was set to later take place as well. Although motor production from India had failed at being profitable in the past, Ratan Tata found an advantage in this situation. He dropped out of cramped market like textiles and cement and lead India into the automobile market.

11.2.3 Step 3: Self-Independence

Self-independence is the fact or state of being self-ruled and having the freedom to do as one wishes. Both Michael Dell and Ratan Tata run their company the way they choose to and to great success.

Michael Dell	Ratan Tata
His ideas are his own; he was one of the first to come up with selling computers without the need of a middle man. By doing so, he could sell each machine over the phone directly to customers at a 15% discount to established brands. This technique, which came to be known as "the direct model of selling," would revolutionize the industry and make Dell a multibillionaire in the process. He did this all by his free will and alone at the start, which at that time was very hard for any upcoming business. In 1996, Michael Dell resigned from his position as CEO. Nonetheless, he remained around and worked closely with Kevin Rollins, who took over the role. Kevin Rollins' vision was to expand Dell beyond PCs. However, Michael Dell refused to support the idea. Dell believed the market was developing rapidly, to his fear was the company would not be able to keep up with such competitive market. Instead, he insisted on acquiring storage bags. In this example, Michael dell shows his independence and creates a niche through trying to avoid competition.	He displays his motivation in his multiple accomplishments. One of the ways in which he exemplifies motivation is in the education he acquired prior to establishing himself in his career. He worked his way up into his family company. He received a BS in architecture from Cornell University in 1962. He later went on and did an advanced Management program from Harvard University Business School in 1975. He is an optimistic risk taker. During an interview he stated the following; "I don't believe in taking right decisions, I take decisions and then make them right." This statement reflects on Ratan Tata's ability to overlook challenges and think ahead in terms of trial and error. He prepares for what may come so that the organization moves in a different path with a different strategy to accomplish a goal. He showed foresight and strategic acumen with the mergers and acquisitions, whether Daewoo, Tetley Tea, Corus, or Jaguar and Land Rover. These were across different countries and different industries, and in consolidating the Tata global brand, it became an ambassador for India.

11.2.4 Step 4: Empathetic Listening

Empathetic listening is the ability to understand the emotional makeup of other people and give a patient hearing to the message being communicated. This means one who is empathetic treats others with caution and consideration of their emotional reactions.

Michael Dell	Ratan Tata
One of Mr. Dell's golden rules is listening to the customer. A person who listens to the customer must also fill the customers' expectations, therefore, being a trustworthy person. A person who just tells the customer what he wants to hear but does not back it up with actions leads the customer to quickly become suspicious. Additionally, we find that Michael Dell's product, the Dell name brand, is very trustworthy. It would be an insurmountable task to be extremely successful, like Dell, without being trustworthy.	Although the production of the car mentioned previously failed in the past due to its poor quality, Ratan believed in Indian Engineers to produce quality cars. He led the country to the motor industry. In doing so, created jobs for engineers who were underestimated in terms of productivity and performance. He gave them an opportunity to redevelop a car that happened to be a great success and the organization was able to reclaim its status in the market.

11.2.5 Step 5: Building Social Skills

An individual with social skills is proficient in managing relationships and building networks. Ratan Tata proves to be socially skillful in building relationship and networking through public speaking forums. Michael Dell builds relationship through addressing entrepreneurial summits.

Michael Dell	Ratan Tata
Michael Dell builds and develops relationships through public speaking. During his public speaking sessions, he shares his knowledge, strength, and weaknesses with startup entrepreneurs. Dell believes that startups bring new ideas, talent, and fresh thinking into the company. This means that, in addition to sharing his knowledge, he also walks away from these sessions having learned something he can apply to the development of Dell Inc. Michael Dell is self-regulated. He stands strong on what he believes, and is not easily influenced to make impulsive decisions. "If It Isn't Broke. Fix It Anyway," is the mindset of Dell. This is the key reason that his business is still going strong today. He changed his company from just selling PC, however, to be more on the line how Amazon does business. He knew that his company needed to change to stay in business and did so to still be one of the best known in the United States.	Ratan Tata has a very strategic way of executing his social skills. He invests in companies and holds public speaking conferences where he invites managers from the companies in which he invests. Mr. Tata also speaks at many universities. During these conferences, he shares his business knowledge and strategies to grow and maintain a successful business. Tata establishes and maintains them while being open minded to the challenges related to business. Ratan Tata has high social skills. There are series of news reports and pictures of him being present at the sight during the terrorist attack in Mumbai in 2008. He met all the employees and guests at the Taj Mahal hotel in person and declared spot bonuses. He ensured that all employees would receive a pay check till the hotel was renovated. The Bhavishya Kalyan Yovanna plan is funded for Tata employees and subsidiaries. Employees are eligible at the time of death or disablement due to accident or authority wise.

11.2.6 Step 6: Stress Tolerance

Stress tolerance refers to the wide spectrum of techniques and psychotherapies aimed at controlling a person's levels of stress. The purpose is improvisation of everyday functioning.

Michael Dell	Ratan Tata
His stress tolerance skills are excellent. He doesn't let grapevine communication or poor sales stress him out. He believes no one works harder than an entrepreneur starting a business and entrepreneurs have a passion for what they're doing, and so work doesn't feel like work. It's energizing and fun. It might seem like crazy hours to someone else, there's nothing else you'd rather be doing.	Ratan Tata's stress management is really well. He has a mindset that with every turning point, if good or bad, one can learn from the outcome and improve from it. So many people, whether employees of the company or those who have met Tata, had much to say about his efforts. This is credited to him being a motivator. Tata had asked McKinsey to do a study on the Tata portfolio and McKinsey had suggested that the Tatas should get out of steel. However, Tata had disagreed and continued to be in steel. This boosted the morale of the employees. Then he set up an impossible target and worked with them to achieve it. He played a strong role in encouraging motivation. Though, he has not been the only one.

11.2.7 Step 7: Impulse Control

Impulse control is an ability to control one's primary negative reaction to a situation. Many situations indicate that an action after a thought process is more feasible.

Michael Dell	Ratan Tata
In case of Michael Dell, throughout his years working at Dell, there were many times that other teams were working on innovative projects and those projects either failed or had to be scrapped. It takes a great leader to motivate the teams to work better on their next product. In April 1993, John Medica, who has led the development of Apple's Power Book, was put in charge of the Notebook division at DELL. By the time he took over, one product has already been canceled and the development of other products was taking longer than expected. After a realistic assessment of the situation, it was decided by Michael Dell that only one of the products under development—the Latitude XP—would be competitive in the market. The Company canceled several products that were in the developmental stage and focused the entire team on the Latitude XP. This cancellation demotivated the engineers who had spent a lot of time and energy developing the products that had been canceled. To motivate them, Michael Dell reinforced DELL's strategy to the notebook group and encouraged the team to pull together to make the Latitude XP a success. He did this by his great skills as a motivator and controlling impulses.	As a strategic and rational analyzer, he believes that a company does not become global by simply participating in geographical markets around the world. The objective of globalization is to become globally competitive, leverage global opportunities, and have required global capabilities. In 1991, he thought they were in too many businesses and spread too thin. Tata instituted a restructuring of management in order to allow the company to work more fluid. He structured the group profile into businesses and not individual firms. By the end of the 1990s, a new group structure was in place and a clear new mindset had evolved under his leadership. To summarize, he succeeded in changing the company again for future success. Tata's leadership style is to suggest ideas and offer encouragement and motivation, not to lead the charge. Foreseeing the expansion of capital markets, which meant easier access to money for new projects, Tata helped draw up a group strategic plan in 1983. Among other things, it emphasized venturing into high-tech businesses, focusing on select markets and products; judicious mergers and acquisitions; and leveraging group synergies.

11.2.8 Step 8: Flexibility Skills

Flexibility skills refer to the ability of being flexible in a situation and adaptation to change.

Michael Dell	Ratan Tata
Another example for an opportunistic mindset and flexibility skills is when Michael Dell was 16, he got a summer job selling newspaper subscriptions to *The Houston Post*. The newspaper gave its sales people a list of new phone numbers to be called. Dell thought that this was an inefficient method for acquiring new business. On the basis of feedback that he received from potential customers, he soon noticed a pattern. He found that there were two kinds of people who bought subscriptions to *The Houston Post*: people who has just moved into new houses or people who register their names and addresses in the country courthouse for getting a marriage license. Soon, Michael, along with some of his high school friends, collected the names and addresses of such couples and started targeting them through personalized letters offering them a subscription to the newspaper. Even after he went back to school, Michael continued with this work. Soon thousands of subscriptions poured in and he earned $18,000. This exceeded what his teacher earned in a year.	Tata continued with many mergers and acquisitions including Daewoo of Korea and Jaguar Land Rover. His mostly innovative foot was the creation and production of the model, Tata Nano. It was originally priced at $1,600 to be the least expensive car in the world and is currently $3,000. Tata did all this against odds, competition, and difficulties. He came out superbly ahead and very successful. Tata has surpassed expectations, lived by dreams not relative norms, pushes when possible, emphasizes teamwork, uses every resource available, and also enjoyed his work.

11.2.9 Step 9: Problem-Solving Ability

There could be three scenarios for problem-solving ability:

1. Solving a problem for a client
2. Supporting those who are solving problems
3. Discovering new problems to solve them

Those problems faced can be large or small, simple or complex. A fundamental part of every individual's role is finding ways to solve them.

Michael Dell	Ratan Tata
Dell isn't a quitter and efficiently resolves the complex problems. His company was doing well. By mid-1993, Dell Computer Corp. seemed to be spiraling out of control. Stock prices had plummeted from $49 in January of 1993 to a mere $16 by July. Dell's chief financial officer (CFO) resigned. Dell took that hit and made a huge turn around by hiring Mort Topfer, a seasoned executive from Motorola, to handle day-to-day operations. Next, he tapped the talents of Kevin Rollins, an organizational expert from Bain and Co., to run the American operations.	Tata Indica failed in its first years as a car company. In 1998, Tata and his top advisors went to Ford for a buy. The CEO of Ford told Ratan Tata that it was a favor he was doing by buying out Tata motors. Tata went back to India and a few years, now owns Jaguar and Land Rover.

11.2.10 Step 10: Maintenance of Optimistic Behavior

Optimism is a temporary state of mind or temper having a cheerful mood.

Michael Dell	Ratan Tata
He is excited and passionate about his work and seems to be in a great mood. He's looked at as a great leader and fast problem-solver.	Ratan Tata was known to be very optimistic. He is known to push people, always looks for a way to motivate those around him and stress free.

11.2.11 Step 11: Anger Management (Maximize Happiness)

Michael Dell	Ratan Tata
Dell had met with Howard Shultz of Starbucks during the period of turbulence. He implemented strategies to increase the turnover and maintained positivity. His anger management skills are exemplary.	The 6.7 billon Corus deal is the proof of the kind of goodwill the Tata Group has created for itself. The Corus management was happy to support the deal with Tata Group, with reassurance that there would be no layoffs and no problems with pensions

11.3 PHILIP KNIGHT

Phil Knight—the former CEO of Nike—owns three restaurants, fitness center, beauty salon, laundry service, jogging facilities, day care center, and other amenities. Philip Knight and Bill Bowerman were two visionaries who wanted to reinvent athletic footwear at low cost with high quality. Better, faster, and lighter product was their vision. Knight's partner and cofounder of Nike, Bill Bowerman, spent a long career as the coach of the American Olympic track and field team. Knight took full advantage of the opportunity of access to Olympic athletes by supplying Nike shoes through Bowerman. This initial step was the foundation for the Nike megabrand (Smithson, 2016).

It has not always been easy for Nike. There have been instances where even though the company won lawsuits, changes that resulted made Nike a more trustworthy character on the world stage. Among accusations that Knight had to respond to were lying to consumers about the conditions in Asian factories. Human rights groups complained that Indonesian workers were getting paid $2.46 per day, which was well below the minimum wage of $4. Eventually, Nike raised its workers' wages. The firm was also accused of child labor, overtime labor, corporal punishment, and sexual harassment. As we can see from these accusations, Knight, at least for a time, suffered from a reputation for being untrustworthy.

Knight, however, is a strategic, rational thinker who could recognize opportunity in nonconventional ways. This out-of-the-box thinking was visible in his marketing strategy, which was not based simply on advertising through conventional media, like television, newspaper, billboards, and flyers, but also included advertising directly through the athletes who wore his shoes (Oregonian/Oregon Live, 2016). For him, getting athletes to endorse his shoes was the best way to advertise. In order to leverage his advertising budget, Knight athletes wore Nike shoes. Many of the athletes who have helped to make Nike the brand it is today include Michael Jordan, LeBron James, Tiger Woods, and Kobe Bryant (Smithson, 2016).

Knight is a good motivator of himself and others. Sports motivated him to design a shoe brand for top athletes. In the process, Knight created jobs for impoverished people in far off lands, as well as jobs for individuals in retail worldwide. For a short time, between 1986 and 1987, the Nike brand was outpaced by its competitor Reebok. Knight responded with more vision and innovation and regained the top spot in athletic ware by developing the "Nike Air."

Emotional intelligence has a direct correlation with success. Individuals are able to actively communicate with others in their workplace tend to be more generally accepted and admired within their company. This section is on EI of Phil Knight.

Many leaders have unique strategies that allow them to differentiate their organization from others and increase the productivity of their employees and peers. As a leader, Phil Knight firmly believed in letting his employees do things in their own way. He didn't like to forcefully guide people into doing things the way that he wanted because he felt that this technique would only stifle the workers and demotivate them from being innovative in their means of accomplishing tasks. He believes that environment plays a big part on the work ethic of his employees and has stated that he likes to create a culture at Nike that can positively affect performance. He wants to make sure that everyone is on the same page at Nike and instead of doing so through directly interacting with every employee. He sets the precedent so that employees know what they are expected of and how to act even without his direct guidance. He doesn't micromanage his employees.

Phil Knight has demonstrated that he is a very self-independent individual in many different ways. One of the things that really make him stand out as a self-aware person is the fact that he often does interviews where he openly speaks on personal topics. Knight even wrote a book about his life where he discusses everything from his early insecurities as an entrepreneur. He discussed how he doubted in himself early on and even though he had a vision, he didn't have full confidence that he was going to be able to reach his goal. He also openly discusses personal topics of the death of his 34-year-old son, Matthew Knight, which completely threw Phil Knight off course and dramatically affected his outlook on himself and on life.

Power hasn't affected Phil Knight. Gathering information from his speeches and interviews, it is clear that Phil Knight publicly conducts himself in a very balanced fashion. He is very fluent at speaking and demonstrates a very enthusiastic demeanor that can be hypothesized as being the driving force behind his lasting success. Besides conducting himself in a professional and wise manner, in every interview he has done, he is noted for giving words of inspiration to others who hope to be successful as well. Someone with that kind of generous and polite can definitely be admired for his self-regulation.

Phil Knight is an incredible business savvy entrepreneur Stevenson (2016). He is an optimist who has made numerous statements about the challenges he's faced as an entrepreneur and the motivation for success that has gotten him through those challenges. In one of the interviews, he was questioned about his motivation to keep progressing despite his early challenges with sales. Knight was assertive in stating that earlier on his career he really didn't enjoy sales. The turning point in his thought process happened in Hawaii. That trip made him realize the numerous occasions that his love for the business is what keeps him going regardless of the obstacles he faces. He decided to go on that trip alone and is now sitting in the position of one of the most influential and financially magnanimous people in the world.

It is inferred that Phil Knight is very well-rounded socially. In 2004, when Knight's son, died from a scuba diving incident in El Salvador, he received condolence letters from every employee in Nike and everyone with whom he met through his endeavors. Nike brings in over 60,000 different employees worldwide. The commendable aspect is that there is such a huge population within the company and he got letters from every employee. This proves that Knight is a very socially adept person. It was noted that Knight is a very likeable person, who is well appreciated by everyone in Nike. In addition, something that stands out about Phil Knight's social skills and overall likability is his generosity. Phil Knight has donated $400 million to Stanford University, which will be used to pay for over 100 full ride scholarships for hardworking students who qualify. Phil Knight does well at internalizing and handling his stress. On the death of his son, he could not function for a while. It took him 9 months to recover. Despite losing a loved one, he was still able to run the world's leading sports apparel company (Rudulph, 2016).

Phil Knight understands that he is a man of importance and yet he doesn't allow that to influence the way that he thinks of himself. He is self-aware and has proved himself to be humble and level-headed when reflecting on himself. Phil Knight has a very interesting relationship with his employees. Along with his gentle, humble, and polite aura, Phil Knight operates on a merit and punishment system. He believes that employees working hard within his company should be rewarded and complimented, whereas those who do not should be penalized. The reason behind this is because he likes to create competition within his company. He feels that to be the most efficient way to optimize the production within his company is to influence others and to motivate themselves with their peers. This culture is reminiscent that of a sports team that is built on not only competition with other teams but also competition within the team.

Proof of Phil Knight's ability to be adaptable can be found in his business strategies. In the past, when Nike and Adidas were major competitors, Phil Knight decided to use celebrity marketing for his apparel. At the time, this marketing strategy was not frequently used. Major stars, like Kobe Bryant, were given sponsorships for wearing Nike items. Phil Knight seeing the opening in the void left by Adidas' stagnation, decided to pioneer celebrity marketing and take his company past the heights that Adidas was able to reach. Phil Knight has shown that he has the ability to adapt when necessary.

Phil Knight has always been an optimistic. When it comes to business, he was always positive. He has enjoyed the process of building Nike from the ground up and turning it into the global titan it is now. The air of positivity and hope is what kept him and his team going. His belief of success is what led to him achieving it.

Nike's mission statement perfectly shows what Phil Knight set out to do. He wanted to maintain the quality of the products for the athletes. He also stressed the importance of having a relationship with their customers. It's a philosophy that started with Phil Knight and continues in the company to this day.

11.4 SIR RICHARD BRANSON

Sir Richard Branson is the founder and chairman of the Virgin Group. The Virgin Group controls more than 200 companies in 30 countries. His vision is exemplified by his belief in the importance of commercial spaceflight. He is opportunistic because he hires who will fit in with Virgin's entrepreneurial culture. He is foresighted and he is trustworthy; he understands the risks involved in shaping the world through business. One example of his trustworthiness is his offer to refund the money to anyone who has purchased future spaceport passage because of the October 2014 crash of Virgin Galactic, a space-bound test flight. He is a serial innovator with a sharp eye for the latest technology and a knack for upsetting the status quo. Branson's business interests span casinos to banking, gyms to phone networks, and retirement care to high-speed trains and book publishing. Some ventures flopped and were quietly forgotten, including Virgin bridal stores and Virgin Cola (Chang, 2014).

Richard Branson is a self-aware, assertive, and self-independent individual. He is an extremely bold individual and not afraid to express himself. He is a risk taker; he finds himself trying new things and challenging himself to do things better. He is an adventurer going to new places. These things affect him as an individual and President of Virgin Group.

Richard Branson pursues his goals with energy and persistence. Motivation for him isn't money or the things a big business provides for the owner of the company. Instead, he solely based his motivation on being able to provide great service and great products to customers. He doesn't let himself get caught up in managing things. He believes in giving time to appreciate employees. He also receives input on what customers think and feel about the company as that he believes is vital for organizational success.

Richard Branson believes that social skills is proficiency in managing relationships and building networks and is an ability to find common ground and build rapport. He has two views on social skills and being social. Social skills are platforms to enhance our live conversations and not replace them entirely. He believes that there's no substitute for making a new contact than in person. The implied meaning is that as a society, one shouldn't allow technology and forms of communication to take away our socials skills of meeting with individuals. For Branson, being face to face is very important. The second view is about the business aspects of social skills. Connecting with organizations to promote a product/commodity is essential. He believes in writing emails, and conducting presentations is a key to social skills in terms of the business connections.

Branson has many suggestions for keeping high self-esteem, independence, and assertiveness. Believing in our ideas and being the best is a philosophy followed by Branson. He has numerous amounts of businesses within Virgin Group and keeps himself updated with technology and fitness measures. This demonstrates flexibility and problem-solving ability.

He has three aspects to keep in mind when considering stress tolerance. He finds a routine that works, minimizes guilt feelings, and enjoys work. In case an individual may not be able to finish work, there should be a feeling comfort with the amount achieved. He should be able to take a moment or moments away from the task without having guilt. Optimism and happiness on the job make sure that negative stress is away. His entrepreneurial achievements are unparalleled. Branson started his business career at the early age. He was 16 years old when he established magazine *Student,* which become an instant success. He was knighted in 1999 for his "services to entrepreneurship." Virgin Group is classed as a private limited company that has exceeded expectations from its original business venture and has its hands in music to transportation, travel, financial services, media, drinks, books gaming, and fitness. Virgin has created more than 400 branded companies worldwide, employing approximately 50,000 people in 30 countries.

The Virgin Group is structured more complex and could be assumed as operating as a single business entity. In reality, however, each of the Virgin brand companies operates as a separate business entity. Branson still retains control of the 400 companies. Occasionally, he enters into licensing agreements for the brand name. Virgin Group makes a significant amount. It's not from cash flows from its investments, particularly since a number of large Virgin businesses do not turn a profit. The amount is generated from the fees it charges companies for lending them the Virgin name. The Branson Family's wealth, therefore, is dependent on the value of the Virgin brand, which is intimately linked to Sir Richard Branson himself. The point of connection of the companies to use the Virgin trademark is Branson's role as chairman and shareholder and his management role as the face of Virgin in publicity, public, and government relations. In the case of the Virgin Group, this means that the style of Sir Richard's leadership cannot be separated from the activities of Virgin Group and the effective teambuilding within the organization. The major contributor to the Virgin Group's success is the inventive leadership style of Richard Branson. In examining his style, his ability to influence and skills to build shared ideas among his employees are renowned. One of the ways of Branson is through his sense of equality and fairness in how he treats people and by promoting flat, nonhierarchical structure to run his business.

Richard Branson is renowned for his vibrant yet competitive leadership style. Many of Richard Branson's companies are good examples of startups in the face of entrenched competition. Although the experts advised him not to take a risk of starting a new venture, Branson found golden opportunities in markets in which customers have been ripped or underserved where confusion reigns and the competition is complacent. Branson's strategies are based on individual informality and information. Branson broadens and elevates the interest of their purposes and when they stir their people to look beyond self-interest for good on the group. Branson evidently demonstrates flexibility and success in adjusting to change in organizational culture to bring in new businesses and move into a new sector while bringing his people with him.

He is self-aware and believes in trusting individual to learn from mistakes. It's the leadership skill of being able to think differently that sets them apart. He has positive company culture and has developed the level to be trusted with managers. Organizational culture plays an important role within any company. It is a mixture of customs and practices and the beliefs and attitudes that these are based on that make up the way of working and the approach of an organization. The culture of an organization is also often likened to the personality of an individual entrepreneur. Virgin group describes culture and brand as making a difference and edge. Virgin stands for value for money, quality, innovation, fun, and a sense of competitive challenges. These traits are often used to describe Richard Branson. The company aims to deliver a quality service by empowering its employees, facilitating and monitoring customer feedback to continually improve the customer's experience and through innovation. It is evident that Virgin's values and approach to business appeal to the customers and create an adventurous spirit in the organization that has contributed to its success, which has enabled it to branch out into other sectors. The Virgin Group has a distinct culture, which is characterized by its founder's individual values, personality, and personal style. The company reflects his ambitions that are given below:

a. Drive for success
b. Informal anticorporate approach

Virgin has been able to use organizational culture to foster loyalty, commitment, and hard work within its employees by offering freedom and empowerment and by giving them a sense of being part of something cool and different while providing social activity. Virgin holds onto the value, symbols, and rituals that have guided them for several years and supports existing practices. Organizational culture is developed through effective leadership and empowered strong development programs. He does not emphasize on qualifications for hiring individuals in lead positions. His philosophy ensures that individuals who want to work at senior level have the soft skills and strong leadership skills required to unite and direct staff. His interest in life comes from setting challenges. Most of the time, these challenges are large and apparently unachievable. He makes all effort to try to rise about the challenges of life. He believes in living to the full and attempts to taking on newer challenges. He believes in business leaders who need to be passionate while making a strategic decision, building teams, and motivating employees to give their all. He believes in inspiring individuals and develops great ideas. He claims that finding gaps in the market and creating products that make a real difference to an individual's life can only be accomplished with passion for work. Branson avoids making decision in isolation because he believes that each decision has some degree of impact on the ability to adopt other future opportunities.

When a decision doesn't work out as planned, Branson credits his background in competitive sports, especially tennis, for the discipline, teamwork, and leadership skills it can teach. He believes that playing tennis is like business as it moves quickly. If an individual dwells on the past for even a few minutes, opportunities will have passed and the moment will be lost. Individuals have to get into the right frame of mind in order to perform the best and need to be able to put setbacks behind instantly. He firmly states that it's critical to move on from the last mistake and focus on the next challenge.

Richard Branson found an entrepreneur way to provoke positive change in the world. His leadership style is his persistent determination to accomplish his goals, despite a few obstacles in his way. Regardless of some negative circumstances, mainly external, he has been persistent in shaping of the vision for his company. His unique ability to infuse values to those he hired is the reason for Virgin's continuous success and growth. He has been known to be empathic and self-aware, which has allowed him to instinctively understand how customers and employees feel and estimate the organization's emotional state. He believes it is important that business leaders have an eye for talent and ability to get the most out of their employees. He believes that no organization can be successful because of its founder. It takes a leader to lead to build a successful organization. He claimed that employers need to hire people who have the necessary skills, experience, and drive. They should be a good fit culturally for the business. He looks for managers who are eager to have fun at work and will pass that on enthusiasm on to other employees in the company, supporting a positive work environment.

Successful business leader masters the art of delegation in helping to reduce employees' workload and given opportunities to ambitious employees. Branson is a famous advocate for the autonomy style of leadership. He gives employees the freedom and responsibility of big projects and puts his trust in their decisions. In putting trust in employees' work force and allowing them to make important decisions, employees will feel more responsibility for the brand and recognize that the work they do is important and each employee feel more dedicated to the brand itself. He believes in the art of delegation in finding the best possible people and giving them the freedom and encouragement to flourish.

His philosophy is to give individuals a space to thrive. Once an individual is associated with a group, he or she establishes his or her self-esteem and self-belief to some extent on his or her belonging to that group. Group failures and successes would be faced as personal to the individual. He believes that followers are inspired by the leader to identify with the group aims and ethical approach. This is achieved by connecting the follower's self-belief to the mission statement of the organization and goals of the group.

According to Branson, it is vital that leaders are able and willing to listen and learn. This is because nobody—no matter how senior they are—has monopoly on a good idea or good advance. He claimed that learning and leadership skills go hand in hand. Branson considers that the best leaders are great listeners. It's important to listen carefully to everyone involved in a business venture, from individual team members to investors who allow the whole project to get off the group. Listening allows entrepreneurs to make the most of the skills of those around them. It also encourages good relationships and helps everyone to be together in brand development. Branson believes in speaking less and contributing more. He is a good listener and notes while listening because it helps him to gather his thoughts and ask questions (Jasper, 2014).

Branson's success was not always predictable. He believes that the ability to adapt and determining priorities is incredibly important. In case of facing challenges, he believes in having a contingency plan, assess its importance, and reorganizes priorities accordingly. An example is in 1992, Virgin Music was struggling financially. The company was sold and Branson was disturbed immensely by the loss; however, it remained determined to stay in the music business in order to start again.

Branson supports many humanitarian causes. For instance, in May 2008, he traveled to the Messer-Mare to open a new school. Branson maintains a daily blog to discuss and sustains information on travel, music, and humor. He has more than 11.5 million followers across five social networks. The sprawling business empire that makes up Richard Branson's Virgin investment group consists of about 400 operations, a tangled web of enterprises owned via a complicated series of offshore trusts and overseas holding companies. Branson's finances are difficult to penetrate because of their complexity and opaqueness with few of his large companies wholly owned by Branson himself. His big-branded firms such as Virgin Atlantic, Virgin Money, Virgin Media, and Virgin Trains have other major shareholders. In some cases, he simply licenses the brand to a company that has purchased a subsidiary from him, and these include Virgin Mobil USA, Virgin Mobil Australia, Virgin Radio, and Virgin Music. In return as the license holder of the Virgin Brand, he receives annual fees that can amount to hundreds of millions over time. By forging partnerships with cash-rich allies, Branson has established new businesses without depleting the group's reserves and spending little to establish new ventures in sectors such as Mobil Telecoms. However, initiatives come straight from Branson, who prides himself on his ability to spot a gap in the market. He is not a number or a details man and has the everyday running of his firms to a group of executives.

He went into business in 1966 after leaving school at 16, publishing the *Student* magazine, from the basement of a rented flat. He rapidly expanded into the world of pop music starting a mail-order business that sent records through the post to tens of thousands of teenagers and set up Virgin Records, a chain of shops with the first one opening off London's Oxford Street in 1971. Two years later, he launched Virgin Record label after clinching the rights to Mike Oldfield's Tubular Bells and attracted a growing roster of artists. In 1984, Branson diversified, leasing his first 747 to fly to New York from Gatwick, to upstart airline Virgin Atlantic; this was soon competing with British Airways at Heathrow (Mazumdar, 1999).

Amid rumors that Branson needed cash to underpin part of his business at the turn of the millennium, he announced in 2000 that Virgin Group had sold 49% of the airlines holding company to Singapore Airlines for more than €600 million. In 2005–2006, Branson was busy assembling the Virgin Media Group that today competes with BT and Sky for entertainment, phone, and broadband customers. The formation of Virgin Media is a classic Branson business venture: he owns a tiny stake in the business that is listed on the NASDAQ exchange in New York, but derives tens of millions by licensing the brand name. He is not on the Virgin Media board, and Chief Executive Neil Berkett runs the company. Branson has also his share of flops. There was a series of them in the mid-90s, including Virgin Brides, Virgin Cola, and Virgin Cosmetics. He has never been a friend of the City. The relationship soured in the late 1980s when he listed his Virgin Music business on the stock market. An outraged Branson took the company private, buying out institutional shareholders who he claimed did not understand the business. In 1992, he made a mint when he sold the company for €560 million. Another transport group launched Virgin Train in 1997 and 49% owned. Virgin Active, which runs 122 UK health clubs, is 49% owned by private equity firm CDC, following a deal last year. Branson doesn't sit on the board of any of the companies within the Virgin Group, underpinning this claim to be entrepreneur rather than a businessman in the conventional sense.

Richard Branson's charismatic way of leadership is one that comes from how he influences those in his organization. He shows clear skills in his ability to read the emotions of others and assess the mood of his own culture. He has tremendous skills in how he can adapt his style and approach to the particular situation or contort. His drive and determination to succeed has been a key element of his success. His success in becoming and remaining an effective leader of Virgin is largely due to his willingness and ability to empower individuals within the organization. Branson has shown sensitivity to the needs of others such as need of recognition, growth, and achievement. Through his attention to employees and encouragement of ideas and initiatives, Branson has the support of his subordinates. His authority of Virgin is extended by his flamboyant charismatic personality and attention-grabbing behavior, both of which increased his visibility and appeal to staff and the public. Although unique to Branson himself, this style of leadership is one that works very well within the Virgin group.

11.5 WILLIAM CLAY FORD JR.

William Clay Ford Jr. is the Executive Chairman of Ford Motor Company, serving as CEO of the company from October 2006.

Ford is categorized as foresighted and trustworthy. In 2006, before the economic meltdown took place, Ford went to the banks and borrowed as much money as he possibly could, which was in excess of $20 billion. In subsequent years, the credit market basically froze shut. The timing for borrowing was excellent. During the 2009 economic meltdown, two U.S. automakers, General Motors and Chrysler, had to take a Federal government bailout to survive. Ford became the only U.S. automaker that did not take the federal bailout. Ford wanted to rescue the family business; so, in 2006, he hired Alan Mulally, formerly a Boeing Executive, as President and CEO of Ford Motors to restructure the company. Under Ford and Mulally's leadership, Ford improved quality, lowered costs, and delivered new products.

During the company's so-called dark period from 2006 to 2009, one of the things Ford accomplished was to take all product developments around the world and combine them into one global product development effort, which saved time and money. He was a strategic and rational analyzer, which is depicted in his hiring Jim Farley as group vice president, who previously worked for Toyota and had rich experience in global marketing. Ford thought a combination of completely revamping product development and having a top global marketing person in charge could propel Ford Motors forward. Based on research, Ford quickly found a weakness of Ford Motors being its poor fuel economy and was determined to turn that weakness into strength. As an environmentalist, Ford has been a strong advocate for sustainability in Ford Motors. He foresaw that energy efficiency and environmental friendliness would be crucial to the auto industry in this decade. He believes that one day cars and the environment actually come into harmony (Bonini and Kaas, 2010). He continues to endorse that transportation itself is transforming with the emergence of alternative-fuel and electric vehicles, connected and self-driving vehicles, and ride-sharing services (Burke, 2014). Ford's company has been involved in such efforts as well. He has been a great motivator. His going green strategy was debatable when he joined Ford Motors. However, he did not give in, and after much persuasion and motivation, successfully changed the culture in his own company. He had also visualized being the fuel economy and technology leader in the auto industry.

11.6 HERBERT KOHLER

In 1940, Herbert Kohler Sr., John Michael Kohler's grandson, took over the leadership of the Kohler company. As a CEO, Kohler is constantly analyzing his company and seeking new strategies in how he could remain a leader in the industry. During World War II, Kohler changed his production channels from manufacturing enameled plumbing fixtures to producing torpedo tubes for submarines being built in Manitowoc, Wisconsin. In 1948, the company diversified again. It began to manufacture stand-alone industrial engines. This led the company to launch its successful Global Power Group. In addition in 1975, Kohler constructed a strategic corporate model that created a fundamental baseline of where the company should be currently and where he expected it to grow too. Each time that Kohler created a change in his production has allowed him to remain successful and be an outstanding leader in his industry (Colby, 2004).

Adding more originality and color to kitchen and bath products became the running advertisements in the 60s. Those years were known as the bold look of Kohler. This symbolized the culture at Kohler that it was the leader in design and technology in bath and kitchen fixtures. With technological advancements, it designed luxurious whirlpools. This transformed bathrooms into retreats of relaxation. This created worldwide recognition and gave Kohler the status of being innovative and opportunistic in the style and décor American washrooms (Colby, 2004).

Over the years, Kohler was constantly looking for new opportunities to expand his business. In 1984, Kohler purchased the Sterling Faucet Company. This brought synergistic marketing facilities and direct access to growing rental markets. By expanding his company and increasing his presence in bedroom and bath furniture, he has given himself the opportunity to expand his company globally (Colby, 2004).

One of Kohler's main successes is that he has been a visionary leader. He has not limited himself to specific products. Instead, he leads his company in the direction of new markets and opportunities. This is essentially his vision. He adapts and changes his company in order to remain competitive in the industry. Throughout his stewardship of the company, Kohler has been consistently identified as a company that has provided and maintained a single level of quality regardless of price. It has been recognized as a company whose consumers can trust with providing a high standard product that is continuously being improved. Kohler's motto is to focus on the consumer because they will be the ones using his products. This has singled Kohler out from the rest of his competitors in the industry (Moore, 2004).

11.7 FREDERICK W. SMITH

Frederick Smith is the founder of Federal Express (FedEx) and remains its corporate head today. Smith identified the need for reliable overnight delivery in the early years of information automation. Through the years, Frederick Smith has proven himself very trustworthy. With the knowledge that he gained from his various paths through life, he has not given up. Even when the odds were against him in the early years and especially the start-up of FedEx, Smith always defied the odds. His first 26 months in business racked up over $29 million in losses and his investors were disappointed. Smith did not give up and let his investors' hope and money go down the drain. Rather, he reformed and refocused his efforts and propelled the company forward and eventually re-earned his investors' respect. He never recognized defeat.

Another way that Smith has shown to be trustworthy is how he has remained true to the stories and comrades he served with in the military. He runs FedEx with a huge sense of respect for and from others. Smith believes the key ingredient in the success of his company has been the corporate philosophy that emphasizes treating workers fairly. In FedEx, managers are trained to foster respect for all employees, and the performance of manager and employee is monitored.

Smith was told that his new model for overnight shipping would not work; but in the time-honored style of innovation and visioning, he listened to his own council and was not deterred. In the end, he single handedly changed the way the world does business. Today, FedEx is present in more than 220 countries and territories, operates 634 aircraft and over 90,000 vehicles, and employs more than 300,000 team members worldwide. More than 10 million shipments are delivered daily by FedEx. Smith's motivation was quite simple: he believed that with his knowledge, he could change the way that people were doing business. He believed he could change the economy and the world in a positive way, and he did.

As a FedEx employee, social skills are extremely important. These skills will help a FedEx employee with the tasks he or she will face, which include being diverse, having an open mind to other insights or other ways of life, and finding a common ground that means seeking out a common thing that will help to connect employee and customer. FedEx workers also have to focus on practicing "the golden rule" that simply means treating others as you'd like to be treated. With that also comes showing empathy and sensitivity that means trying to understand a situation better and showing consideration, and lastly being a good listener, which is most important because not only is it beneficial in sales but also to be an empathic, sensitive person; you have to listen. Suppose if you were on the phone with someone who was in charge of your package but wasn't the best listener and he or she ends up shipping it off somewhere else; it will be upsetting and frustrating not only for the customer but also for the employees' representation of the company.

In regard to providing these services, the techniques they use on a daily basis for emotional intelligence include knowing yourself which is to increase self-awareness of emotions and reactions, choosing yourself which is to shift from unconscious reaction to intentional response, and eventually giving yourself which aligns the moment-to-moment decisions with a larger sense of purpose.

Just like any other business FedEx is always facing challenges. Challenges are the need for something that needs great mental or physical effort in order to be done successfully, or the situation of facing this kind of effort. The world's leading delivery services giant is facing many challenges in an uncertain global economy. With slowdown of world trade, economic problems in Europe and Asia, and the low economics growth in the United States, FedEx's bottom line continued to be threatened, according to Richard Smith, managing director of the FedEx Express. Its major challenge now is to deal with other deliver companies.

11.8 ANAND MAHINDRA

Anand Mahindra has been described as an insightful person. He understood India's economy and visualized its improvement. He studied the Indian automotive revolution from its conception and then guided his own company to its current position as a world leader in agricultural equipment sales. It all began when he changed the affordability of the sports utility vehicle (SUV) to suit his Indian customer needs, which for him meant changing the economy with the Scorpio SUV.

Without a clear vision, Mahindra's accomplishments would have been impossible. He understood the value of striking while the iron was hot. Where others in his industry failed, he was successful because of his tenacity and self-belief to keep going. He saw the potential and nursed a struggling economy to become the world power it is. His vision was only sharpened by lessons of failure from the past. His vision for India is a much brighter one than the many people could imagine. Thus, Mahindra and the Mahindra Group has become a leading company for tractor farming equipment in the world.

He recognized new opportunities that related to an emerging open market and he capitalized to lead his company into other fields including aerospace and hospitality. He realized that his company lacked needed technology and financial resources; so Mahindra partnered with Ford Motors in India and gained a strategic advantage for spreading into new markets.

Anand Mahindra is a motivator in every respect. He took a downed Indian economy and led by example with trust and smart business decisions. After a failed partnership for India, Mahindra learned from his experience and realized he needed to develop products that could hold their own in competitive marketplaces. So, with determination in hand, he sculpted a long future of successful innovations by starting with just one successful venture—the Scorpio small SUV specifically designed for the Indian market.

He is one of the world's fifty greatest leaders by *Fortune* magazine and featured in the magazine's 2011 listing of Asia's twenty-five most powerful business people. Anand has also been noted as the "Entrepreneur of the Year" for 2013. However, he doesn't want to be a role model and his parents told him don't see any one, any single person as a role model.

Anand Mahindra believes that people have to know the value followed by the individual. He emphasizes the importance of maintaining a congruence between who one actually is and what is being done. He thinks business schools and leadership institutes will miss the mark if they try to remake individuals into someone different from who they actually were when they entered. He believes it's not worthwhile trying to emulate someone else, no matter how brilliant. He said that the only way that he could lead effectively is by seeing himself as a conductor of a very larger and talented orchestra.

His father has been a guiding force and never forced him to do anything specific. He gave his son space to do things as per his interest and choice. His job as a leader is to inspire challenges and encourage people to see and follow dreams.

11.9 NARAYANA MURTHY

Narayana Murthy is the cofounder of Infosys, a business consulting and technological/outsourcing corporation. Infosys has been a great company and coming on top of its competitors for good reason. He worked in different prestigious companies around the world but decided to return to India to start his own company—longtime leader of the software-development company, Infosys Technologies. He became one of India's, and the world's, most highly esteemed managers. Though a wealthy man and a prime mover in India's booming software-outsourcing industry, he continued to live modestly and practice "compassionate capitalism," a philosophy that used free-market systems to create a better life for society as a whole. Murthy also believed in contributing to his country as a whole.

He has the capacity to be aware of, control, and express one's emotions, and to handle interpersonal relationships judiciously and empathetically. Narayana is a strong supporter of India's anticorruption movement and led a crusade for better corporate governance. More than his management and strategic implementations, it was the values that he stood for that helped him and his company reach where they are today. Murthy always had a clear vision who has taken a small enterprise to make it a strong hold on the international market.

He was born into middle-class family with limited resources but that did not stop him from pursuing his goals. His father couldn't afford tuition and housing fees for him to attend the prestigious Indian Institute of Technology, and so he joined a local engineering college. He started a company named Softronics. When that company failed after about a year and a half, he joined an organization named Patni Computer Systems. After working for a while, Murthy founded Infosys in 1981 with six other software professionals.

He was the first CEO in India to give equity to his professionals. His company was the first in India to introduce stock options starting from janitors to the senior vice president. It was ensured that everybody was given stocks in the company. Also, the company allowed for communication from within the company from highest ranking employee to lowest. Mail was sent to senior people and they responded. The Infosys Foundation has addressed the basic needs of poor individuals by building hospitals and donating equipment to hospitals. They have also built 35,000 libraries in rural India, created scholarship for 5,000 children, rehabilitated sex workers, and contributed to cancer research (Mazumdar, 1999).

Murthy has the ability to communicate, persuade, and interact with other members of the society, without undue conflict or disharmony. He has passion, will to persevere, gives priority to the long-term interests, has high levels of optimism, aims for higher aspirations, and is a team player. India would have never been the way it is without one man—Narayana Murthy. He espouses that one of the leader's core jobs is to raise the confidence of the followers. He believes that tough time and challenges are essential parts of the life and they will come out better at the end of it. According to him, a leader has to sustain followers' hopes and their energy levels to handle the difficult days. His leadership skills made a lot of difference in bringing growth to his company and also bringing the new IT wave into India. He is aptly addressed as the father of the Indian IT sector because of his immense individual contributions in pioneering outsourcing to India in the IT sector. This has helped the Indian economy immensely and gained him respect and laurels from both Indian citizens as well as worldwide audience.

He was willing to take risks. He started Infosys with a small sum of money, he borrowed from his wife, and it went on to become a huge successful company. Infosys has a de-risking strategy where decision-making is inclusive and made by several people. Every decision has support in order to solve the problems encountered. He believes in a life of simplicity. Even though he has massive personal wealth, his lifestyle remains modest. He lives in a simple two-bedroom flat in Mumbai.

He has created a company that promotes transparency and community. According to an article by CNBC Author Benjamin Wachenje, the most significant change to the management of large companies in the United States and Europe over the past 25 years has been the outsourcing of back-office processes. Much of that work has ended up in India, at Bangalore-based tech companies such as Infosys and Wipro, and at Tata consultancy service in Mumbai. No man did more to spark that revolution than Narayana Murthy, the visionary founder of Infosys, who is regarded as the father of Indian information technology. In building a multibillion-dollar software and IT services firm, he showed that Indian companies could compete with the best in the world.

Murthy stresses the concept of being a team player. He also likes the value system a lot. Value systems help build confidence/enthusiasm. An interesting view Murthy has is what he thinks a successful person is. He says a person is successful if he or she can bring a smile to other people's faces. It's a great way to look at "success" in his opinion. If you bring a smile to someone's face, you're most likely doing something good, which can be interpreted as successful (Kris, 2005).

Adaptability is an important skill for a good leader. Murthy knows this that is why he decided to take a flexible approach in leading. This will help the company to keep growing. One thing he did was adopt a flexible pricing policy. Murthy also noticed a couple of problems India had and saw that they were long aspiring problems. Healthcare, education, nutrition, and shelter are some of these aspiring problems. Murthy knew the importance of fixing these problems and started trying to fix and improve on it.

Stress is a challenge a lot of people come across with and managing it is very important to keep on moving forward. Murthy not only tries to manage his stress and helps his employees become less stressful. Long hours in the workplace can take a toll on the employees, which is why he's alright with taking a nap once in a while to help catch up on sleep. Murthy also likes to see his employees happy about their job and smiling (Kris, 2005). He believes that having employees comfortable at work builds a better environment in the workplace.

11.10 REID HOFFMAN

Reid Hoffman took business to social media and started a born global firm, LinkedIn. Hoffman inspires those who want to create something significant on their own. Hoffman's first innovation was his own start-up called Social Net, an online dating site, and the PayPal, an online payment company, where he became a member of the funding team. There was a moment when Hoffman wanted to create a new online company as he stated, actually much easier to build a great company when the capital money is down because real competition isn't Google and Microsoft. It's all the other start-ups and everyone trying to find the rocket ship. So, when lots and lots of companies are being financed, it's just a brutal battle. In the Silicon Valley, Reid Hoffman gathered some of his colleagues whom he worked with and started building his company. LinkedIn, a networking site for business professional, became the start-up business. Less than 6 months later, LinkedIn was launched on May 5, 2003.

Hoffman used his network to assemble a team of engineers from Apple, Fujitus, and a former classmate from Stanford, who was the founder of GamePro. The team decided to build an online dating site called SocialNet.com and raised $1.7 million but never went mainstream due to lack of advertisement. In 2000, Hoffman separated himself from SocialNet.com before it was sold to MatchNet.com. Peter Thiel convinced Hoffman to sit at the board of his company he cofounded in 1998, called Confinity. The company initially focused on mobile-phone encryption, but gravitated toward online payments. Hoffman joined the team ensuring threats to larger websites, such as eBay, Master-Card, and Visa, would not migrate and eventually prevent his site from being shut down. Later, X.com merged with Confinity and became PayPal. In 2002, PayPal (PYPL) went public, raising $70 million on its first day of trading. The new stock price plummeted with the rumor of eBay's entrance into the finance market. Eventually, Hoffman decided the best course of action was to let eBay acquire the company for $1.7 billion, and Hoffman became an instant millionaire.

Hoffman is opportunistic. He launched the first business-oriented social network. LinkedIn has more than 187 million registered users in 200 countries, and the company itself went public in 2011, raising a staggering $4.3 billion of going public. LinkedIn allows users to maintain a list of professional contacts through connections. LinkedIn users can invite anyone to connect, whether or not the individual is a member.

Reid Hoffman is known as the digital world's best-connected networker, making his fortune as the cofounder of LinkedIn, a partner at Greylock, an early investor in Friendster and Flickr, a board member of Zynga, Airbnb, and Mozilla, and approached in 2004 by Sean Parker to invest in a new startup called the facebook.com. Hoffman became one of the most prolific and successful investors in the past decade, investing more than eighty technology companies. What a visionary!

Reid Hoffman is an American entrepreneur, author, and venture capitalist also known as the cofounder and executive chairman of LinkedIn, a social network used mainly for professional networking, As in March 2015, Hoffman, with a net worth of $4.7 billion, is ranked as number 341 on the list of the richest people in the Business Industry. Hoffman wanted to change the world because technology is the new era nowadays. He realized he was very interested to become an entrepreneur to get great opportunities.

In the article by *The Wall Street Journal*, Reid Hoffman was actually planning to teach a course about Entrepreneurship at Stanford University. Students had the opportunity to sign-up for his course to learn on how to start their own business. The statement is described as realistic self-assessment, a continuing process which managers evaluate on their performance of responsibility, improvement that needs to be required, his failure, and what he learned from it. Hoffman mentions building connection, which is the key application. One needs to build network by having connections and good relationship. He is aware everyone has flaws, learns from his experience, and can recognize other's strength. Hoffman doesn't judge and appreciates their strength and weakness. He will comment on a person's mistakes and will also notice his or her unique strength. He now teaches courses mostly at Stanford University.

Hoffman emphasizes a two-way relationship that lets the company and employees work together to reach a goal and building a long-term relationship. Reid Hoffman believes managers shouldn't treat employees as family because employer either won't or can't fulfill a high expectation. Employers shouldn't be treated as if they are free agents; in most workplace people do consider each other as family. In other words, the term family for them means a positive environment supporting each other, treats each other with respect. However, there's always a con that can lead people to emotional and would take advantage of not completing the job because they will feel like the managers will be okay with it. In most cases, if anything happens, the managers and employees can turn against each other and face the consequences. Another reason, not everybody is comfortable to be treated as family because they like to keep things separate, family is family and work is work. Even though Hoffman doesn't believe in treating employees as family members, he still respects them and show that they are appreciated. Hoffman believes in treating employees as a sports team. This does not mean that he will be harder on them but he wants them to learn how to work together and help one another out where they are weak. He thinks if you treat your employees as if they are family or friends, then they may want to take advantage of that. This doesn't mean that because he doesn't treat them like family, he is unpleasant to them; he just feels that treating employees as teammates helps build the relationship between him and the employees, as well as employees and other employees. Hoffman wants his workplace to be a very positive environment and has as less negativity as possible. This allows workers to work better.

Hoffman wants to inspire many entrepreneurs to start up their own business. Reid Hoffman wrote another book *The Start-Up of You*, which offers guiding support to entrepreneurs about starting a business, business strategy, and more. Reid Hoffman believes building networking is important. Networking can build a traditional relationship and alliance. Gathering together can build more communication and support. In order to do so, both need to have a mutual valuable time and face-to-face common action and mutual support. LinkedIn is a professional networking site created by Reid Hoffman (Wilkinson, 2015). The main purpose of this site is to connect people with each other who are looking for work or looking to hire someone. LinkedIn has grown to become the world's largest site used for professional networking. Reid Hoffman is the cofounder and executive chairman of LinkedIn. It is the largest professional networking site with almost 400 million users. It allows users to create profiles and document networks of people they know and trust professionally. After 14 years of establishing LinkedIn, Hoffman decided that he will be selling it to Microsoft. LinkedIn makes it easier to connect with others professionally. It has some what changed the way professional networking is done. LinkedIn is a very popular site that is used by people seeking jobs or people who are hiring.

In an interview, Hoffman stated he learned from the failure of Social Net, which is his first company. Hoffman realized that one cannot become successful without enduring a few failures. It is from those failures he learned more about himself and what he is capable of. Normally people are afraid to admit to themselves and others that they fail. People sometimes look at failure as a bad thing. However, even though Reid Hoffman was disappointed that everything did not go as planned, he definitely didn't see failure as something negative. He was somewhat welcoming of failure. He stated that one must fail in order to succeed. Self-awareness was crucial in accepting and admitting to others that he failed. Hoffman would not hide his failure to anyone. He was very open to his friends and family because his failures did not cause him to give up on what he wanted to create. Hoffman welcomed failure as a way to push himself. Because of the failure of his first company, he realized more about himself and had better understanding of his strengths and weaknesses.

In order to run a successful company, one must be very motivated. Self-motivation is an important quality for someone to have. Reid Hoffman is very motivated, especially when it comes to LinkedIn. He's motivated to use LinkedIn to change the way people do business or network. If Hoffman was not motivated, then he would have stopped trying to create networking sites when his first one failed. He hopes that his motivation rubs off on people around him. Hoffman stated that he's motivated by thoughts on how the world works, how people work, and how entrepreneurship works—and from those factors he wants to discover truth.

Hoffman does not only motivate himself, he also try to motivate his employees. Hoffman wants his employees to enjoy their job and reach their goals at the end of the day. He realizes that employees play a great part in the success of his business. Because of him being self-motivated, he tries to motivate his employees, family members, or anyone who is around him. He realized that if one cannot push self to reach goals, then one will be less likely to succeed.

Hoffmann even tries to help his friends when it comes to business. If his friends need business advice, he will willingly give them and speak about his experience and hope that his friends can learn from that. This shows that he's very empathic and willing to help anyone. Hoffman acknowledges that every employee plays a role in the success of a business. He rewards his employees and encourages them as a way to motivate them. Apart from the business, Hoffman cares about the world as well. He tries to give back. He wants to use his talent and money to make the world better and help solve the humanity's problems. An interviewer stated that Hoffman is among the most selfless and externally generous person he have met.

Some people do not like to be in the public light and like to remain behind the scenes. This does not necessarily mean they lack social skills. Hoffman stated in an interview that he doesn't like to be known, he would rather be anonymous. Although this is the case, Hoffman is very much in the public's eyes. He wants everyone to know the face of LinkedIn and somehow create a relationship with his users and employers. He feels like this is the best way to operate a business. Hoffman is very social. He has done a lot of networking that requires one to be social. His job is based on him having social skills. Hoffman does a lot of interviews and public speaking. He uses his fame and success as an example to teach up and coming entrepreneurs the ropes. During his interviews and public speaking, he seems very comfortable in front of a crowd and camera. He isn't shy to communicate with his audience. He has been doing this for years. He has great body gestures and eye contact during interviews and public speaking. He strives to keep his public speaking as interesting as possible. He keeps the crowd attention. Hoffman's job has a lot to do with social skills and he likes that. He likes doing interviews and public speaking.

He is very confident in himself and the business he created. He gives himself self-motivational speeches. He writes down motivational quotes to live by. He is also confident in his abilities to run a successful business. He does not doubt himself. If he decides to do something, he will do that; if somehow he fails, he will use that as a lesson learned.

He is very open and verbal with the people around him. He does not sugarcoat anything, he is very direct. He is friendly and approachable. He wants people to be open to communicating with him as he is with them. During his interviews, it is shown how well he is communicating with others.

Hoffman is considered to be a very adaptable person. He does well with adapting with changes. This is shown when he created his first site. This site was unfortunately not a success; however, Hoffman did not throw in the towel (give up). He continued working on another site that he believed would be a success (LinkedIn). This shows that Hoffman is very flexible and adapts well. He used the knowledge gained while creating his first site LinkedIn, which came out as a success. Hoffman stated that in running a business, adaptability is a skill someone should have. It is very necessary. If one is not open to change, then he or she will not be able to grow. He views change as something positive.

Running a business can get stressful at times. People deal with stress differently. Some people let stress get the best of them, whereas others are better at managing stress. Hoffman performs well under stress. Hoffman is a positive person in general; so he just views every obstacle that comes his way as a good challenge. He is a very calm and collective person. Sometimes the stress can be too high; however, he doesn't let the stress get the best of him. He thinks if someone takes stress on, then his or her mind will be clouded and will not be able to think straight, which will affect that person and his or her business negatively. Hoffman stated in an interview that some days are more hectic than others but his stress tolerance is high and as time goes by he learns how to deal with things better. Throughout his time running a business, he has down quite well when it comes to stress.

Hoffman is a very positive individual. Hoffman is a very happy individual who always has a welcoming look on his face. This is a good quality he possesses. He is happy with what he has accomplished. Even though Hoffman is a billionaire, he chooses to not live a luxurious life. Hoffman is more focused on things that matter rather than spending money to buy the latest things. He lives in an average size house with his family. He doesn't feel the need to be flashy with his money or what he has accomplished. He rather saves his money and uses it for good. He wants to benefit the world in any way he can. He has a good heart and is always ready to help other people.

Hoffman is very optimistic, confident, and believes that he can fix the problems the business world is having through enabled networks. He wants to use LinkedIn as a way to do so. He's always looking to find solutions to problems. Overall, it is clear and evident that he is generous. Anyone who is around him will notice this about him. His mood is always positive that it rubs off on the people around him. He is generally a well-grounded individual.

11.11 LARRY PAGE AND SERGIN BRIN

Organizing the vast amount of information in the world was seen as a great intellectual challenge; however, it was an amazing opportunity by Google cofounders Larry Page and Sergy Brin. At that stage, they had no idea how Internet searching could be monetized at the time.

A visionary, Brin is also referred as an enlightenment man. Brin believes in thinking ahead and planning for the future. He has a vision and trains his employees as well. His employees trust him because everything is documented and he, his partner Larry Page, and other associates treat everyone equally. Brin and his partner trust each other because they have been partners since the very beginning and now consider themselves best friends. Brin motivates his employees to work hard every single day. They work every day around the clock. He knows how to treat people. He is a phenomenal innovator and draws people to work for him. Talented individuals want to work for Google and Brin because he treats them with respect.

Larry Page's best quality is his vision about Google as a change agent for the world. Over the years, Google's ability to organize the world's information and make it universally accessible and useful has been constantly redefined and improved. Page affirmed that Google has a responsibility to use its resources and influence to make impossible things happen. He plans and makes decisions thinking about the next 5–10 years, not this year or next. His ambition, self-motivation, accomplishments, and perseverance positively affect Google employees' self-esteem, create hope, reflect trust, build positive emotions, and rise optimism. Page ensures Google employees have dental and healthcare, retirement, transportation, meals while at work, 18 weeks paid maternity leave, and much more.

During the earlier years of the company, Google was a place where only ideas mattered, not emotions. This notion is a reflection of Larry Page's style of interaction with others. When Mr. Page and Mr. Brin had initially met, it was a day of fierce arguments. While their debates were not shouting matches, they were a series of blunt points by one side, and then the other, with a little name-calling thrown in. However, they bonded over this type of interaction and their friendship never deteriorated from it, leading Mr. Page to style this type of interaction with his employees thus creating an argumentative atmosphere for the company's senior management.

After a disaster in management in the year 2001, which will be discussed later on in this report, Page was forced to step down as CEO and became president of products. For the next 10 years, he was rather unhappy and reduced his day-to-day interactions and dealings with the company. During this time, Page had learned and realized that the argumentative nature that he once viewed as a strength for the company is a problem. Nothing gets done when people in the same team could barely tolerate working together, and the company's high ambitions were impossible to achieve with all the conflict. When he reclaimed his position as CEO in the year 2011, he held a retreat with major executives, announcing that there would henceforth be zero tolerance for fighting.

On January 12, 2010, Google Inc. had revealed that it faced cyber-attacks originating from China that resulted in the theft of intellectual property from Google. After investigation, the company had obtained evidence to suggest that a primary goal of the attacks was accessing the Gmail accounts of Chinese human rights activists. Not only that but third parties routinely accessed these accounts via phishing scams and malware placed on the users' computers. Brin personally supervised Google's investigation, even moving his office into the building where Google's security team was operating. After these revelations, the company decided to lift all censorship as defiance to those forces of totalitarianism.

Mr. Brin was instrumental in the decision of the company to lift all censorship from its Chinese search engine. He argued that because services and information are our most successful exports, if regulations in China effectively prevent us from being competitive, then they are a trade barrier.

In college and graduate school, Mr. Page had been able to connect with people over external extractions, cool technologies, dreams, and visions of the future. In his heart, he is a passionate utopian who believes that technology has overwhelmingly improved the livelihood of people and will only continue to do so. At Google, he kept this interaction with employees on this level and managed without regard to feelings.

If there was any empathy, publicly, displayed by Sergey Brin, it is his philanthropic activities. Mr. Brin's story is a rags-to-riches one and does what he can to give others the same chance to experience their version of his story. For example, he donated $1 million to the Hebrew Immigrant Aid Society, for he would like to see anyone be able to achieve his or her dreams.

During the early days of Google, Larry Page demonstrated how little empathy he had for his employees and made one of the worst managerial decisions as a result. In July 2001, Larry Page decided it was necessary to fire Google's project managers. Since Google only hired the most talented engineers and the fact that he hated the concept of delegation, he figured the extra layer of supervision was not necessary. In fact, he thought of it as a hindrance. Mr. Page felt that the things he wanted to be done were not getting done and blamed the project managers. He suspected that Google's project managers were moving engineers away from tasks that he deemed important.

After Mr. Page had informed his HR team of his desire for such a drastic change, many were very resistant and made many attempts to reason with him to change his mind. Google's at-the-time HR boss Stacey Sullivan, Chairman Eric Schmidt, Executive Bill Campbell, and many others opposed this decision. Mr. Campbell, in particularly, got into a very big argument with Mr. Page over the plan and tried to prove his point by bringing engineers to Mr. Page's office. The engineers offered their perspective and expressed their preference to have a manager. To them, a manager is someone who could end disagreements and direct his or her teams/

Wayne Rosing, VP of engineering, was given the task to break the news of Mr. Page's decision. All engineers and project managers stood outside Mr. Page's office to hear the statement: All engineers will now report to Rosing and all project managers were out of the job. The news did not wash over well, and the engineers and managers demanded an explanation. With little emotion, speaking in his usual flat, robotic tone, Mr. Page explained that "he did not like having non-engineers supervising engineers. Engineers should not have to be supervised by managers with limited tech knowledge."

The decision did not stick. However, there were many lessons learned here. Google started hiring managers again, but they must also be engineers if they wish to oversee the most intricate projects. Mr. Page was forced to step down for Eric Schmidt as CEO, and spent the next decade soul-searching.

When Sergey Brin met Larry Page, he was outgoing and energetic. Mr. Brin was known among professors, in Stanford, for his habit of bursting into their offices without knocking. He would bring a much-needed extroversion that Mr. Page lacked to Mr. Page's startup-turned-global-technology company. Here, Mr. Brin excelled at branding, strategy, and developing relationships between Google and other companies.

During Google's early years, Larry Page tended to communicate through empathic body language. He'd lift an eyebrow in a way that would make one know he thought one's idea was stupid. If someone said something that made him angry or uncomfortable, he would respond in a quieter tone and would not be able to look at that person while he did it.

Sergey Brin invests much of his time in exercise and really enjoys it. Mr. Brin goes for more active sports such as trapeze and gymnastics. While he has never outwardly expressed worry regarding his chances of developing Parkinson's disease, he does take measures to prevent it. Although exercise can be a great stress reducer, it is also a risk reducer for Parkinson's disease.

Sergey Brin and Larry Page created an American multinational conglomerate, Alphabet Inc., to better manage and organize its subsidiaries operating in different industries. The establishment of Alphabet Inc. was prompted by the desire to make all the services provided by Google cleaner and more accountable, allowing greater control of unrelated companies. The founders expressed their overall excitement in this new chapter in the life of the empire they created via blog post, believing they are now in a better position to improve the lives of many people.

11.12 JEFF BEZOS

Amazon's CEO Jeff Bezos, whose mantra to serve his customers whatever they demand, has made Amazon the Wal-Mart of the online world. Bezos's greatest accomplishment has been the transformation of Amazon from just an online bookstore to Amazon, the online everything enterprise. His strategy and rational analyzing ability have cracked one of the business' great mysteries about figuring what customers want before they may actually demand it.

Amazon, which has a reputation for frugality (Burrows, 2003), has developed the cultural norm that frugality drives innovation. Bezos motivates his employees to embrace the unknown–to take risks and to experiment. However, he has created tools to reduce the cost of experimentation. According to Bezos, if one reduces the cost of risk while increasing risks and leveraging what one learns in the process, then what one ends up with are increased revenues because of the number of innovations produced. This culture of rationale risk taking connects directly with our next theme, acceptance of risk and potential failure. It was the amazing growth rates of the Internet that caused Jeff Bezos to quit a job in New York, move across the country to Seattle, and start Amazon.com in a garage. He immediately grasped the opportunity to use the technology of the Internet to offer customers a vast selection of products at the lowest possible prices.

The purpose is to show how a CEO's characteristics can show directly through his or her company in a negative or positive way. Through our research, we discovered how Jeff Bezos' behavior reflects on his employee's perception. Jeff Bezos is a very smart man with a relentless work ethic. He lacks qualities that would make him a great CEO, while showing qualities that allow his company to continue to grow.

Jeff Bezos is an American entrepreneur born on January 12, 1964, in Albuquerque, New Mexico. Bezos often displayed scientific interests and technological proficiency when he was young. He was a high school valedictorian and was a National Merit Scholar. While at Princeton, he was elected to the honor societies Phi Beta Kappa and Tau Beta Pi. He also served as the president of the Princeton chapter of the students for exploration and development of Space (Anders 2012).

After reading a report that projected annual Web growth, Bezos drew up a list of 20 products that could be sold on the Internet. He narrowed the list to five most promising products: compact discs, computer hardware, computer software, videos, and books. Bezos eventually decided that his venture would sell books over the Web, due to the large worldwide market for literature, the low price that could be offered for books, and the tremendous selection of titles that were available in print (Burrows, 2003). He chose Seattle as the company headquarters due to its large high-tech workforce and its proximity to a large book distribution center in Oregon. Bezos then worked to raise funds for the company while also working with software developers to build the company's website. The website debuted in July 1995 and quickly became the number one book-related site on the web.

Jeff Bezos is a very confident person and thrives on being the best. The early days at Amazon were characterized by working twelve hours a day, seven days a week, and being up until 3:00 a.m. to get books shipped. Jeff Bezos is committed to his work and believes in improving his company. During the recession, Amazon sales grew 28% and he created the Kindle. He knew that majority of people during the recession had limited shopping privileges. So he placed a low price on the Kindle, $79 for the classic Kindle, an everyman reader. For $99 you can buy a slightly fancier Kindle Touch and for $149 you can add cellular functionality with the Kindle Touch 3G. Jeff Bezos knew that people still wanted to buy during the recession, but didn't have the money for the expenses. Jeff Bezos' decision to create a product that has similar qualities of the iPad for a cheaper price was a smart business choice.

He loves people counting on him and so it's easy for him to be motivated because millions of customers are counting on Amazon.com. We've got thousands of investors counting on us. And we're a team of thousands of employees all counting on each other. This shows that Jeff Bezos is motivated when having a lot of pressure on him and his company. He wants people counting on him in order for his company to grow.

Jeff Bezos is hardworking, dependable, and organized. He is independent and loves to focus on the task at hand, how to execute it, and how to prosper. Bezos is willing to take risks, however, only after careful calculations and thorough research on the subject. Just like Amazon, Jeff Bezos' personality is intriguing to the new generation of entrepreneurs.

Bezos noted that Amazon often begins its staff meetings with thirty minutes of silent reading. The company also forgoes PowerPoint, Bezos says, which is easy for the presenter, but difficult for the audience. Bezos noted that slides generally communicate very little real information, primarily bullet points and numeric data. However, the necessity to communicate thoughts in full sentences and paragraphs requires presenters to think more deeply and forces a deeper clarity. This example shows how Jeff Bezos wants his employees to be able to verbally talk to each other without today's technology. Jeff Bezos also states the benefit of the memos, is that they force presenters to go beyond the numeric facts of an issue or statement to include the story around it. He also stated a general rule that memos should be kept to one page so that organizations can maintain a laser focus and act quickly. From this example, it concludes that Jeff Bezos believes in communication and wants his employees to be well organized.

Jeff Bezos is hyperintelligent, ultradriven, and obsessed with detail. Bezos expects everyone around him to be the same. Jeff Bezos always had a relentless work ethics and thrives on being the best (Penenberg, 2009). His decision to create a product that has similar qualities of the iPad for a cheaper price was a smart business choice. Jeff Bezos is motivated when having a lot of pressure on him and his company. He wants people counting on him in order for his company to grow.

His disregard for the conventional business dress code shows that Bezos is a low self-monitor. This could be inferred because Bezos doesn't change the way he behaves, in this case, the way he dresses, depending on who he is around him. Jeff Bezos is hardworking, dependable, and organized. He is independent and loves to focus on the task at hand, how to execute it, and how to prosper. Bezos is willing to take risks, but only after careful calculations and thorough research on the subject (Hartung, 2013).

Jeff Bezos is someone who believes in feedback. When it comes to the customers of amazon, anyone can send him an email: jeff@amazon.com. He reads every single one of them to see what people say. If there is a negative email, he sends it in an email to his employees with a question mark in the subject line. From there, his employees have to come up with a resolution. After *The New York Times* article came out that spoke about the many troubles at Amazon, Jeff Bezos responded saying that he was "horrified" by *The New York Times* August 2015 article recounting callous behavior on the part of Amazon executives, company founder Jeff Bezos warned today that any employees found lacking in empathy would be instantly purged. They would begin grading them on this and 10% of the employees who are least empathic would be fired. In order to achieve the goal, Amazon introduces a new internal reporting program called Empathy Track, which will be able for employees to rate each other on their lack of humanity. So, from this example, we can see how Jeff Bezos was able to challenges that were taking at Amazon.

Jeff Bezos believes that the fundamental measure of his success will be the shareholder value he creates over long term (Anders 2012). He uses a data-driven approach to help him make decisions. It allows him to take risks, to innovate; day by day he reaffirms his security in his belief that this is the right thing to do. He won't focus on the details for the next quarter, focusing on what's going to be good for the customers; thinking that this type of aspect for our culture is rare. The Kindle again is the example of this he internalized hundreds of data points that millions of buyers would want a crisp e-reader that could download any book in sixty seconds or less. Not getting bogged down by the mechanics, right compressions, or the transmission speeds for the book files, letting the engineers be free to build it as they saw fit. Here is how he uses motivation for himself and his workers. He's concerned about his employees, and so he would prepay 95% of their tuition for in demand fields such as airplane mechanic, nursing, or whatever else because skills are very important in amazon. The whole plan for that was to enable choice. He wants his employees to prove him wrong, motivating his workers by the idea that our work is good enough when it can prove him wrong. He doesn't care how the work is done. His thinking is that as long as work is done it doesn't matter how or where as long as it's on time and up to his standards. Allowing most of his employees like customer service workers to work from home or any place they are familiar with.

Jeff Bezos is quiet philanthropist, despite the very active Bezos family foundation (Patric, 2010). Self-reliance is a concept that he really believes in. Assuming his beliefs came from his early life, his biological father and mother were teenagers by the time he was 4. The idea of charity in association with Jeff only brought up the idea of stinginess; some of his critics say that lemonade stands donate more than him. This was due to the fact that he doesn't give enough to his hometown charities. He is very calculated when it comes to the act of giving money away as it takes way too much time that is equivalent to the time needed to run a business. Another way he has come close to donating is through the stock of the foundation in his parents' name.

Some of the issues the foundation tackles are health. He gives a gift of $10 million donation to the Fred Hutchinson Cancer Research Center. It was to kick-start a program for the expansion of a certain uses of immunotherapy for breast, ovarian, and prostate cancers. Doing the similar thing, his parents gave fifteen million to Princeton University. Their alma mater helped to make Bezos Center for Neural Circuit Dynamics. It focuses on the new field for research measuring neural connectivity and mining that data to better understanding a neurological illness. There has been a donation of $20 million to the research of immunotherapy. Millions of grants are given; both large and small were donated in the name of charity. They even have a Bezos Scholars program. He is also a supporter of world reader—the nonprofit that one of his employees started. It brings reading to parts of the world where it was assessable and unattainable donating $300,000 to start it and $500,000 in the years that follows.

Jeff Bezos is often portrayed in press coverage as a charismatic, ambitious, and a shrewd businessman. He has also been characterized as a fun-loving guy with great sense of humor. He has very good social skills in both verbal and nonverbal ways. He holds interactive conversations with his peers and fellow employees. He may be known for as the mean boss; however, he is known for being friendly in person, wise, and intelligent beyond his years. During discussions, he can be seen as easy to get along with, and even this image he has to a certain degree at times rebuttal it or defend it. In the public eye, he is seen as someone people either wants to be or wants to defeat. Jeff Bezos' intrapersonal ability allows him to communicate with his self, by asking himself questions in order to make certain decisions. An example of this is when he quit his job in New York on Wall Street, to start Amazon in Washington. He knew what he wanted and he act on it by making very important decisions.

Jeff Bezos uses his interpersonal skills to interact with others properly (Deutschman ,2004). This is generally used by him and the ability of his employees to get along with each other while getting the job done. He devotes his full attention to the conversation. He is aware to a certain degree meaning he knows himself, self-reflecting through his childhood on how he was, remembering the lessons of his past to help him in the present day. During interviews of all types, he acts in a demeanor of actually self-awareness though at times this can be questioned by how he is seen by treating other people.

One of the most integral parts of his business is embracing the chance of failure most times one is going to fail. However, one succeeds it makes it all the while worth. He is very calculating often thinking in terms of what could benefit him; this even goes into how he handles people. He believes that pushing them makes his workplace friendly but at times very confrontational. It can at times insulting in hope that he can get the best results. His interviews prove to be very sincere, where he mentions the ways to handle stress, his childhood, and what he thinks on matters of the political climate. However, once he's in the business room, the atmosphere changes.

In terms of stress management, Jeff Bezos stated that he laughs a lot. He goes on to say stress primarily comes from not taking action over something that one can have some control over. So, if he finds that some particular thing is causing him to have stress, that's a warning sign for him. He finds that as soon as he identifies the problem, and makes the first phone call or the first email. He believes in taking steps addresses that situation, even if it's not solved.

On adaptability in business, he doesn't change his management style so often nor does he change his business plan. The way he adapts is through the mind of an analysis. Analyzing the situation looing all possible outcomes to help him accomplish his goals on the job it would be customer's satisfaction using data and work metrics. He uses his foresight to be able to not have a herd mentality, which is one of his strongest characteristics if he needs to go slow he will, despite the maddening of the crowd. Jeff's adaptability in terms of flexibility and problem-solving ability is traits that make him the person he is today. He adapts to different situations and inferences over the course of his life. He sometime thinks of the worst possible solution, then do the complete opposite. He also thinks that when things get complicated, consider what's best for whoever is affected.

His general mood is always optimistic and happy. As stated above, he is characterized as a fun-loving guy with great sense of humor. He is known to be light hearted, laughing, and joking. He's fun to be around and his laughing also plays a big part for his likeability.

References

Anders, G. (2012), "Jeff Bezos gets it", *Forbes*, 189(7), 76–86.

Andrew H. (2016), Nike co-founder Phil Knight: I was told I wouldn't make it. How I did it anyways. Available from http://www.cnbc.com/2016/08/04/nike-founder-phil-knight-on-success-and-failure.html. Accessed on December 08, 2016.

Bar-On, R. (2000), "Emotional and social intelligence: Insights from the Emotional Quotient Inventory (EQ-i)", In R. Bar-On and J. D. Parker (Eds.), *Handbook of emotional Intelligence*, San Francisco, CA: Jossey-Bass.

Bar-On, R. (2004), "The Bar-On Emotional Quotient Inventory (EQ-i): Rationale, description and summary of psychometric properties", In G. Geher (Ed.), *Measuring emotional intelligence: Common ground and controversy*, New York: Nova Science Publishers, Inc, 115–145.

Bartram, D., Robertson, I. T., and Callinan, M. (2002), "Introduction: A framework for examining organizational effectiveness", In I. T. Robertson, M. Callinan and D. Bartram (Eds.), *Organisational effectiveness: The role of Psychology*, Chichestor, United Kingdom: Wiley, 1–12.

Beinhocker, E. D. (2000), "Robust adaptive strategies", *Sloan Management Review*, 40(3), 95–106.

Bonini, S., and Kaas, H. W. (2010), Building a sustainable Ford Motor Company: An interview with Bill Ford, Mckinsey Quarterly. Available from http://www.mckinsey.com/insights/sustainability/building_a_sustainable_ford_motor company_and_interview_with_bill_ford. Accessed on February 2015.

Boyatzis, R. (1982), The competent manager: A model for effective performance, New York: John Wiley and Sons.

Burke, K. (2014), Bill Ford predicts 'radical transformation' of auto industry, Automotive news, July 8, 2014, retrieved on February 19, 2015.

Burrows, P. (2003), Bezoz: How frugality drives innovation, *Businessweek*, 4081, 64–66.

Cherniss, C., and Goleman, D. (2001), The emotionally intelligent workplace, San Francisco: Jossey-Bass.

Colby, R. (2004), Herbert Kohler, Jr.", *Forbes*. Accessed on March 14, 2015.

Cosh, C. (2013), "Innovation that's above and beyond," *Maclean's*, 126(50), 12–14.

Deutschman, A. (2004), "Inside the mind of Jeff Bezos", (cover story). *Fast Company*, 85, 52–58.

Chang, K. (2014), Virgin-Galactic-is-Rattled-by-crash-but-Undeterred, The New York Times, November 1, 2014.

Dell, M. (2004), Thinking out of the box. Accessed on October 2, 2014.

Dell, M. (2008), Entrepreneur India. Available from http://www.entrepreneur.com/article/197566. Accessed on October 2, 2014.

Dyer, J., and Gregersen, H. (2013), "The secret to unleashing genius", *Forbes*, 191(12), 1.

Eisenhardt, K. M. (1999), "Strategy as strategic decision-making", *Sloan Management Review*, 40(3), 65–72.

Goleman, D. (1995), Emotional intelligence. New York: Bantam Books.

For LinkedIn Founder Reid Hoffman. (2012), Relationships rule the world. Available from https://www.wired.com/2012/03/ff_hoffman/. Accessed on December 08, 2016.

Casnocha, B. (2014), 10,000 Hours with Reid Hoffman: What I Learned. Available from http://casnocha.com/reid-hoffman-lessons. Accessed on December 08, 2016.

Hammett, R. D. (2007), "Personal excellence: The development and validation of a new measure of emotional intelligence", A dissertation Texas A and M University-Kingsville and Texas A and M University-Corpus Christi.

Hartung, A. (2013), Why Jeff Bezos is our Greatest living CEO, (cover story) Forbes.

Jasper, C. (2014), "Branson empire reverberates from shock of shattered space-craft." Bloomberg Business Week.

jobs.nike.com. (n.d.), Benefits. Available from http://jobs.nike.com/article/benefits. Accessed on December 08, 2016.

Low, G., lomax, A., Jackson, M., and Nelson, D. (2004), "Emotional intelligence: A new student development model", A paper presented at the 2004 national conference of the American college personnel association in Pennsylvania.

Malekar, S., and Mohanty, R. (2009), "Factors affecting emotional intelligence: An empirical study of some school students in Mumbai", *International Journal of Management in Education*, 3(1), 8–28.

Malekar, S., and Mohanty, R. (2011), "Constructing an emotional intelligence radar for Indian school students", *Educational Research*, 2(1), 790–802.

Malekar, S., and Mohanty, R. (2012), "Constructing an emotional intelligence radar for Indian professional college students", *International Journal of Scientific Research in Education*, 4(2), 115–130.

Moore, T. (2004), Herbert V. Kohler | 20th Century American Leaders Database, Hbs.edu. Accessed on December 14, 2014.

Nelson, D., and Low, G. (2011), "Emotional intelligence - Achieving academic and career excellence", *Pearsons*, 165–174.

Patric, S. (2010), Amazon.com whiz Jeff Bezos keeps kindling Hot Concepts. *Investor's Business Daily*. P. A04.

Penenberg, A. L. (2009), "The Evolution of Amazon", (cover story), *Fast Company*, 137, 66–74.

Petrides, K. V., and Furnham, A. (2006), "The role of trait emotional intelligence in a gender-specific model of organizational variables", *Journal of Applied Social Psychology*, 36, 552–569.

Spencer, L., and Spencer, S. (1993), Competence at work: Models for superior performance, New York: John Wiley and Sons, 9–15.

Smithson, N. (2016), Nike, Inc. Vision Statement and Mission Statement - Panmore Institute. Available from http://panmore.com/nike-inc-vision-statement-mission-statement. Accessed on December 08, 2016.

Mazumdar, S. (1999), The Pride of Bangalore - Infosys is a software success and not just in India," Newsweek International, 52.

Nike founder Phil Knight on story and culture behind his sports apparel juggernaut - Sportsnet.ca. (n.d.), Available from http://www.sportsnet.ca/more/nike-founder-phil-knight-story-culture-behind-sports-apparel-juggernaut/. Accessed on December 08, 2016.

Oregonian/Oregon Live, A. B. (2016), Phil Knight comes home, accompanied by 'Shoe Dog,' for a victory lap. Available from http://www.oregonlive.com/business/index.ssf/2016/05/phil_knight_comes_home_accompa .html. Accessed on December 08, 2016.

Philip H. Knight (n.d.), Available from https://www.entrepreneur.com/article/197534. Accessed on December 08, 2016.

Rudulph, H. W. (2016), Interview Insider: How to Get Hired at Nike. Available from http://www.cosmopolitan.com/career/interviews/a42012/interview-insider-nike-career-jobs/. Accessed on December 08, 2016.

Available from http://www.businessinsider.com/nike-founder-phil-knight-profile-2015-8/#phil-knight-was-born-on-february-24-1938-he-ran-track-at-the-university-of-oregon-and-graduated-in-1959-with-a-degree-in-journalism-after-serving-in-the-army-for-a-year-he-went-back-to-school-to-earn-his-mba-from-stanfords-graduate-school-of-business-1.

Stevenson, A. (2016), CNBC. Available from http://www.cnbc.com/2016/08/04/nike-founder-phil-knight-on-success-and-failure.html. Accessed on August 04, 2016.

Kris, S. (2005), "Murthy, N. R. 1946-." International Directory of Business Biographies. Ed. Neil Schlager. Vol. 3. Detroit: St. James Press, 2005. 165–167. Gale Virtual Reference Library. Web. March 23, 2016.

Wilkinson, A. (2015), What Elon Musk and Reid Hoffman Learned From Failing Wisely. Available from http://www.inc.com/amy-wilkinson/why-the-best-leaders-fail-wisely.html. Accessed on December 08, 2016.